Baedeker

G000125634

Bali

www.baedeker.com

Verlag Karl Baedeker

SIGHTSEEING HIGHLIGHTS ✶ ✶

Lush green rice terraces, impressive volcanic landscapes, endless beaches, sunny groves of palm trees, smiling people, mystical temples and sheer exoticism – the small island in the east of Indonesia offers all this and more. Experience Balinese shadow theatre, wayang kulit, and let the colourful masks used in traditional dances such as the legong and kecak cast their spell on you.

Pura Ulun Danu
Dewi Danu, the goddess of the waters, is venerated in this temple.

12 ✱✱ Mengwi
Pura Taman Ayu enjoys a picturesque setting in a lotus flower lake.
► page 205

13 ✱✱ Ubud
Bali's artistic heart, set in the midst of peaceful rice terraces, tropical forests and wild gorges ► page 237

14 ✱✱ Peliatan
Painters, woodcarvers and the widely-known Agung Rai Museum ► page 209

15 ✱✱ Bedulu
The great destinations for outings here include the Elephant Cave of Goa Gajah, the spring sanctuary of Yeh Pulu and the world's largest bronze drum.
► page 157

16 ✱✱ Gianyar
Traditional palace and extraordinary temples in Blahbatuh ► page 184

17 ✱✱ Klungkung
Kerta Gosa, with its unique paintings, is a reminder of Klungkung's former importance as a seat of Bali's supreme court.
► page 188

18 ✱✱ Candi Dasa
Popular holiday resort with the Bat Caves of Goa Lawah
► page 173

19 ✱✱ Kapal
Impressive meru in Pura Sada, the founding temple of the Megwi
► page 186

20 ✱✱ Denpasar
Bustling capital of the island, where Balinese culture and Western influence collide
► page 177

21 ✱✱ Bukit Badung
An eldorado of luxury hotels and water sports with the sea temple of Pura Luhur Ulu Watu set in an extraordinary location
► page 165

22 ✱✱ Penida
Ideal for surfers and divers
► page 214

23 ✱✱ Lombok
Bali's smaller neighbouring island
► page 197

3 Kubutambahan
2 Singaraja
1 Bali Barat National Park
4 Bedugul
5 Negara
7 Besakih
6 Tampaksiring
9 Bangli
8 Amlapura
10 Tenganan
11 Tabanan
13 Ubud
14 Peliatan
16 Gianyar
18 Candi Dasa
12 Mengwi
15 Bedulu
17 Klungkung
19 Kapal
Lombok 23
20 Denpasar
22 Penida
21 Bukit Badung

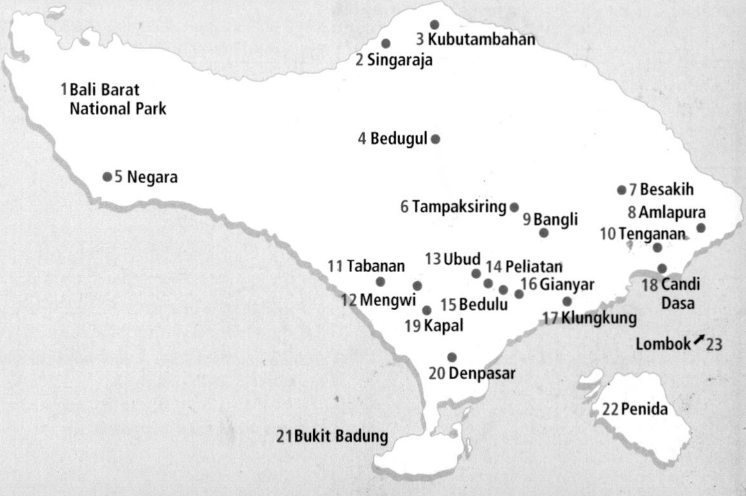

BAEDEKER'S BEST TIPS

Here, we have collected together the most interesting Baedeker tips in this book. Experience and enjoy Bali at its most beautiful.

◼ Design your own jewellery

Those in the know in Bali have rings, necklaces and even belts produced according to their own specifications. Working from a sketch or a photo provided by the customer, silversmiths create made-to-measure objects. There is just one drawback: it takes about 1–2 weeks to complete an order. ▶ page 118

◼ Proper behaviour when visiting a temple

Visitors wearing mini-skirts or shorts are not welcome in a temple. The solution is to wear a selendang, a cloth that the temple guardians hand visitors to be wrapped around the hips. It is even better to have your own clean selendang at the ready. ▶ page 164

◼ Fresh from the sea

Freshly caught fish and seafood are prepared in Jimbaran's innumerable beach

Beauty secrets
Natural ingredients are used for all kinds of wellness treatments.

restaurants. The delicious meals are enjoyed here in open, palm leaf covered huts, the atmosphere either regal or rustic. It is especially pleasant here at dinner time, with candles and Chinese lanterns creating an enchanting mood. ▶ page 171

◼ Oasis for cyclists

Even if the way the locals drive takes some getting used to for foreigners, Nusa Dua is an oasis for cyclists. Here it is possible to get around on a bike on well-developed paths that lead through park-like areas, past hotels and even to the occasional small Balinese village. A very relaxing way to travel. ▶ page 173

Fascinating diving grounds
– but do not underestimate the dangers

◾ The underwater world of Gili Tepekong

Gili Tepekong, Gili Biaha and Gili Mimpan off the coast at Candi Dasa can be reached by boat. The area is considered to be excellent for diving, but some caution is in order; only experienced divers should venture into its depths. ► page 176

◾ For body and soul

There are a large number of small spas and beauty salons in Kuta. They offer excellent massages and relaxation programmes at modest prices. ► page 196

◾ A visit to the spice garden

Pepper, vanilla, ginger, cinnamon and cocoa: Balinese spice gardens will whisk you away to an aromatic world of intoxicating fragrances. Exotic shrubbery and vegetation abound; take a sniff here and a whiff there, sample strange fruit with a completely unknown name or sip a cup of freshly prepared cocoa. Ready packaged spices, coffees and teas can be purchased afterwards. ► page 230

◾ The art of the double ikat

The women of Tenganan are the only masters in the art of weaving cloths with threads that have been pre-dyed in such a way as to produce a traditional pattern. The parts that are not meant to be dyed are tied tightly in knots (ikat). Ikat cloths are precious works of art whose production takes many months. ► page 236

◾ Yoga, dance or Balinese cooking

Ubud is a stronghold of exciting courses, workshops and seminars on Balinese culture. The local tourist information office can provide a list of events, which is also posted in cafés and restaurants. The programme ranges from one hour lectures to events lasting several days as well as courses attended weekly. ► page 241

Enchanting textiles
The cloths produced in double-Ikat process are said to possess magical powers

Legong dancer
mystifying and graceful
► page 54

BACKGROUND

PRACTICALITIES

Price categories

Hotels
Luxury: from £96/$190
Mid-range: £32–96/$64–190
Budget: up to £32/$64
for one night in a double room

Restaurants
Expensive: from £12/$24
Moderate: from £5.50/$11 to £12/$24
Inexpensive: from £2.40/$6 to £5.50/$11
(3 courses, without drinks)

A feeling of total wellbeing
Baths with exotic blossoms and grasses
▶ **page 122**

Basakih
The figures along the steps are decorated for special festivals.
▶ **page 163**

Tanah Lot
The Hindu temple is perched on a crag in the ocean close to the shore.
▶ **page 231**

Background

CLEAR AND CONCISE, EASY TO FOLLOW, AND HANDY FOR QUICK REFERENCE; HERE ARE THE FACTS WORTH KNOWING ABOUT BALI, THE PROVINCE AND ITS PEOPLE, ITS ECONOMY AND POLITICS, ITS ART AND CULTURE, ITS SOCIETY AND EVERYDAY LIFE.

ISLAND OF THE GODS

Once a year thousands of Balinese gather on the beach in Sanur at sunset. The festively-dressed multitude gazes out at the water and, every now and again, people glance over to the small altar adorned with flowers and crowned by a canopy.

As the sun's rays grow weaker and the crowd swells with the arrival of hundreds of people dressed in white and yellow, the first individuals begin standing up and walking toward the ocean. They carry small boats woven from palm fronds with offerings of rice, a few coins, and tropical blossoms: blue ones for Vishnu, red ones for Brahma and white ones for Shiva – the three major deities of Hinduism. As if acting on a signal, they lay their offerings down on the sand, pause for a moment in silent prayer, then return to their place and sit down again. It is the eve of Nyepi, the Balinese new year celebration, and the people have assembled on the beach of Sanur to solicit the goodwill of the spirits of the sea for the coming year.

Gods, Spirits and Demons

There is sense for the spiritual dimension in everyday life in Bali. All over the island, even in the middle of the loud, bustling tourist mecca of Kuta, the Balinese live in harmony with the cosmic mandala, honour the

Friendliness
The warmheartedness and calm poise of the Balinese is legendary.

gods, and are fully aware that there is something more than just the cares and joys of this present life. The family is of major importance to every Balinese and traditionally they live in an attractive homestead with various sleeping and living rooms, including an area where the lady of the house makes offerings to gods and ancestors first thing in the morning. Everyone who sets foot on the tropical island feels its magical atmosphere. Contributing factors to this are the numerous festivals and ceremonies that enrich village life throughout the whole year and which foreign visitors are welcome to attend. In addition, the Balinese world of dance, often marked by spiritualism, is full of vitality. Bali is the sweet smell of tropical blossoms and incense sticks, and the sounds of gamelan orchestras. Its verdant rice terraces sparkle in the sunlight, and its deeply spiritual people exhibit

Procession
Festively dressed worshippers with elaborate offerings can be seen regularly.

Rice
is considered to be a gift from the gods in Bali.

A paradise of spices
Whoever likes to cook should take home a supply from one of the many spice plantations.

Wayang Kulit
The figures used in Indonesian shadow theatre are usually cut from buffalo leather.

Temple
Each temple celebrates its odalan on a different day; there is always a celebration going on somewhere.

Wellness
Spoil yourself: a Balinese spa is a real experience.

a bubbly cheerfulness and a desire under no circumstances to dwell on annoying problems. There are innumerable temples: in fact more temples have been counted on the island than homes, and particularly on national holidays these places come to life, becoming the scenes of various ceremonies. Bali offers volcanoes and dark lava beaches lined with palm trees, has lush tropical vegetation, and boasts a range of hotels that could have sprung out of a catalogue of international furnishings.

Beautiful Landscapes and Decorative Arts

If only for its religion, Bali is different from the other approximately 13,000 Indonesian islands. The volcanoes Batur and Agung, set in enchanting landscapes ideal for hiking and trekking, are considered to be the abode of the gods. Tourists appreciate the many seaside re-

sorts and their beaches, from the black lava sand in the north to the mangrove-lined beaches in the south of the island. In point of fact, all of the tourist centres are on the coastline with the exception of the artists' town of Ubud. Visitors are enthralled by the wealth of luxuriously proliferous vegetation. Thanks to the large amount of precipitation, many varieties of palm thrive, as do lush, blossoming frangipani trees and orchids in all sizes and colours. Dense forests, on the other hand, can only be found in the west of the island, primarily in Bali Barat National Park. Numerous rivers flow through the island and contribute to the constant irrigation of the rice terraces. The

Barong
portrays the eternal struggle between good and evil.

Balinese are unique craftsmen: for them, the wish to create something stems from their desire for inner and outer harmony. Museums provide a good overview of the diversity of art objects, but only the displays in the shops and a visit to those engaged in the decorative arts can familiarize the visitor with the great variety of woodcarving, painting, weaving art, wickerwork, jewellery and batik art. And so it is, at the latest on the return trip home, that every visitor to Bali discovers how a stay on the small Indonesian island only arouses the wish to return again as soon as possible.

Facts

Bali's unique character has always fascinated its visitors. Lush tropical vegetation and artfully arranged rice terraces, innumerable shrines, rich decorative arts, colourful markets and the famous temple dances hold a magical attraction for holidaymakers from all over the world throughout the entire year.

Nature

Bali was not always an island. About 10,000 years ago, before the last Ice Age, it was connected to Java, Borneo and Sumatra. The melting of the continental ice mass and the resulting rise in sea level made Bali an island.

Origin

According to a theory of the British Zoologist Alfred R. Wallace (1823–1913), a boundary line (the Wallace Line) dividing the Asiatic and the Australian continental shelves runs through the strait between Bali and Lombok (Lombok Strait). Wallace based his theory on clearly determinable differences in flora and fauna.

Wallace Line

The highest mountains in Bali are the volcanoes Gunung Agung (3142m/10,308ft) and Gunung Batukau (2276m/7,467ft), the latter of which has been active again since 1999. On the neighbouring island of Lombok the Rinjani volcano is the highest elevation at 3726m/12,224ft. Almost all of the rivers and streams that flow through Bali run essentially in a north-south direction. They have their source for the most part in the central portion of the island and carry so much water that they are capable of supplying an extensive irrigation system with countless canals.

Mountains and rivers

The geology of many Indonesian islands is marked by numerous volcanoes, quite a few of which remain active to this day. Pronounced dissection is typical of volcanic landscapes as a result of the flow of lava after a volcanic eruption. Relief inversion occurs frequently in the course of the centuries, whereby elevations, hills or even new mountains develop out of what were originally depressions through the erosion of the rift's flanks.

The last major eruption occurred in March 1963, when Gunung Agung, after a long period of inactivity, ejected millions of tonnes of ash, burying whole villages. Gunung Batur, which almost always has a column of smoke above it, has again been experiencing minor eruptions since 1999.

Volcanism

A number of lesser islands belonging to the province of Bali (total area: 5561 sq km/2147 sq mi) are located south of the main island – separated by the Badung Strait (Selat Badung) – these include Nusa Penida (the largest), Nusa Ceningan and Nusa Lembongan as well as the small Turtle Island or Pulau Serangan, lying to the south of Bali right across the mouth of Benoa Bay. Situated off the coast of Bali's northwest is the uninhabited island of Pulau Menjangan. All are part of the Lesser Sunda Islands.

Lesser islands

← *As a food, rice plays a central role on Bali. A large number of rituals accompany its cultivation, from sowing to harvest.*

ISLAND TOPOGRAPHY

5561 sq km/2147 sq mi of earth of volcanic origin: Bali, the most western of the Lesser Sunda Islands, lies in the Indian Ocean between Java and Lombok. Its highest elevation, 3142m/10,308ft, is Gunung Agung, an active volcano. Gunung Agung, considered sacred by Hindus, last erupted in 1963.

① Central Bali

The central part of Bali is dominated by four separate volcano complexes, the highest of which is Gunung Agung (3142m/10,308ft) in the eastern part of the island. The Gunung Batur (1717m/5633ft) massif with a large crater lake forms the transition to northern Bali. Towering upwards further west are two more volcanoes: Catur (2096m/6877ft) and Batukau (2216m/7270ft). A mighty sight to behold, the volcano complex takes the form of an approximate V-shape that opens up to the south, the open side thus facing the capital Denpasar.

② South Bali

The south of Bali is the most fertile part of the island. It is characterized by humid alluvial plains made fertile by volcanic ash. These lie on the windward side of the central volcanic mountain range that slopes down to the south, and enjoy high amounts of precipitation throughout the year, providing ample moisture to the region. The most intensely cultivated areas of the island are here; for example rice cultivation take place in the area.

③ West Bali

Deep valleys between mountain ranges created during the Tertiary Period characterize the narrow western part of the island, most of which is included in the national park. In a sheltered position leeward of the mountains, it is considerably drier here than in the island's southern regions.

④ East Bali

The central Balinese mountain ranges stretch down close to the island's edge, determining the landscape in the east. Agung, the major volcano with a central peak and foothills sweeping in a north-south direction, dominates the landscape, as does the Batur volcano, whose massif forms the transition over to Central Bali.

⑤ Wallace Line

The so-called Wallace Line runs between Bali and its neighbouring island, Lombok. It is the biogeographic dividing line between Asian and Australian flora and fauna.

On the rim of Gunung Agung's crater

Fishing with a volcano
for a backdrop

The Wallace Line
runs between the
islands of Bali
and Lombok.

© Baedeker

The Bali starling or Bali mynah, a protected species, in Bali Barat National Park

Idyllic evening atmosphere on Kuta Beach

Artfully arranged rice terraces in the south of the island

Climate

Two Seasons Unusually for the Southeast Asian region, the prevailing weather conditions on the island of Bali are quite **stable**. The climate is dominated by two seasons, a »dry season« from around April to October and a »rainy season« from November until March. The climatic factors that play a role here have their origin on the Australian continent.

Precipitation Strong winds coming in from Australia beginning in November collect moisture over the ocean and then blow as a monsoon in the direction of Indonesia. These are partly responsible for the abundant rainfall that in Bali reaches its maximum in January. The lowest precipitation is recorded in August when hot, dry winds blow in from the north. But even in the half year of winter it is quite possible that while not one cloud is seen in the skies above southern Bali, elsewhere on the island it may rain for days.

Temperatures On the other hand, there is hardly any variation in the daily average highest temperature, which lies between 29.7°C/85.5°F and 31.6°C/88.9°F all year round on the coasts and in the flat interior of the island. This heat feels pleasant, relieved as it is by the constant cool breezes blowing in from the sea. The temperature in the hill country, however, is on average around 5 degrees lower, and in the early morning the difference can be even greater. Night time temperatures in the flatlands sink down to 8°C/46.4°F. The ocean water temperature is almost **like a warm bath** all year: the average temperature is around 27.9°C/82.2°F in April and it reaches 29°C/84.2°F in December.

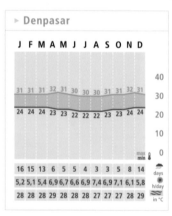

The average **hours of sunshine** between April and October is 6.9 to 7.5 hours a day, though during the remaining months it can be reduced because of cloud cover to as low as two hours at times. The relatively high **humidity** can occasionally be a bother to visitors from more northern climes. It rises to 80 percent in February, but sinks to only 5 percent in August and September. Those who feel uncomfortable in high humidity conditions should therefore travel to Bali between May–June and September–October; during the other months when the temperature is high the moist air can be almost unbearably oppressive.

Flora

Hardly any island of the Indonesian archipelago is so intensively cultivated as is Bali; wherever you look there are rice fields (also known as paddy fields – *padi* is the name of the growing rice plant). Even the smallest patch of earth manages to yield **up to two rice harvests per year**. But there is also another Bali to be found, for the most part in the west of the island in the Bali Barat National Park: tropical jungles made up in the lower regions of high-grade woods such as mahogany, and in the higher elevations of slender, tall-growing pines and diverse varieties of dipterocarp (Greek: two-winged fruit). Stretching out in the south are forests of palms, which give way to the large and small rice fields of the harmonious appearing landscape gently rising towards the interior. The southern coastal regions, on the other hand, may seem at first glance to be quite unimpressive. For its part, East Bali, where the mountains reach down close to the coast, still possesses reserves suitable for agriculture. The flora becomes thinner in the mountainous regions, where hardy, low-lying shrubs and plants dominate the landscape. This then gives way to a barren zone of black lava rock.

A wealth of rice fields and forests

> **❓ DID YOU KNOW ...?**
>
> ■ ...that to the Balinese, rice is much more than just a basic foodstuff? It is ceremonially offered to the gods in colours of red, black and white. Each rice field, each rice terrace, has many shrines, some even a temple. The laying out of a new rice field resembles a ritual festival based on traditional rites. The Balinese celebrate the fact that practically all year round the crop that has such significance to them can be planted and harvested in a single cycle.

The mighty banyan (Sanskrit: nyagrodha) tree, a variety of fig tree typical of Southeast Asia, is considered to be sacred. The ficus bengalensis in Bali reaches a height of up to 30m/98ft and possesses a broad crown whose branches are supported by numerous aerial roots. Banyan trees seldom grow alone and because they suppress other varieties of trees they can form whole forests.

Banyan tree

The banyan tree is considered to be **worthy of veneration** because Siddharta Gautama achieved a state of enlightenment in southern India under such a tree and is said to have later entered Nirvana as the first Buddha. Almost every village in Bali has one if not more banyan trees.

Bali's lush flora serves first and foremost to provide the population with food. Pineapples, bananas, vegetables, coffee, coconuts and betel nuts thrive on plantations. The betel nut, especially popular with the older generation, is a stimulant that acts on the parasympathetic nervous system and induces a heightened sense of awareness. It also possesses aphrodisiac properties. For consumption, small pieces of the not fully ripened **betel nut** are wrapped in a betel pepper plant

Agricultural crops

leaf brushed with lime and then chewed. The attraction of this narcotic is that although it has a euphoria-stimulating effect, it does not diminish the ability to work. However, with continuous use, it stains the teeth, saliva and lips red; furthermore, tannins in the betel nut can induce chronic inflammation of the oral cavity and increasing evidence suggests that they are carcinogenic, linked with oesophageal cancer. Although Balinese **coffee** is an important export commodity, the cultivation of tobacco, tea and spices has only secondary significance and because of the small amounts produced these crops are destined only for the local market. Great importance is attached to coconut palm and fast-growing bamboo, both being popularly used as building materials. There are less orchids here than in other Southeast Asian countries; **lotus blossoms**, on the other hand, are plentiful.

Lotus blossom

Fauna

Land fauna Balinese land fauna is no less diverse. Although many years ago the Bengal tiger was common in Bali, they are now considered to be extinct – at least none have been seen for a long time. Still calling the place home, however, are some smaller varieties of crocodile, monitor lizards, iguanidae and turtles. There are also snakes in the regions grown over with jungles, including poisonous varieties. There are great numbers of **monkeys living in the wilds** of the Balinese forests as well as many species of **tropical bird**. Along with quite a few varieties of parrot and finch, Bali is the last refuge of some 200 remaining specimens of the **Bali mynah** or Rothschild's mynah, a bird about 25cm/10in in size, white except for blue markings around the eyes and black-tipped wings and tail, which is threatened with extinction and is therefore rigorously protected. Bats and flying foxes are held to be sacred and are venerated.

Ill. p.150 ▶

Geckos The gecko (in Bali: tokeh), a Southeast Asian descendant of the lizard family, is an endearing, completely harmless little animal seen primarily in the evening and night time hours that has proven its usefulness in exterminating insects. Geckos like to gather in numbers around lamps and lanterns, call attention to themselves with quacking noises, but then disappear at the slightest attempt to approach them.

Domestic animals Among the domestic animals, the apparently slow and ponderous **water buffalo** is used as a beast of burden as well as to cultivate the rice fields, where hundreds of small ducks dive and feed on the bottom. Other domestic species often encountered include the **pot-bellied pig** and the **banteng**, a species related to the wild ox, as well as geese and chickens. Pig husbandry is of some significance in Bali but because the rest of Indonesia is Islamic sucking pigs and pork must be exported to such far-flung places as Hong Kong.

The ocean surrounding Bali is **rich in fish**. The catch consists primarily of tuna and perch. Fishing is not very intensely pursued because, according to Balinese belief, the ocean is the abode of many evil spirits and demons. One denizen of the deep, however, is revered as sacred, namely the black and white banded sea snake.

Nature and Environmental Protection

Environmental protection has only recently been attributed **greater status** in Bali. Problems with the environment, brought on not least by the flood of tourists, have become all too apparent. Just by walking through Denpasar, for example, a certain discrepancy becomes apparent. On the one hand, the Balinese are (as all Asians in general) very particular about cleanliness and hygiene in their own private spheres, but on the other hand, they allow the piles of

Pot-bellied pigs are considered a delicacy on Bali.

rubbish to grow ever higher and broken glass to accumulate on the beaches, posing a potential hazard for people going barefoot. In the absence of organized refuse disposal, trash is still fly dumped and ignited; waste water is simply piped into the ocean. Governmental campaigns have had little effect. The number of waste bins, at least, is being increased at the sites frequented by tourists.

Traffic The problems caused by the growing amount of motor vehicle traffic on the island is visible to the naked eye. At times, in Denpasar for example, thick exhaust fumes make a walk something of a strain. One of the causes of this particular problem is the distinctly bad habit of leaving the motor running while waiting. The high (and greatly increasing) number of motorbikes, an important form of transport for the Balinese, poses a marked environmental problem. Awareness of the need to develop a sensible way interacting with the natural environment is often sadly lacking. Many think nothing of changing their motor oil without bothering to collect the used oil. However, slowly but surely, a process of readjustment in Balinese thinking on these matters is taking place; in fact, methods are being considered for proper waste disposal and how to avoid generating so much.

Population growth A less obvious problem is that caused by the growing population on the island. Large families with a dozen children or more are the rule rather than the exception in Bali. In order to feed them all, more and more primeval forests are being cleared for agricultural purposes.

Soil erosion One of the unpleasant results of this not often taken into consideration is an increase in soil erosion. The forest loses part of its function as an important factor in a balanced climate. Fortunately, there have been no devastating floods and other natural catastrophes – apart from erupting volcanoes.

Future prospects The greatly increased sea traffic between Bali and Lombok and the Gili Islands, and the cleaning of the ships' motors that goes along with it, present no small danger for the coastlines. In addition, anchors often destroy parts of the beautiful coral reefs.

Population · Politics · Economy

Origins Indonesia is a **multi-national state**, which can be seen alone in the number of languages and dialects – more than 250 of them. The majority of the population, however, belongs to the Malaysian-Polynesian (Austronesian) family of nations, often called Protomalaysian or Old Malaysian. Originally, Bali was inhabited by nomadic peoples – as were some other Indonesian islands, too. A strong growth in population started around 3000 BC when peoples who had up to that point been living in southern China left their hereditary homeland and spread out over large parts of today's Southeast Asia. During the course of this migration, the extent of which can only be guessed at today, those groups familiar with the open seas reached, among other places, the Indonesian archipelago. These people had a close association to nature, and venerated their ancestors along with spirits and demons – indeed, elements of this religious belief are still retained today in the basic Balinese view of the world. A second major migration began shortly before the start of the Christian era. The Protomalaysian (Old Malaysian) people were joined by the Deutero-malaysian (Young Malaysian) people, who gradually merged completely with the original inhabitants of the island. Other peoples who settled in Bali and on its neighbouring islands (e.g. Chinese), however, have remained minorities to the present day.

Population At present around 3.4 million people live on the island of Bali. The annual rate of population growth has successfully been limited to 1.8% thanks to a **birth control** programme propagated by the Indonesian government (slogan: »Dua Anak Cupuk« = »two children are enough«). A problem is the fact that a male successor is still consid-

Facts and Figures Bali

Location
► The westernmost of the Lesser Sunda Islands (latitude 80° 30' south and longitude 115° east)
► Area: 5561 sq km/2147 sq mi

Indonesia
► Capital: Jakarta
► Administration: 30 provinces, 2 special regions and capital city district
► Form of government: presidential republic
► Parliament: House of Representatives (DPR) with 550 members and the House of Regional Representatives (DPD). Together they form the People's Consultative Assembly (MPR).
► Head of State: Susilo Bambang Yudhoyono (since October 2004)
► Red and white national flag. The national coat-of-arms displays Sang Radja Walik (Garuda) with extended wings holding a shield with the Five Principles (of State) (Panca Sila, see p.76).

Province of Bali
► Capital: Denpasar
► Administration: Bali is divided into eight administrative districts (kabupaten): Badung, Bangli, Buleleng, Gianyar, Jembrana, Karangasem, Klungkung and Tabanan. The smallest administrative unit is the quarter (banjar); these are joined together to form city districts or villages (desa), each headed by a mayor (walikota).

Economy
► The most significant economic factor is tourism: revenues approx. 1.5 billion US$/year; almost half of the working population is employed here.
► 65% of the island's area is used for agriculture (rice, vegetables); exports include coffee, coconuts, spices and pork.

© Baedeker

PHILIPPINES
Pacific Ocean
MALAYSIA
INDONESIA
Bali & Lombok
Indian Ocean
AUSTRALIA

Population
► Approx. 3.4 million persons
► Population density: 610 inhabitants per sq km/1580 per sq mi (compared with 367 per sq km/951 per sq mi in England)
► Population growth rate: 1.8%

Religion / Language
► Almost 95% Hindus; in contrast to the rest of Indonesia, Hinduism was able to maintain its ground against Islam in Bali.
► Balinese is increasingly being replaced in everyday life by Bahasa Indonesia, Indonesia's official language. English is common.

Bali Administrative Districts

Singaraja
BULELENG
JEMBRANA
BANGLI
Negara
KARANGASEM
TABANAN
Bangli
Amlapura
Tabanan
GIAN-YAR
Klung-kung
BA-DUNG
Gianyar
KLUNGKUNG
Denpasar

Advertising campaigns promote small families.

ered indispensable in Balinese society, above all to assume the father's religious responsibilities. The result is that the island population still continues to grow considerably and it seems there will be a time in the foreseeable future when Bali is overpopulated and the products of the island's agriculture alone are no longer sufficient to feed the Balinese people.

Urban migration Another problem in Bali is a certain amount of urban migration that has brought more and more people to the south of the island, in particular to the densely populated city of Denpasar, which is dominated by tourism. Here, people assume, the chances of earning a living are better.

Education Since 1984 there has been **general compulsory education** for the length of six years in Indonesia and thus also in Bali, followed by, when aptitude merits, a high school education (3 years junior and 3 years senior high school). Children start school between the ages of six and eight. Education at a state school is free. Denpasar has a university and two polytechnic colleges. Members of the Balinese upper class attend at least one of the colleges in the Indonesian capital of Jakarta or an institute of higher learning abroad. A **reduction in the rate of illiteracy**, which in 1971 was still around 40% in rural areas, has been achieved through stricter control of school attendance.

Health care The health care system in Bali is only modestly developed. Although in recent years there has been an increase in the number of doctors'

Bali Map

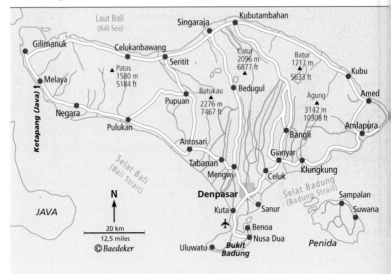

practices, the only hospitals are in Denpasar. However they are extremely poorly equipped and suited at best for primary care. Outside Denpasar there are heath centres (puskemas) maintained by the state in the cities, as well as medical out-patient clinics that are capable of handling the usual illnesses and minor injuries. The costs for medical treatment are borne by the Indonesian state, but medicine must be paid for by the individual. The treatment of severe diseases and serious injury due to accidents, on the other hand, is well-nigh impossible in Bali; such patients are usually transported to Jakarta. There are a couple of good Australian clinics in Denpasar that tourists can consider using. There is no well-developed rescue system approaching Western standards; particularly in the island's interior, the wait for a rescue vehicle can be a long one.

Politics

Ever since the severe economic crisis that began in Thailand in 1997 and spread out over all of Southeast Asia, Indonesian's state and society (at present 242 million inhabitants) has found itself in a phase of fundamental upheaval. In Indonesia in particular this has resulted at times in violent unrest, and though the island of Bali has by and large been spared a similar fate, it has been indirectly affected by the events in the region.

Ibrahim Suharto, the head of state who enjoyed absolute rule since 1967, was removed from office after bloody violence broke out in Ja-

Indonesia's current situation

karta. However his successor was also unable to solve Bali's economic problems and thus relieve the tension between people and government. With the economic crisis that began in 1997 and the overthrow of Suharto in 1998, a **process of democratization** could be observed. This led to Indonesia's first free and democratic elections in 2004. 24 parties were up for election; the strongest party, with 22%, was Golkar, a union of convenience of representatives of various sections of society. The PDI-P (19%) came out of the election as the second strongest party and assumed the role of the opposition in parliament as the »Indonesian Democratic Party – Struggle«. Although more than 90% of the population is of the Islamic faith, the Islamic parties garnered few MPs.

Tsunami At Christmas 2004 Indonesia suffered what was probably the greatest natural catastrophe in its history. An enormous tidal wave from a powerful seaquake, a so-called tsunami, hit the coastline of the Indonesian province of North Sumatra and Aceh, leaving death and destruction in its wake. 240,000 people died in the flood and villages and infrastructure were flattened.

Bali's history Bali gained its independence as far back as the 16th century, during the earliest times within Java's political sphere of influence. In the period when Java was being Islamized (up into the 16th century), Bali became a **refuge for Hindus**. In the 17th century, Bali also ruled over the island of Lombok and the eastern tip of Java. The Dutch had been trading in opium and slaves in Bali since 1826, and in 1839 Danish trader Mads Lange opened a trading post on the island at Kuta; in 1841 Bali's rajas signed treaties recognizing Dutch sovereignty. Between 1906 and 1908 Bali's states fell to the Netherlands – the Balinese opting for the suicidal fight to the death, the *puputan*, rather than surrender to the Dutch forces – and were annexed into the Dutch East Indies. The island was occupied by the Japanese during the Second World War from 1942 to 1945 and gained the status of an autonomous territory in 1946. In the same year, the Dutch returned to reimpose their sovereignty on those pre-war holdings that had not become a part of the newly formed Republic of Indonesia. The Balinese, having just become independent of foreign control, fought desperately under Ngurah Rai to remain so, but were brutally crushed. As the result of international pressure however, the Netherlands relinquished control in 1949 and Bali was incorporated into the Republic of Indonesia in 1950.

Economy

General Indonesia is a newly industrializing, so-called »threshold country«
information that for a long period participated in the economic upswing in the
about whole Southeast Asian region, until the onset of the severe financial
Indonesia and economic crisis. Since early 1997, when economic turbulence

emanating from Thailand severely affected the whole region, Indonesia's economic future has become more uncertain than ever before, even though the Indonesian economy was previously enjoying almost unfettered economic growth: annual growth rates of up to 8% were the rule. The fall in the price of export oil alone cast a shadow on the steadily upward trend of development (as a member of the Organization of Petroleum Exporting Countries, OPEC, Indonesia suffered especially badly). The World Bank linked their offer of aid to the condition that the banking industry – whose policy of unrestricted credit was seen to be one of the causes of the development – would be subject to fundamental reform. The president at the time, Jusuf Habibie, however, not only considered himself forced to accept the reforms but also to decree an emergency that resulted in a drastic reduction of state expenditure (with particular effect on the subvention of food). In turn, distrust grew in the population. Habibie was accused of opposing reform, not least because of his good relationship with Suharto, the ex-head of state, and was eventually voted out of office. Because of developments in the rest of Indonesia, Bali's economy also suffered, even though the agriculture dominating on the island was not affected to the same extent. The decline in Bali's tourist numbers was also only temporary; the advantageous exchange rate soon drew an increased number of visitors.

Rice cultivation continues to play a central role in Balinese agriculture. The development of the cleverly devised irrigation system for the **predominately terraced rice fields** dates back to the 6th century. Bali, one of the nation's smallest provinces, provides an impressive

Rice cultivation in Bali

Rice has left a great impression on Bali's culture and landscape.

5% of Indonesia's total rice harvest. This is mainly wet rice, i.e. rice grown on fields first artificially flooded with water. The water is drained away only after the hand-planted seedlings achieve a certain maturity. When the leaves of the stalks start to turn yellow, the rice is harvested – again by hand – and then threshed, after which it is ready for milling.

Sekaha and subak (cooperatives) A special feature of Bali's agriculture is the union of farmers of one or more village districts (banjar) in **cooperative organizations** called »sekaha«. These in turn are divided into groups, the »sekaha mena-nam« responsible for planting the fields, the »sekaha panen« for the harvest and the »sekaha me jukut« for weeding. A fourth group, the »sekaha bajak«, is responsible for ploughing. Revenues earned through the sale of the agrarian products are equally divided among the members of the sekaha, with a portion put aside as a reserve. In wet cultivation, the cooperatives are called »subak«. In southern Bali, they were presumably formed in the 16th century at the suggestion of the ruling princes of the time. The farmers in the north did it on their own initiative: at that time, not all farmers in a given banjar had their own irrigation canals so the others declared themselves willing to share their water. It is then the obligation of each member of the subak to not only contribute services to the association (e.g. dam building, monitoring and maintenance of the irrigation system), but also to pay a so-called water tax. The subak principle was there-fore created out of **village solidarity**; even today common law is still observed over, say, Indonesian positive law. A subak should not be considered just as a division of labour for rice planting; it is also a social group in which the Hindu religious conceptions of its mem-bers play an important role. Accordingly, the assembly of all subak members, for example, determines the scheduling of religious festi-vals and ceremonies honouring the rice goddess Dewi Sri and the water deity Vishnu (in South Bali, instead of Vishnu, the sea god Baruna is honoured; he has the task of keeping all vermin away from the rice). Every subak has its own temple (pura bedugul) standing among or on the edge of the rice fields. The farmers' major festival during the course of the year is the harvest festival (ngu saba), for which all subak members contribute offerings. Those who shirk the duties and obligations set forth by the association are imposed with a fine payable in kind (in many subaks, the fine is 1kg/2.2lb of rice to be delivered to the association). The head of a subak is a leader chosen by the general assemblage. He distributes the available water to the members, mediates disputes and leads the meetings. A com-prehensive reorganization was supposed to have taken place during the Dutch colonial period, but while the irrigation technology was made more efficient by the new masters, the organization of the sub-ak remained untouched. Since the early 1980s, a cooperative organ-ized on the model of the sekaha distributes loans to the farmers guaranteed by the Indonesian state bank.

Kuta is renowned for its wide beaches and good surfing conditions.

Other farm products

Other agricultural products are vegetables, rubber, tea and coffee (more than 10% of all of Indonesia's coffee is grown in Bali). The cultivation of vanilla is also lucrative; Indonesia is considered the second most important supplier of this flavouring after Madagascar. Recently, a small wine-growing area was established in the northeast of the island, though the quality of the product is still modest.

Fishing

Fishing tends to play a secondary role in Bali. The profits are so small that many fishing families live below the poverty line and depend on state welfare. For that reason, fish are mostly imported from Java. The Balinese belief that demons live in the ocean stands in the way of any serious intensification of fishing.

Tourism

The island of Bali is undoubtedly Indonesia's best developed region for tourism. Since the mid-1970s, tourist enclaves with hotel facilities reaching international standards were built, primarily in the south of Bali (Nusa Dua, Kuta, Legian, Sanur). From year to year, the revenues from tourism play an increasingly important role in the total national accounts. A stopover in Bali on flights between Europe and Australia is popular. Several million tourists visit Indonesia each year; an exact number cannot be determined because of the number of people from neighbouring Asian countries visiting their relatives is included. Between 1.5 and 2 million of these tourists come to the island of Bali, for the most part from Australia, Japan, the USA, Germany and the Netherlands. About 60,000 British visitors arrive on Bali's shores annually. The numbers declined in 2002 and 2005, but are now on the increase once more.

At prayer

Religion

Religious denominations Approximately **95% of all Balinese are Hindus**; other religions such as Buddhism, Islam and Christianity play only a minor role in Bali. This means the province has an **exceptional position within Indonesia** because, taking the country as a whole, about 87% of the population are Sunni Muslims. In the course of time, however, Buddhist elements have found their way into the Hindu-Balinese religion (Agama Hindu Dharma). Hinduism came to Bali from India by way of Java in the first century. There are only marginal differences between the Balinese version and its Indian original, though a **much less strict caste system** is practiced in Bali.

Hinduism

Balinese version of the world religion Hinduism is one of the world's four great religions. A total of about 850 million people profess this belief. In contrast to the monotheistic belief in one god, Hinduism, like Buddhism, Confucianism and Taoism, is a monistic religion orientated toward a depersonification principle. For some decades now however, a denomination has been gaining strength in Bali that noticeably approaches monotheism, recognizing one god with whom everything had its beginning: the **Sangyang Widi**, the »all-encompassing god«. The fundamentals of Hinduism developed over the course of millennia, but it presents no firmly structured religious principle. One of the original elements, which remains an essential part of Hinduism to this day, is Brahmanism, and this in turn took its basic concept from Vedism, an ancient Indian religion.

So what does a Hindu believe? Having become a human being, he has earned a place on the middle rung of the symbolic stepladder. Initially, he is caught in the eternal cycle of birth, death and rebirth of the soul (Samsara), which no living being escapes unless, after many non-quantifiable lives, he achieves entrance into Nirvana. In which mortal frame the soul of the Hindu is reborn is not predictable; a further existence as a human is possible, but that of an animal, plant or a celestial or hellish creature equally so. It is possible to influence the cycle, however: good or bad deeds (karma) are rewarded or punished in the next life with a better or worse existence. The goal of every Hindu, however, is to no longer need to be reborn, to enter Nirvana and thus break the cycle of birth–death–rebirth forever. To achieve this goal, it is important to observe the »**Three Paths of Salvation**« (Tiga Marga). The first prescribes offerings to the gods and demons and their manifestations; the second consists of the striving for knowledge and insight, respect for other people, especially priests and the elderly; the third provides for escaping the embrace of the five elements through the path of turning inwards (meditation), which is the only possible way to a union with the divine principle.

Eternal cycle of birth, death and rebirth

The Hindu also has a relatively solidly structured image of the cosmos based on mythological and philosophical concepts as well as simple observation of natural processes. The world, formed from the basic matter of the universe (prakriti), is in a constant cycle of development and destruction. These phases are separated from each other by a pause phase, a state of rest. Man sees himself as a small world (buwana alit) in a larger world (buwana acjung); he is therefore himself a part of the macro-cosmos.

Cosmology

The lotus (lotus: nelumbo) is the symbol for the concepts of Balinese Hinduism; it is regarded as a likeness of the world. In Bali, the **eight-leafed lotus (padma)** is portrayed more often than the four-leafed lotus (panca dewata). The eight direction gods – Vishnu, Sambu, Ishvara, Maheshvara, Brahma, Rudra, Mahadevi and San(g)kar – are arranged clockwise around the god Shiva in the centre. The deities are attributed with colour, personality and body organs, along with many other auspicious qualities and meanings; four of them stand for the four points of the compass: Vishnu for the north (kaja), Brahma for the south (kelod), Mahadevi for the

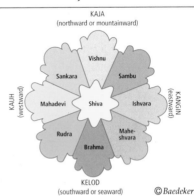

Hindu World System

KAJA
(northward or mountainward)

KAUH (westward)

KANGIN (eastward)

Vishnu

Sankara   Sambu

Mahadevi   Shiva   Ishvara

Rudra   Maheshvara

Brahma

KELOD
(southward or seaward)

© Baedeker

BUILT-IN BELIEF

The small boy stood in the gateway, made a beckoning gesture and said, »Come in, Mister! Please. Come in!« He took a step to the side of the narrow wall opening to clear the way leading into his parent's family compound (kampong).

The entrance to a Balinese family kampong is as narrow as possible and just behind it stands yet another shoulder-high wall, making a real obstacle course. Narrow openings and protective walls are an essential part of the family compound. **Because lurking outside are evil spirits, demons and other scary characters.**

Belief articulated in stone

If unwelcome guests of that ilk cannot be eradicated completely, then they should kindly stay outside.

Religious belief is the bedrock of Balinese architecture and is perhaps the most fitting explanation of why traditional family compounds are built in this manner in Bali. The family kampong consists of houses called »bales« and is surrounded by a solidly-built outside wall. It not only serves to ward off undesired, invisible guests, but is also the visible symbol of the cohesion of the Balinese extended family.

Uniformity of Balinese Villages

Visitors to the island may feel alienated by seeing exactly the same universal arrangement of buildings everywhere. Kampongs are lined up one after the other in a Balinese village with all of the door openings facing the same side. Inside the rectangular enclosing wall, the indispensable family temple invariably stands on the same spot and the arrangement of the individual buildings is almost a stereotypical repetition; at least no essential differences can be seen at first glance. Rich or poor, the family temple, living and sleeping buildings, kitchen, rice granary, shelter for domestic animals and

bale for a variety of ritual occasions are arranged with dependable uniformity on every rural premises. Only one feature distinguishes a family's higher rank in the social hierarchy. Wealthy Balinese have one additional bale in which ceremonies prescribed by Hinduism are held.

The number of houses for living and sleeping is determined by the size of the family living in the compound. The most prestigious, always situated directly next to the family shrine, is that of the grandparents who enjoy the greatest esteem in the family. Occasionally unmarried girls and young women also live in the grandparent's bale. Without exception, the children of each sex sleep separately. It is the rule and not the exception in Bali, at least in the rural areas, that the whole extended family sleeps under

one roof, so to speak. More often than not, three or even four generations live in a single family compound. After a wedding, the freshly married bridal couple moves into the kampong of the groom's family.

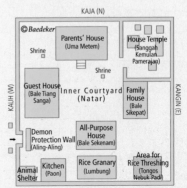

west (kauh) and Ishvara for the east (kangin). The lotus blossom can be found in Bali in a variety of forms as a **symbol for the Hindu-Balinese religion**, e.g. carved in stone or as one of the most sacred elements of batik art.

Castes

From birth on, every individual belongs to a caste (Indian: »varna«). The transition from one caste to another is, on principle, only possible through the process of rebirth, that is, in the next life. Although the origins and sense of the caste system remains a mystery to this day, it is assumed that the members of the first caste sought to preserve their ethnic, cultural and social traditions within a firmly structured unit (clan, village), unadulterated by influences from outside. Over the course of the centuries, however, a complicated system developed out of these four castes through mixed marriages and the admittance of persons alien to the castes who gradually superseded the traditional division. Originally there were only four castes: Brahman (priests), Ksatrias (warriors), Wesias (farmers and craftsmen) and Shudras (labourers). Those who did not belong to a caste were largely ostracized by society and considered in India as a »paria«, an »untouchable«. This is a classification not adopted in Bali, however, where only four castes are known. Although marriage into another caste is possible, there are problems attached to it. What has remained is the traditional high standing enjoyed by the Brahmans. That is mostly because princes, intellectuals and officials belong to this caste.

Sacred animals

Unlike India, Bali has no sacred animals. The pious Balinese Hindu (with the exception of the Brahmans) is allowed to eat beef.

Hindu pantheon

In the Hindu concept, all forms of life (plants, animals, humans) have a place on the stepladder. The highest step belongs to the gods and deities that inhabit the pantheon on **»Mount Meru«**; underneath them are saints, kings and, at the lowest level, spirits and demons. There is a multitude of gods and deities. The »divine« trinity **(Trimurti)** is considered the most important: Brahma, Vishnu and Shiva. **Brahma**, the creator of the world, was once the highest god in Hinduism. Today he has about the same status as Shiva and Vishnu. **Vishnu** is the upholder of the world, who took on human form as Krishna. **Shiva** is considered the destroyer and undoer of the world. In Bali, one of his many manifestations is called **Sangyang Guru**. Shiva is often portrayed as alingam (phallic symbol). The wives of Brahma, Vishnu and Shiva are named Sarasvati, Lakshmi and Shakti; they symbolically stand for knowledge, happiness and sacred power. There is an important difference between the traditional Indian Hinduism that has monotheistic characteristics and that followed by most of the believers in Bali. They believe in **Sangyang Widi**, a god who holds the all-encompassing divine principle within him. He is the supreme deity in Balinese Hinduism and corresponds to the incarnation of all three main gods. The rice goddess **Dewi Sri** is one of the most important goddesses. Her name has Sanskrit origins and means something like »goddess of brilliance«. At the time of the year's first rice harvest, she assumes the form of grains of rice (nini), which in turn are venerated as the personification of Shiva. **Dewi Danu** is also veryimportant; first and foremost within her sphere of influence is Lake Batur, and she is also venerated as the ruler of other lakes. Two of Vishnu's numerous manifestations are the god **Dewa Sedana** and his wife **Dewi**. They are considered to be the god and goddess of prosperity and wealth and are therefore especially eagerly worshipped at temple festivals. Further down in the hierarchy are gods whose responsibilities include

Representation of the rice goddess, Dewi Sri, on the edge of a field

natural phenomena and the forces of nature: Indra (rain), Surya (sun), Soma (moon), Vayu (wind), Agni (fire), Varuan (masses of water), Yama (death), Kama (love), Kubera (riches), Skanda (war) and Ganesha (elimination of obstacles). There are some gods among the lower orders that to a greater or a lesser extent intervene in the course of the world, playing either a good or an evil role.

The lowest rung on the ladder of Hindu belief is occupied by spirits and demons, a multitude of which are to be found far below the level of the gods and deities. Although spirits and demons are loathed manifestations, some of them have the extremely important task of keeping even worse spirits away from temple grounds.

Spirits and demons

Religious Traditions

There is a great diversity of religious customs in Bali, but they all have one thing in common; they are always a welcome excuse for a festival, celebrated either within the family circle or, as is usually the case, together with the other villagers. The rituals, usually of Hindu origin, that are held before or after a transition to a different stage in life are especially important in the lives of the Balinese. Strictly speaking, the **transition from one phase in life to the next** corresponds to a »small death«; the beginning of a new phase in life, on the other hand, to a »small rebirth«. The people in Bali call these transitional points »manusia yadnya«.

Life in Bali is marked by many festivals

Pregnancy and birth The purpose of the various ceremonies carried out during the first months of pregnancy is to keep evil spirits away from the embryonic life and allow the good ones to enter the body of the new addition to the human race. Sacrifices in the temple play here a major role, which can only be offered by relatives and close friends because the mother is consider unclean during pregnancy and cannot enter a temple or set foot on a rice field. When the child is born, ritual prescribes the placing of the kanda mpat, his »four mythical brothers and sisters« (uterine water, placenta, umbilical cord und blood) in a painted coconut shell next to the bedroom door. The god Rare Kumara, for whom a separate place of offering is prepared, watches over the child from above the bed. Bands and bracelets and anklets are put on the baby's wrists and ankles that are meant to keep evil spirits at bay. On the 12th and 42nd day after birth, the mother and child must undergo a further cleansing ceremony of Brahmanic origin. Before the 210th day (the first birthday according to the Balinese calendar), the child is carried everywhere; its feet are not allowed to touch the ground. A great festival is held on this day and the child is set on the ground for the first time, officially crossing over the boundary between divine transcendence and mortal existence. The child and its »four brothers and sisters« are given new names to confuse the spirits.

Puberty Normally after entering puberty, both boys and girls are subjected to the **ritual of tooth filing** (matatah). This involves a Brahman priest filing the four upper incisors as well as both canine teeth (which belong to the gods) into an even line; the lower teeth remain unfiled because they belong to the demons. This eliminates the six evils (greed, jealousy, stupidity, lust, anger and lack of self-control) that are tolerated in the child but not in the adult. The procedure of tooth filing is very painful; nevertheless, this ritual of initiation is considered to be an extremely important step in the life of a (Hindu) Balinese that must be taken. Moreover, young people are only then considered marriageable. In many regions in Bali today, tooth filing is only done symbolically.

Circumcision The ceremony of circumcision is now only performed on boys whose parents profess Islam (particularly on the neighbouring island of Lombok). A few ethnologists are of the opinion, however, that tooth filing, as a ritual of initiation, has a similar function.

The teeth are all reduced to equal length in the tooth filing ceremony.

Strictly speaking, marriage is only possible between members of the same caste. There is the possibility of getting around this: the groom must abduct the bride – with her consent – and hide out for seven days. After this period of time, the caste constraint is lifted. With marriage, the Balinese man gains the right and responsibility of performing in future all of the rituals his parents had performed up to this point in time. As a sign that he is now a fully-fledged member of society, he assumes responsibility for the well-being of the gods honoured in the family's house temple. The family gathers several times during the year for this purpose, with all family members travelling to their native village for the occasion.

Death is an important transitional rite of the Hindus. It is the passage from the material and sensual world. The body, originally provided with breath by Brahma, is now seen as a **shell for the soul** and disintegrates after death, reverting back onto its five components, the elements earth, air, fire, water and ether. These again enter the world of the gods and demons. Visitors will search in vain for cemeteries along Western lines in Bali because the dead are cremated according to Hindu ritual, although the body of the deceased is first buried for a period of at least 42 days; Brahman priests are embalmed according to strict regulations and lie in state until a date determined by an astrologist using complicated calculations. After the minimum period of 42 days, which often extends to several months or even years, the mortal remains are disinterred and prepared for cremation. If little remains, a sandalwood doll is used symbolically in place of the corpse. Whether the time that the soul must remain in the body is short or long is determined by the relatives' financial situation because cremation of the dead is an expensive matter. To facilitate the soul's escape from the body, an open bamboo tube is placed in the mouth.

Cremation

Celebration

The cremation of the dead is probably the most extravagant celebration in Bali, serving as it does to make possible the smooth passage of the deceased to another, better world. The preparations can take weeks, even months.

Preparations and procession

After the body has been exhumed three days before cremation, it is cleansed and wrapped in clothes and laid in a transport coffin, richly adorned with flowers and a number of ritual accessories, that is used to carry the corpse in a **colourful procession** from the home of the deceased to the cremation grounds. But the event in no way resembles a silent and solemn funeral procession; rather it is a joyful event. Even though the death of a close relative causes sadness and pain, the Balinese live in the hope that the deceased will be born into a better existence in his next life. Often the body is transported in a cremation tower (bade), a pagoda-like structure up to eleven stories high. The relatives of the deceased are not the only ones to follow the coffin; almost all of the villagers join the procession. A gamelan orchestra provides the funeral music, which transports the crowd to a state close to ecstasy. On the way to the cremation grounds, the bearers of the cremation tower will suddenly turn in circles or even abruptly strike out in another direction; this is meant to confuse the spirits. Often the deceased's first-born sits on one of the lower floors of the cremation tower, which, because of its flimsy construction, is not particularly safe.

Coffin forms of the different castes

Upon reaching the cremation grounds, the body is removed from the transport coffin or bade and placed in the cremation coffin. To which caste the deceased belonged can easily be seen from this coffin. Brahmans (e.g. priests) have them in the form of a black and white spotted bull. If it looks like a lion or a stag, then the deceased belonged to the Jaba or Wesia caste. Members of the Ksatria caste have cremation coffins in the form a black bull for men and white bull for women with a colourful snake or dragon figure carried ahead of it. The cremation coffins of the members of the Pasek caste are an ex-

Cremation after death is one of the most important ceremonies: the fulfilment, as it were, of the sacred duties of every Balinese.

ception; while the coffins of the aforementioned castes are capable, as it were, of rising into the skies (the Hindus envision the lion with wings and the bull is considered to be the mount of the god Shiva), they are cremated in a coffin based on Gajah Mina, the elephant-headed fish.

Finally, the coffin is set on fire and while the soul rises into the air through the **cleansing fire**, the mood of the crowd rises to the verge of rapture. Then the transport shrine is also set on fire. After everything has burned, the relatives gather the ashes and lightly singed pieces of bone and lay them in a small litter that is then carried in a procession to the sea (or a nearby river) and committed to the water.

Cremation

The elaborate ritual is not nearly over with the cremation, however. On precisely prescribed days after the cremation follow yet other, not so elaborate ceremonies meant to help cleanse the soul of the dead from all wickedness and evil.

Temple Festivals

Odalan festivals on temple anniversaries

Every temple in Bali annually celebrates its anniversary or birthday, i.e. the anniversary of its original consecration. The whole village takes part in these odalan festivals. As a rule, the preparations take weeks or even months. The exact time, however, that particular preparations may begin – for example making the offerings – is decided by skilful calculations that a Brahman carries out according to the Javanese-Balinese calendar. The **gods are symbolically invited** to the temple festivals, coming down from the Pantheon and taking a seat in the precinct of the holy temple (bale paruman) that has been prepared and specially cleansed for them. From there, they can monitor how precisely the prescribed rites are followed.

Three days of festivals

The temple anniversary festival **lasts three days**, each day serving to fulfil a particular task. On the first and most important festival day, the gods are received in the temple, which has been cleansed and decorated with colourful cloths, and provided with offerings. So that the gods won't be annoyed by the odd demon who may possibly be wandering around, the villagers butcher a pig on the first morning and its meat is placed at a suitable spot ready for the demons. Then the Brahman priests take small figures of sandalwood out of the gedong – a small, closed building in the inner courtyard of the temple – and take them with dignified steps to a small pavilion where they are cleansed with holy water (tirtha), dressed and displayed. When the time approaches for the gods to arrive, the priests light a pot of incense. The rising smoke is meant to serve the gods as a symbolic stairway from heaven. Accompanied by the booming of an ever louder clanging gong, the gods begin their descent. The crowd of people, who arrived earlier in the temple precinct with elaborately stacked layers of offerings, is now fascinated and participates in this absolute highpoint, becoming reverently quiet. The gods are now ready to be honoured. For this, they use the help of the priests. The crowd is sprinkled with consecrated water; lotus blossoms are taken between the fingers tips, raised three times above the brow and finally let fall. Symbolic washings of the face and torso follow. Women bear offerings in the form of skilfully stacked fruit and food into the temple where they are accepted by the priests and symbolically presented to the gods. These offerings are usually picked up again in the evening, the gods having taken the spiritual essence of the fruit by then. The gods then have the opportunity to observe the three days of festivities that is now begun with great exuberance. They are entertained as much by the cock fights, shadow theatre performances

Magnificent offerings at a temple anniversary celebration

(wayang) and musical background provided by the gamelan orchestra as the villagers. On the second day, the village is cleansed of all the wickedness and evil left over from the previous year. On the third day, the evil spirits are driven out, naturally with the help of the gods, and the temple and village are prepared for the waiting new year. Late in the evening, the gods are bid farewell. The clothing is taken off the sandalwood figures and they are then taken back to the gedong. The festival ends with the closing of the inner gates of the temple; the inner precinct will only be opened to the public again during the next temple anniversary.

History

When did Hinduism and Islam come to Bali? What effect did the influence of the Dutch East India Company have? Who was the first Indonesian president after independence? And how many victims did the 2004 tsunami in Indonesia claim?

Prehistory and Early History

500,000 years ago	Oldest evidence of humans on Java (Homo erectus)
200–100 BC	Migration from the Southeast Asian mainland

The oldest evidence of human life in Indonesia was uncovered on the island of Java in the form of remains of early human beings (**Java man**; *c*500,000 years ago), which have been classified as Homo erectus. Several fossil skulls of so-called Solo man were found in the 1930s; they resemble Neanderthal man. Traces of Palaeolithic cultures on Sumatera (Sumatra), Kalimantan (Borneo) and Sulawesi (Celebes) show a similarity to those of the Southeast Asian subcontinent, which was connected by land to a greater part of Indonesia during the Ice Age. Several waves of people emigrated from the Southern Asian mainland during the second and first centuries BC.

Influences from India

6th–7th century	The Hindu Empire of Srivijaya had control over a large part of what is now Indonesia.
9th–10th century	The Hindu religion increasingly gains in importance in Bali.
from 1037	Javanese versions of both Hindu epic dramas of creation, the Ramayana and Mahabharata, are formed during the rule of Raja Erlangga.

The Hindu Kingdom of Srivijaya existed in the seventh century in southeastern Sumatra. Its centre was near the present-day city of Palembang and it controlled the flow of trade in the Malacca and Sunda straits. Indian culture and religion influenced the leading classes of society on the main island of Indonesia. An **ingenious irrigation system** was developed in Bali. Alongside the language already existing in Bali, the use of Sanskrit spread.

Hindu Kingdom of Srivijaya

The Javan princess Mahendratta of the Mataram Dynasty married the Balinese prince Udaya around 1000. **Bali and Java were united** under the rulership of their son Erlangga (1016–42) and experienced

Mataram and Singharasi dynasties

← *A water nymph seducing a demon (scene from the Hindu epic, Ramayana) painted on cloth* a cultural heyday at that time. In 1284, Kertanagara, the last of the East Javan rulers of the Singharasi Dynasty, conquered Bali; however he soon lost it again. The seat of the government of the Hindu empire was moved from Mataram (central Java) to East Java. **Hindu thought** emanating from here increasingly gained in importance in Bali.

Majapahit Empire The Majapahit Empire, the last great Javanese empire, spread out over large parts of Indonesia between the 13th and the 16th century. The initial basis for a system of administration was created in Bali. In the 15th century, merchants from the Middle East began spreading **Islam**. The decline of the Majapahit Empire began in the first half of the 16th century. The son of the last prince fled with his followers to Bali where he founded the **Gelgel Dynasty**. Sultanates were founded in Bantam in West Java and in Demak in East Java.

Colonialization

1487	With the discovery of a sea route to India, Europeans advance for the first time into South Asia.
1602	The Dutch East India Company begins colonizing the Indonesian archipelago.
1839	Bali is placed under Dutch control.
c1900	The Dutch gain sovereignty over all of Indonesia.

European influence Afterthe discovery of the sea route to India (1487), the Europeans pushed into South Asia. The Portuguese began building fortresses in the early 16th century in the east of the Indonesian archipelago, not least to challenge Oriental merchants in the lucrative spice trade. About one hundred years later, the Dutch also gained a foothold there, initially establishing bases on Java. The **founding of the Dutch East India Company** followed in 1602, which greatly expanded its sphere of influence under Governor-General Jan Pieterzoon Coen, the founder of the city of Batavia (1619; today's Jakarta). Following the fall of the Gelgel Dynasty in Bali, the island disintegrated into a dozen independent principalities. There were continual armed conflicts between the individual rulers. The regency of Klungkung was established in 1686. The independent Balinese rajas recognized the Dewa Agung of Klunkung as having the highest ceremonial rank. The Dutch East Indies fell to Great Britain during the Napoleonic Wars in Europe. From 1811 to 1816, Stamford Raffles, the founder of Singapore, held power in Java. In 1816, the East Indies were returned again to the Netherlands. The colonial power then became involved in bitter struggles with insurgents.

A Balinese prince with his entourage

In the1830s, the colonial administration started building up a well-devised plantation economy with payment in natural produce replacing the forced labour practised until then. It was also dictated to the farmers in Bali what their main crops were to be, namely **rubber, coffee and tea**. The traditional cultivation of rice, on the other hand, was neglected, which subsequently led to famine. After Bali became subject to Dutch rulein 1839, a Dutch expeditionary force landed in 1846 and placed part of the Island under its administration. As of 1870, Indonesia was opened up to European capital and enterprise. In 1882, Singaraja became the official seat of the Dutch administration. On 26 August 1883, the volcano Krakatau (part of an island group between Sumatra and Java) erupted. Tens of thousands of people fell victim to this tremendous natural catastrophe. The **discovery of oil** on Sumatra (1885) led to the formation of »Royal Dutch Shell«, which was later to become one of the world's largest oil companies. The Dutch gained control of all of Indonesia around 1900. The plundering of a Chinese merchant sailing ship provided the Dutch with a welcome excuse to expand their power over Bali. A blockade was imposed on the southern part of the island, which was also placed under colonial administration, and war was declared on

Effects of the plantation economy

◀ Dutch sovereignty

the Prince of Badung. In September 1906, Dutch soldiers undertook a further punitive expedition against Bali, during the course of which they also attacked the civilian population. The Balinese royal family, together with members of the upper class, resolved to seek death in a ritual suicidal assault (called a *puputan*) against the Dutch.

Independence movements

Two years later, all of Bali was declared a **Dutch colony**. In the early 20th century, several independence movements, influenced by Islam, began a struggle against the Dutch colonial power, among them the »Budi Utomo« (»Pure Endeavour«) and the »Sarekat Islam« (»Union of Islam«). The Indonesian Communist party was established around 1920, and in the subsequent period, freedom fighters joined together in the »Partai Nasional Indonesia« (PNI), formed in 1927 by **Raden Ahmed Sukarno** (▶Famous People).

Asian influence

In the firsthalf of the 20th century, Chinese immigrants were able to gain key positions in commerce and business. This led to clashes with the Malayan population. In 1938, the historic principalities were re-established in Bali, but they were not to achieve their former importance. Japanese troops occupied the Dutch East Indies during the Second World War, and Europe's position of supremacy in Bali was ended.

Independent State

1945	Independent declaration of the Republic of Indonesia by Raden Ahmed Sukarno and Mohammed Hatta
1946	Bali is the scene of bitter battles of resistance by Indonesians against the Dutch.
1950	Dissolution of historic principalities and establishment of governmental districts. Sukarno becomes president of the new Republic of Indonesia.
1959	Denpasar made capital of Bali.
1966	General Suharto takes over power.

Indonesian independence

The Indonesian Nationalists were able to organize and establish a state and declared Indonesia's independence on 17 August 1945. **Sukarno became the first president** of the new republic. Initially, the capital was Yogyakarta (later Jakarta). The Dutch attempted in 1947 and 1948 to regain their sovereignty by force. Under pressure by the UN and the USA, however, they were forced to recognize Indonesia's independence (first of all as the »Republic of the United States of Indonesia«) at the Hague Round Table Conference of 1949. Indonesia, however, remained tied to the Dutch crown until 1954.

Indonesian President Achmed Sukarno (right) and General Suharto (left) after a session with the country's military and civilian leaders (1966).

Sukarno institutionalized his system of a »Guided Democracy« in 1959. He endeavoured to achieve a balance between the various domestic powers (religious groups, parties, military). The state also guided the economy, paying especially close attention to limiting the influence of foreign companies. Despite this, the country was shaken by internal conflict, which reached its height in the **Darul Islam rebellion**. Dutch New Guinea came under Indonesian control in 1963. A little later, Sukarno became involved in a confrontation with the neighbouring state of Malaysia (temporary resignation from the UN, 1965–66), and increasingly worked together with the communists as well as seeking support from the People's Republic of China. A communist initiated revolt took place in the autumn of 1965, which General Suharto was able to crush; for several months, communists and Chinese were the victims of bloody persecution. In March 1966 the military government led by Suharto seized power and ousted Sukarno. The new leaders put an end to the policy of confrontation and attempted to end social and economic injustices with aid from Western countries. Relations with the People's Republic of China were suspended in 1967. Indonesia took part in the founding of the »Association of South Asian Nations« (ASEAN), and, in 1968, Suharto had himself elected **president**. The Indonesian government propagated a national family planning programme for the whole country; its motto, »Dua Anak Cukup« (»two children are enough«) was in-

»Guided Democracy«

Suharto seizes power

◄ Ill. p.26

Megawati Sukarnoputri at an election campaign meeting (1999)

tended to contribute to the lowering of the birth rate. In 1969, the controversial incorporation of West New Guinea took place, today the province of Iran Jaya. The general elections of 1971, 1977, 1982 and 1993 brought victory to the »Sekber Golkar«, a coalition of civil servants, technocrats and military men loyal to the government. Disregarding international protests, Indonesia annexed East Timor in 1976, which had been Portuguese East Timor up to that point. A resumption of diplomatic relations was agreed upon with China in July 1990.

Economic crisis At the beginning of 1997, the whole of Southeast Asia was gripped by an economic crisis originating in Thailand. The Indonesian rupiah lost close to two-thirds of its original value. The old resentments against Indonesians of Chinese descent erupted in the population once again; further fuelled by the dramatic rise in the price of basic foodstuffs, severe unrest broke out in the capital of Jakarta and soon engulfed the whole island nation. Bali was affected only slightly by these events. Although there were some demonstrations in Denpasar, they remained of little consequence. One focus of public criticism though was Suharto's well-established system that refused at first to carry out the state and social reforms demanded by the World Bank. Only after clashes between students and the military, some of which were bloody, did Suharto feel compelled to announce his resignation on 21 May 1998. **Bacharuddin Jusuf Habibie**, Suharto's close friend, took his place, declaring he was prepared to carry out the reforms needed to help get the ailing economy back on its feet. Although the opposition assured their support, they made no secret of the fact that they considered Habibie to be no more than a transitional president. Renewed unrest flared up in November 1998 when the reforms were slow in delivering the desired results. Once again, Jakarta was the centre of the turmoil. Surprisingly, Habibie did not put forward his candidature in the new elections in October 1999 and was subsequently relieved by Abdurrahman Wahid.

The Islamic scholar, Wahid (also called Gus Dur), quickly named **Megawati Sukarnoputri**, the daughter of the nation's founder, Sukarno, as vice president and promised a radical new beginning. One of the signs that made these intentions believable was the granting of independence for the long-disputed territory of East Timor. The favourable exchange rate in 1999 brought Bali an **increase in visitors** of about four percent. Meanwhile, there were fierce clashes on the neighbouring island of Lombok between religious and ethnic minorities, leading to street fighting and looting. Tourists still remaining on the island were evacuated to Bali. In 1999, the Gunung Batukau volcano in Bali erupted. The eruptions were less severe than expected and there were no casualties.

Abdurrahman Wahid's Presidency

The Present

2002	Bomb attack claims 202 lives in Bali.
2004	First free and secret elections
2004	A tsunami devastates Southeast Asia.
2005	Renewed attacks in Bali (22 deaths)
2006	An earthquake and another tidal wave claim several thousand lives on Java.
2007	UN Climate Change Conference takes place in Bali.
2008	Suharto dies on 27 January at the age of 86.

The 21st century was greeted in Bali with the hope for domestic stability in Indonesia as well as further growth of the revenue-bringing tourism industry. The news that East Timor was to be granted independence in 2002 and that the island would from then on form its own nation, the independent »República Democrática de Timor-Leste«, was greeted positively by the international media.

East Timor Independence

Adevastating Islamic terrorist attack caused a huge shock internationally. On 12 October 2002, a bomb exploded in a bar in Kuta, followed seconds later by a second bomb detonated in the popular Sari

Terrorist attack in Kuta

Club, a disco frequented mainly by Australians. 202 people were killed and over 200 seriously injured. Most of the victims were tourists. Members of the **Jemaah Islamiyah terrorist organization** claimed responsibility.

170,000 Indonesian victims of a Tsunami

In 2004, an event occurred that was almost beyond the imagination. On 26 December, **the most powerful seaquake in Indonesian history** took place. A huge tidal wave or tsunami, measuring up to 15m/49ft in height, hit the coastlines: the worst-affected area was Sumatra in the region around Banda Aceh. In Indonesia, about 170,000 people died. But it didn't stop there. Yet another bomb attack by Islamist terrorists cost the lives of 22 people on 1 October 2005, when three explosives were detonated in Jimbaran and Kuta. Some of the extremists identified as the masterminds behind the bomb attacks

Not forgotten –
a floral salute to the victims of the tsunami

are still at large, and government departments in the UK, USA and Australia continue to warn of possible attacks in the future. Those destinations frequented by foreigners are considered to be the most endangered. Java was also hit by its own catastrophe; in May 2006 an earthquake near Yogyakarta resulted in the deaths of 6000 people and hundreds of thousands being left without shelter.

Recognition of Indonesia as a democratic state

In this extremely dangerous time, observers are especially grateful for positive political developments. Since 2004, the Indonesian president has been elected by the people – Indonesia is now officially recognized as a democratic state. The first directly-elected president was the retired general, **Susilo Bambang Yudhoyono**, who took over from Megawati Sukarnoputri, the daughter of the founder of the nation, Sukarno. Sukarnoputri had been in office since 2001.

Bali Roadmap

In 2007, the UN Climate Change Conference, hosted by the Government of Indonesia, took place at the Bali International Convention Centre. Its 10,000 participants included representatives from over 180 countries. The conference culminated in the adoption of the Bali Roadmap, which consists of a number of forward-looking decisions that represent the various tracks essential to tackling climate change. Part of the Roadmap, the Bali Action Plan, charts the course for a new negotiating process to be completed in 2009.

Suharto's death

On 27 January 2008, at the age of 86, Indonesia's second president General Suharto, died of multiple organ failure. He had ruled the republic for 32 years until being compelled to announce his resignation on 21 May 1998. He left office in the face of mass protests over corruption and abuses of human rights, but did not stand trial on health grounds.

Art and Culture

How can demons be kept away from temple grounds? What must be considered when making a Rangda mask? How is a double ikat produced? In which of the typical dances are the feelings and actions of a warrior portrayed? And what are the distinguishing features of a gamelan orchestra?

The Balinese play a special role in the Indonesian republic. The primary reason for this is that, despite quite a number of challenges from outside, Bali has managed to maintain its religious traditions and with them its cultural independence. This does not mean, however, that over the course of the centuries Bali has remained an island totally beyond the influence of foreign cultures, but Hinduism has always remained the most influential religion, even if the form practiced today in Bali is moving towards the veneration of a single godhead more indicative of a monotheistic faith. Given this background, there have of course also been changes in the cultural life, which have eventually had an influence on artistic depictions. Compared with the diversity of representational means that, for example, were used on neighbouring Java before Islamization, Balinese art, especially that of earlier centuries, may seem folkloric, even simplistic. On the other hand, Balinese temples are impressive precisely because of their simple design and decoration. Here, the flat or sculpted representation of motif and meaning are always a means to an end, having only the task of making religion and religious views tangible.

Cultural independence

Temple Architecture

Compared with the colourful splendour of Thai temples, the religious sites in Bali are rather plain, functional buildings. But when a festival is held, Balinese temples are decorated, dressed up to the nines with flowers, colourful strips and cloths. A temple that is anticipating no festival or where one had already been celebrated stands there still and abandoned, quite often locked up.

Richly decorated for temple festivals

The island of Bali is often considered to be one huge temple: the western tip of the island with the port city of Gilimanuk represents the entrance gate, and the mountains in the east (Gunung Agung and Gunung Batur) are symbols for the mountain of the gods, Meru. Most of the temples in Bali, by the way, are aligned toward these mountains (kaja = mountainward), while their entrances face the sea (kelod = seaward). There are more than 20,000 temples (pura in the local vernacular) in Bali. This figure does not include the family temples (sanggah) in every pekarangan or kampong (family compound). The highest ranking temples are the **six »state temples«** (unofficial count), the Pura Besakih being the most important. Other honoured temples are the sea temple, Pura Tanah Lot, and the mountain temple, Pura Batukau. Some natural shrines dedicated to the gods of the mountains, the seas, and the rivers and springs are also highly revered. Temples equipped with places to bathe, not only for the gods

← *It takes an elaborate make-up and dressing ceremony to make the legong dancers look like princesses.*

but also for mere mortals, have a special role (e.g. Pura Tirtha Empul (Holy Water) near Ubud).

Three Temples As a rule, a village community owns not just one but three temples. The **Pura Puseh** is the main temple, dedicated to the god Brahma (the god of creation) and always built on the side of the village facing the holy mountain of Gunung Agung. The village community gathers in the **Pura Desa** (occasionally also called PuraBale Agung, and dedicated to Vishnu, the maintainer of world order) to hold the general religious ceremonies, while the **Pura Dalem**, which is usually outside the village near to the place of cremation, is dedicated to the goddess Durga (one of the incarnations of Shiva, the god of death and destruction) and hosts the ceremonies accompanying cremations. The Pura Dalem temple always faces the sea. The temple facili-

Typical village temple

ties in Bali do not serve all of the inhabitants of the province; rather they belong to either a family, a whole village community, an occupational group or a caste. An exception is the so-called state temple or royal temple. These are used in common by all the islanders.

Temple grounds

A temple in Bali usually corresponds to the layout of a typical kampong or family compound; it always faces the mountain and consists of three courtyards. They are not only considered to be a symbol for the three worlds (upper, middle and underworld), but also indicate the continuing cycle of birth, death and rebirth. The Jaba Tengah (middle courtyard), in which believers gather during a temple festival to prepare and become attuned for the arrival of the gods, is entered through the first courtyard (Jaba Sisi), where primarily non-religious structures can be found. The jeroan, the holiest area of the temple, is almost exclusively reserved for the gods and their earthly representatives, the priests. Normal mortals may only enter to bring offerings.

Structure of Balinese temples

Candi bentar

The first courtyard of a temple compound is almost always entered through an elaborately decorated, so-called **split gate** (candi bentar), whose passageway is relatively narrow. Its form goes back to a legend. When Mount Mahameru, seat of all Hindu gods, was transported to the island of Bali, it fell apart and split into two pieces, creating the mountains of Gunung Agung and Gunung Batur. The candi bentar now symbolizes these two halves of Mount Meru.

Candi korung

The artistic and richly decorated **covered gate** (candi korung or kori agung) in the second courtyard leads into the third part of the temple, the innermost of the temple's courtyards, which symbolizes Mount Meru and, with it, the highest of all worlds in Hindu cosmology.

Aling-aling

A **wall protecting against demons**, an aling-aling, is always erected behind the gate. Evil spirits are supposed to bounce off it because they can only move straight ahead – if they even make it that far because in front of the gate are a number of ferocious-looking demons (raksasa), whose sole task is to scare their own kind to such an extent that they do not even dare to enter the temple grounds.

Bale

A bale, of which there are often several within a temple compound, is a **pavilion** open on all sides. If the bale is in a pura desa (one of the three village temples), it is called a baleagung and serves the village elders as a place to congregate. At larger temple sites there are several bales in which the offerings for a temple festival are prepared.

Gedong

A gedong is either a small, closed structure (gedong penimpanan) or a large building (gedong agung). All that is required to provide shelter for the gods during their visit on earth is stored in a gedong pen-impanan. This can consist of a small statue, as well as an elaborately carved mask or even a kris (dagger). A gedong agung, on the other hand, is where the ancestors are venerated.

Padmasana The seating arrangement for the gods varies. While the richly decora-ted stone throne in southern Bali stands in the northeast corner, in northern Bali it is in a central spot. This is because of the fact that the backrest must always face the holy mountain of Gunung Agun. The **throne of god** also has three parts: the lowest level symbolizes the underworld, the middle the middle world and the top Mount Meru. The highest throne in a jeroan belongs to the god Shiva, who is named Sangyang Widi in Bali and visits earth in this manifesta-tion. If more seating is available, they belong to various gods of dif-ferent ranking. The seats for the gods or deities, by the way, are not symbolic of the respective god or deity, but are considered to be their property.

Meru A **tiered pagoda** in the innermost temple area is called a meru and serves as a symbol for the world mountain of the same name, the home of all Hindu deities. Its several tiers (tumpang) are covered with either palm tree fronds, rice straw or sometimes even corru-gated iron.

Pelinggih Just once a year, namely on the occasion of an odalan festival (see p.42), the god who lives permanently in the temple leaves the peling-gih, a **holy shrine** with one or two roofs. Up to eleven tiers (tum-pang) stand above it, also symbolic of Mount Meru. Additional pavi-lions, shrines, sacrificial altars and pagodas in varying numbers com-plete the facilities.

Kulkul As a rule, the **bell tower** is in the first courtyard. From there, the faithful are called to assemblies and festivals in the shrine by two men, or occasionally young boys, who rhythmically strike a long, hollow log (or, rarely, a gong or metallophone) with beaters.

Sculpture · Painting

Enlivened by Hinduism Whether there existed pronounced forms of sculptural art in Bali in pre-Hindu times, i.e. approximately up to the turn of the first mil-lennium, is not clear. Researchers have until now been of the opinion that ancient Balinese cult sites tended to be rather plain. Recent finds, however, prove that the inhabitants of the island were quite ca-pable of depicting praiseworthy figures – initially of the Buddhist, and later of the Hindu religions – in sculpted form, primarily as re-liefs. Hindus persecuted on the neighbouring island of Java, among them priests and artists, sought refuge in Bali in the 15th and 16th centuries. The subsequent influence of Hinduism on Balinese art expanded its variety of creative means and the use of Javanese elements increased. Since that time, the portrayal of the deities stands in the foreground. In Bali's sculptural art this meant a highly artistic addition to bas and high reliefs through detached statuary along the Indian model. In the subsequent further development of relief carvings, the Balinese love for opulently rampant ornamentation became obvious. It is the repetition of details that allows Javanese-Hindu sculpture to be clearly classified as Balinese relief.

While the tuff walls around a temple, for example, were kept fairly plain up to the period of conversion to Hinduism, they are now decorated on the front surfaces and corners with elaborately worked, detailed embellishments. These consist first and foremost of the hideous faces of demons and witches, whose job it is to frighten away their own kind and keep them from the holy area. In other places, there are scenes depicted from the Ramayana or Mahabharata epics, as well as scenes from the daily lives of the Balinese people.

Sculptures ranging immensely in variety and size are produced in the village of Batubulan.

ries. Further artistic development is barely taking place these days, simply because of the constant demand to replace statuary destroyed by the ravages of time with new ones of a similar type.

Old Balinese Art of Painting

Painting in Bali is plain and still exhibits folkloristic characteristics. There is little evidence of the work of previous eras because the Balinese characteristically paint on less substantial materials such as textiles. The subject matter consisted of scenes that are also familiar in Balinese **shadow theatre** (wayang kulit; see p.67). The colours used (primarily warm tones likes red, orange, ochre yellow and a clear white) were purely of organic origin. One of the most beautiful examples of Old Balinese painting can be found in the Kerta Gosa court hall in Klungkung.

European influences

With the arrival in Bali of large numbers of European-influenced artists around 1930, a change in style, expression and subject matter became unmistakable. One of the most important innovations that painters like **Walter Spies** (▶ Famous People), Le Mayeur, Rudolf Bonnet and W. O. J. Nieuwenkamp inspired was the introduction of central perspective. Balinese painters, who had until then been limited to two dimensions, were introduced to a third. At about the same time, a change in subject matter is noticeable. Up until that point, it had been difficult to differentiate between foreground and background, but now the main person or figure became the focus.

The European artists founded painting schools where they taught young Balinese how to use European painting equipment while at the same time only cautiously influencing expression and style. This approach explains why Balinese painting assimilated European influence while losing hardly any of the strength of its natural expression and originality.

Arts and Crafts

Woodcarving

Even though many wooden objects (e.g. vessels and bowls) primarily had a practical purpose in everyday life, the art of woodcarving in Bali also has a religious and cultural background. The extremely **skilfully carved wooden masks** have become known all over the world. They can be divided into two groups; those that have great religious value and as such are rarely if ever offered for sale, and those that are expressly produced for the tourist trade. The layman, however, would notice no difference – the term (rangda mask) is used for both. In addition, there are a great number of different dance masks used in the performance of Balinese dances.

A number of requirements are attached to the production of a rangda mask employed for religious purposes, particularly those used in the dances. For example, they must be made exclusively from the wood of a pohon pule tree; a priest determines by calculation when the tree can be taken from the forest. When the mask is finished and painted (only with organic colours), it is said of it that holy water (tirtha) flows from it every 32 days.

But a lot of other beautiful things are made from wood. Whole families of woodcarvers live from the production of timeless wooden figures. Since the 1920s, many figures have taken on an overtly slender form. High quality woodcarving comes at a price, by the way, because the Balinese mentality demands only time-consuming production by hand.

Textiles

Even if the origins of **batik production** are most probably to be found on Java, where the highest quality examples of batik artistry are still produced today, the Balinese have developed an extraordinary skill at it. Today there are even schools in the tourist centres in Bali offering special courses in the production of batik.

Artistic patterns are created by hand.

A profusion of beautiful textiles are on offer.

But there is a special process in Bali that, although based on batik, has little in common with it. Cotton threads are used that are dyed only after weaving. To achieve a distinctive, subtle colouring, the batch that is not to be dyed is tied up. The name **ikat** came from this very complex technique and literally means »tied« or »knotted«. A distinction is drawn between warp-ikats and weft-ikats. The difference has to do with whether the warp thread (tied securely to the warp pegs of the loom) or the weft thread (which is threaded through the warp threads with a shuttle) is dyed.

A more complicated ikat process called **double ikat** is used on the neighbouring island of Lombok; in Bali, this process is used only in the village of Tenganan. Here, both warp and weft threads are dyed. The production of a piece of double ikat takes months, if not years. The islanders attribute magical powers to double ikat cloth.

Dance · Music

Expressive dance Balinese dances are an extremely important part of life, both religious and secular. The various kinds of dance usually presented in the form of expressive dance could be termed »lived religion«. No temple festival takes place without a dance performance.

Today, there are also Balinese dances especially adapted for tourists and their cameras. Whether these still have anything to do with tradition is a matter for speculation. In fact, it is increasingly difficult for tourists to find a dance performance that is uninfluenced by commercial considerations: such dances are more likely to be performed in a private setting in the evening or at night. Travellers who stray far off the main tourist routes, for instance, may make contact with locals (usually without difficulty) in a village and have a chance of experiencing unadulterated Balinese dance. Indeed, it is not unusual to be invited to a festival that just happens to be taking place. A schedule of the numerous festivals and celebrations can be obtained from tour operators or at hotel receptions.

The barong dance is undoubtedly the most famous of the Balinese dances and the one presented most frequently. There are several versions of it; these vary, though only in nuances. Actually, the barong dance can be seen to be more of a drama in several acts because of the complete story it tells. Accompanied by a gamelan orchestra, several main characters – disguised in animal masks – take to the stage. In the beginning, a solo **legong dance** is presented (see p.64). The main characters are the **witch Rangda**, who appears wearing a hand-carved mask with the most frightening face imaginable, and **Barong**,

Barong dance

The eternal struggle between good and evil is portrayed in the barong dance.

a figure in the shape of a lion animated by two dancers. While Rangda stands for evil, Barong symbolizes the opposite – which of the two ends up winning the battle remains to be seen.

Baris dance The baris dance is performed exclusively by men wearing various weapons. Originally featuring no single main role, over the course of time a form of the dance has developed that stresses the solo abilities of an individual dancer. The focus of the dance are the various feelings and emotions that are present in a warrior, such as courage and fear, compassion and callousness toward the enemy, elation over the victory and grief over defeat, and so on. The gamelan music accompanying the baris dance follows the movements of the dancers – not the other way around.

Kebyar Dance Perhaps the most symbolic of Bali's solo dances is the kebya dance. The form seen today developed around 1915. Although it is danced by a grown man, its subject is the temptations and moods of a pubertal youth. The costume is of little significance (as a rule, a cloth draped about the hips with a long train suffices); the focus is on the facial expressions and gestures of the dancer, who sits cross-legged on the floor and »dances« only with his upper torso and arms and hands.

Kecak dance The kecak dance, performed only by men, is certainly one of the most impressive ritual dances that a visitor to Bali can experience. At any rate, it is the noisiest. In addition, it is considered to be the youngest of the Balinese dances: its present form first developed in the 1930s. At this time, elements of the Ramayana epic were built into the action. The inspiration for this was given by the German painter Walter Spies (▶Famous People) prior to the shooting of the film *Island of Demons*. Originally, the kecak dance was performed to drive away evil spirits and demons with between 70 and 100 barechested men sitting in a spiral-shaped circle. They symbolize the followers of the monkey Hanuman. The kecak got its name from the sound, a percussive »cak-cak«, chanted by the men, accompanied by conjuring movements of the arms and upper torso.

Legong dance If the kebyar dance is about the moods of a pubertal boy, then the legong dance can be seen as its female counterpart; although physical maturity only plays a role insofar as the girl is no longer qualified to perform as a legong dancer with the onset of menstruation. A perfect body and virginity are the prerequisites for a girl to be allowed to learn the legong dance, at about the age of five. A trained dancer functions as teacher.

As with many Asian dances, the **»language of the hands and fingers«** play an important role in legong. Every movement of the body, every position of the hands and every motion of the fingers have their meaning. Legong is danced by three girls with one of them ap-

An elaborately decorated kris

pearing as a soloist. It tells the story of the son of a prince, Raja La-
sern, who seeks the favour of the girl Rangkesari, ultimately in vain,
and in the end meets his death in battle. Although the girls change
roles during the performance, they do not change costumes. For this
reason, those familiar with the culture find the legong dance hard to
understand, though quite beautiful.

The most important prop in the kris dance is the kris (dagger) itself. **Kris dance**
Inhabited by a guardian spirit, it possesses magical powers and is
therefore the **»holy« weapon of the Indonesians**. Always made by
hand and usually elaborately and imaginatively decorated, the kris is
the pride of every man, especially in Bali, and is a symbol of full
membership in the village community. Craftsmen specializing in its
production are among the most respected occupational groups in
Bali. The correct method of making a kris is passed on orally from
generation to generation. But even then, the most respected smith
cannot start work without first asking a Brahman to name the most
propitious time to begin working the raw metal.

Gamelan

There is no village in Bali that does not have its own gamelan orches- **Typical**
tra; many even have several. The term gamelan, though, is used for a **Indonesian style**
variety of musical groupings. For example, the term gamelan can re- **of music**
fer either to an ensemble of just a few musicians (gamelan legong)
or an orchestra sometimes composed of **up to 30 or 40 players**
(gamelan gong). The gamelan is used for all celebrations in Bali, as
well as with dance, drama and shadow theatres.

The roots of Balinese music can be found on the neighbouring island of Java, although differing combinations, forms and terms for the instruments have developed in Bali over the course of the centuries.

The word »gamelan« comes from the old Javanese language and means »to strike« or »to hammer«. It appears highly likely that about the same time that man learned how to produce bronze in Asia (about 1000 BC), the first instruments were also built from this metal.

Musical basics

In contrast to the music based on octaves subdivided into seven half and whole notes or the twelve semitone scale customary in the West, music practised in Bali in most cases uses a pentatonic scale (Javanese: slendro). There are three scales each with five full notes. These five notes have approximately the same distance from each other; that is, there are no half notes. In addition, the gamelan uses scales with seven, six and four notes, as the occasion dictates. The angklung ensemble used at funerals, for example, uses a scale with only four notes.

Balinese metre is also different from its Western counterpart. As a rule, the rhythm is even and only the tempo varies.

Ensembles and instruments

It is common to all forms of gamelan that the musicians play several instruments equally well so that, in the case of the gamelan gong, 30 to 40 musicians play **up to 80 instruments**. The range of instruments is very extensive. Among the melody instruments are the gender panembung (bronze sheets hung over tuned tube resonators), gongs tuned high, middle and low, bonangs (small gongs called kettles or pots hung in a wooden frame), bamboo flutes and the rebab (a stringed instrument with a curved sound-box). The rhythm is set by drums (gendang) of different sizes and tuning. The variation of the sequence of notes established by the melody instruments is the task of the gender barung (similar to the gender panembung, but with more octaves) and the tilempang, a type of zither.

However this list does not exhaust the range of instruments available – not by a long way. Various instruments are added according to the size of the gamelan, but all are based on the materials of the aforementioned instruments.

The instruments are always produced by hand and here, too, a myriad of rules prescribed by tradition have to be followed. Old instruments are particularly respected and can even be considered sacred. For this reason they are allowed to be played only by a few select musicians and then exclusively on high holidays and major festivals.

Current situation

The melodies have been passed from one generation to the next for centuries. Even today – of course based on formal rules –free improvisation and playing by memory are still practised.

Although in earlier times some core melodies were written down on palm leaves, it is thanks to the German painter and musician Walter

A gamelan orchestra consists mainly of instruments like gongs, metallophones and glockenspiels.

Spies (▶ Famous People) and the American Colin McPhee, both of whom studied Balinese music intensively in the 1920s and 1930s, that quite a few pieces of music for gamelan orchestras were recorded in a form of musical notation especially developed for the purpose. This has since made them available to an interested Western audience.

Wayang · Literature

Even though shadow theatre (wayang kulit) is spread across almost the entire Asian continent, a relatively independent form has developed in Bali. The central role in the performance of the plays, which are sometimes several hours long, is taken by the puppeteer, the dalang, who performs behind a white screen illuminated by the flickering glow of a petroleum lamp. It is his job to bring the flat figures, usually **cut out of buffalo leather** to life. The dalang develops great skills and can manipulate up to ten puppets at a time. The action in the wayang kulit is based on themes from the Indian Ramayana and

**Shadow theatre
Wayang kulit**

The spirits of ancestors, mythological heroes, gods and demons appear as shadows in traditional Balinese shadow plays.

Mahabharata epics (see p.70). It is a permanent feature of temple festivals, but is also sometimes performed during the celebrations accompanying rights of passage. Audiences of all ages, enthralled by the story, sit transfixed in front of the screen, at time breathless with excitement, following the action and dialogue, which is normally in the form of a soliloquy. A gamelan ensemble usually provides the sparse musical accompaniment.

Masked theatre
Wayang topeng

Topeng means mask, and indeed in wayang topeng or masked theatre it is the masks and not the people wearing them that are the important part of the storyline. When the dancer takes the mask out of the cloth in which it is kept and puts it on, he assumes the role the mask represents. The moment of donning the mask is therefore preceded by a certain pause to turn inward and meditate, during which the wearer of the mask works himself perfectly into the role. Although topeng masks are available in souvenir shops, such masks are in no way considered to be appropriate for the performance of a wayang topeng. The real masks are believed to possess a spirit and are sacred; for this reason, their production is tied to strictly prescribed rituals. A wayang topeng's story consists of stories from the times when Bali was still ruled by princes.

Literature

Balinese literature had its origins in Indian works of literature. As in many other Asian countries, Hindu missionaries ensured that stories, tales, fairy tales and legends from India – often only in fragmented form, of course – also came to Bali, whose native population then altered them according to their own understanding. The source of each individual work, however, is usually still recognizable.

Origins in India

The Ramayana is the **most important story of Indian origin**. It is a kind of chivalric poem. Its central theme is the story of the eternal struggle between the gods and demons. The first part was possibly written down in the third century BC. Altogether, the work of that time was composed of 24,000 verses. Unknown chroniclers later added two additional books in which the hero of the story is made into an incarnation of the god Vishnu. There is no single version of the Ramayana and there are regional variations – according to religious perceptions – and a great number of differing interpretations, in which often only a part of the original core of the story can be recognized. The following is the customary version of the story in Bali.

Ramayana

Vishnu comes to earth for the seventh time in the person of Rama and is born as one of the three sons of Rajah Desarata, the king of Ayodhaya (a city on the river Sarayu in northern India). Rama falls in love with Sita (also called Sinta), the daughter of a king, and gains the favour of her father because he is the only one capable of stringing his bow.

However it now emerges that years ago Rajah Desarata had promised to fulfil two wishes of his first wife. Although he would love to see his favourite son made his successor, he must keep his promise and instead declare his second son, Betara, to be his successor. The second demand of his first wife hits him even harder: he must send Rama into exile for a period of 15 years. When Desarata dies and Betara ascends to the throne, Rama and Sita more or less voluntarily leave their homeland, although Betara wants to give up the office and title in favour of his stepbrother.

The beautiful Sita, however, is abducted by the demon king Rawana, who wants to force her to live with him. Rama now recalls the mission in life bestowed upon him by Brahma: to destroy the demon king. Brahma had, however, once assured Rawana that no god could defeat him. The way around this was a deception: to have Vishnu come to earth, born again as a man.

Rama succeeds in defeating Rawana after several successful adventures with the aid of the monkey king Sugriva and the monkey Hanuman. Although Hanuman is at first able to sneak into Sita's prison and bring her the message that Rama is on the way to rescue her, he is taken prisoner by Rawana. Hanuman is able to escape, however, and set fire to the palace with his burning tail. With the support of the sea god, Waruna, one of the monkeys builds a bridge from the Indian mainland to the island of Ceylon (Sri Lanka) to which Rama is able to flee with Sita and his followers. However, Rawana pursues him and embroils him a bloodbath that lasts for six days and six nights, at the end of which, naturally, Rama emerges as the shining winner. Rama and Sita return to their homeland where his step-brother Betara again offers him the office of ruler. But the people are against this as long as Sita has not proven that Rawana had not influenced her with his evil thoughts during the battle. She passes the test; as a sign of her innocence, she emerges unscathed from a pyre of burning wood.

Mahabharata   The Indian story the Mahabharata is even longer than the Ramayana. It is composed of 110,000 double verses and **presumably has a historic nucleus**, the battle of the Pandava (five sons of Pandu) and the Kaurava (49 sons of the blind Rajah Desarata) for the domination of the area around present-day Delhi. Of course, the actual story is also

Balinese dancers during an international Ramayana festival in Denpasar with participants from India, Thailand, Cambodia, Singapore, Indonesia and the USA.

intertwined here by a large number of other stories, mythologies of the gods, heroic legends, love stories and religious and philosophical treatments that are only loosely still related to the core of the story. The Mahabharata was written sometime between the fourth century BC and the fourth century AD. Of the entire work, the section relating the events before the decisive battle between the Pandava and the Kaurava plays the most important role in Hinduism.

Famous People

Who was K'tut Tantri and where did she come from? Which Russian-born German learned to play all of the instruments in a gamelan orchestra and later greatly influenced the art scene? What are the »Five Principles« (Panca Sila) that Sukarno formulated as the basis of Indonesian politics?

Antonio Maria Blanco (1926–99)

The Spaniard Antonio Maria Blanco is one of the most significant **Spanish Painter**
painters who chose to work in Bali. After attending school in the
Philippine capital of Manila, he studied at the Art Academy in New
York and then lived in Florida, California, Honolulu, Oahu, Hawaii
and Japan. Blanco came to Bali for the first time in 1952, where his
much awarded artistic work that mixes **comical impressionistic elements with erotic elements** greatly impressed the son of the Prince
of Ubud, who let him have a former summer residence in the midst
of a spacious garden as home and studio. Blanco left Bali in the early
1950s only to return permanently a few years later. The painter, who
was a perfect master of the art of showmanship, was married to a
Balinese woman and before his death in 1999 had even converted a
large part of his residence in Ubud into a museum.

Vicki Baum (1888–1960)

The writer and harp player born in Vienna, Vicki (also Vicky) Baum **Austrian writer**
came to Bali in 1935 when the Dutch had brought almost all of the **and musician**
island under their control after years of conflict. Fascinated by the
Balinese people, who, unimpressed by their foreign masters, maintained their own culture, Ms Baum was inspired to write a book during her nine-month stay on Bali, *Tale of Bali*, which was published in
1937. She not only succeeded in burrowing deep into the history of
the island and its people, she also **understood the mentality of the
Balinese**. Using the example of a Balinese village, she describes what
influence the Dutch colonial masters tried to exert on the traditional
village life of the people, at which, however, they were only superfi-
cially successful. Vicki Baum died on 29 August 1960 in Hollywood.

Donald Friend (1915–89)

Donald Friend was one of the most important foreign-born artists to **Australian artist,**
live in Bali. Born in Sydney Australia in 1915, Friend was preco- **writer and diarist**
ciously talented both as an artist and a writer and grew up in the artistic circle of his bohemian mother. After studying in Sydney and
London, he served in the Second World War as a gunner in the AIF
(Australian Imperial Force). Much of Friend's life was spent outside
Australia, and he settled in Bali in 1968, remaining there until his return to Sydney in 1980.

Donald Friend's reputation reached a high point in the 1940s when he
was ranked alongside the likes of William Dobell and Russell Drysdale;
however by the time of his death his reputation had dwindled. For
Friend, rejection by the majority of critics was made all the more acute

← *Vicki Baum opened up a view of the exotic culture and history
of the island in her novel »A Tale of Bali«.*

by what was seen as the frivolity and self-indulgence of his work and life. He made no attempt to disguise the homo-eroticism which underlay much of his work and spoke openly about these aspects of his life, depicting himself in his journal as »a middle-aged pederast who's going to seed«. He had a series of relations with adolescent boys; the Vice Squad were known to take an interest in his exhibitions.

Friend was considered a great draughtsman, a skill particularly evident in his studies of the young male nude, and was a formidable wit. The value of his contribution to Australian art, however, remains a matter of debate.

Walter Spies (1895–1942)

Russian-born German painter and musician

Born in Moscow the son of a wealthy and respected merchant family, Walter Spies was one of the painters whose works were greatly influenced by a stay on the island of Bali. Spies lived up to the age of 15 in the Russian capital and then moved to Germany with his family where he attended high school. Spies came into contact with painters in Berlin such as the Expressionist Oskar Kokoschka and Otto Dix, one of the most famous representatives of the New Objectivity, as well as the composer Ernst Krenek. Leaving Germany in 1923 he travelled on a freighter to Java, where he earned a living in the first weeks after his arrival as a pianist in a bar. On 1 January 1924, the Sultan of Yogyakarta named him the conductor of his court orchestra that was formed along western lines. However very soon Spies was making a name for himself by researching music. He not only learned to play all the instruments customarily in a gamelan orchestra, but also eagerly collected Old Javanese (later also Balinese) compositions to save them for posterity. In addition, he made them also accessible to the Western world on instruments tuned to the European key.

Spies first came to Bali in 1925, where he settled permanently two years later. Fascinated by the landscape and the people, he lived there in the palace of the princes of Ubud, who were appreciative of the arts. Later he built his own house, called it »Campuan« and made it into a **meeting-place of numerous artists** who were living permanently or temporarily in Bali (among others, Austrian writer Vicki Baum lived in »Campuan« and wrote her novel *Tale of Bali* there). Spies influenced local artists, but also learned from them, particularly with regard to their mental attitude toward art.

When German troops marched into the European Netherlands in 1940, the German nationals in the Dutch East Indies were interned, Spies among them. While they were to being transferred to British India in January 1942, only a few days before the Japanese invasion, a Japanese bomber sank the ship. There were only a few survivors: Spies was one of those lost. Walter Spies is honoured to this day in Bali. Some of his most beautiful works can be seen in the Neka Museum in Ubud.

Raden Ahmed Sukarno (1901–70)

The founder of the sovereign state of Indonesia, Raden Ahmed Sukarno, was born on 6 June 1901 in Blitar on Java, the son of a Javanese father and a Balinese mother. After attending school in Surabaya and then studying engineering, the 26-year-old Sukarno, gravitating toward politics advocating independence, founded the »Partai Nasional Indonesia« (PNI) in 1927 and placed himself at its head.

Indonesian Politician

Sukarno was imprisoned from 1929 to 1932 and was exiled by the Dutch colonial government to the island of Flores in 1933 and to Sumatra in 1938. Freed by the Japanese in 1942, he worked together with them for Bali's independence. Sukarno's declared goal was to **shake off the yoke of colonial rule**. The greatest difficulty was con-

Sukarno delivering a lecture.

vincing all the provincial princes that it was necessary to take action together to form a unified state. He succeeded on 17 August 1945, when together with Mohammed Hatta, a comrade-in-arms from the underground movement fighting against Dutch, he declared the State of Indonesia. The Dutch eventually recognized Indonesia's independence in 1949. While Sukarno sought to realize the principle of a »Guided Democracy« with a powerful figure at its head, Hatta preferred a democracy in the Western mould.

Sukarno always strived to create and maintain a certain balance between Indonesia's political and social groupings. The basis for this was the Five Principles (**Panca Sila**) he formulated, in which he attempted to create a link between Hindu-Javanese, Islamic and socialist values (belief, nationalism, democracy, humanity, and a just and affluent society). This basis of a dynamic society that should continually discuss its principles, redefining them, can be seen on innumerable memorials, walls and posters throughout the entire country and is meant to remind all Indonesians of their common nation.

During Sukarno's years in power, the influence of the Communist Party increased in many Asian countries. At the close of the 1950s, Sukarno moved closer to the People's Republic of China and around 1963 distanced himself from West-orientated Malaysia. His role remained unclear in a viciously crushed attempted coup staged by the communists in 1965, which was one of the reasons for Sukarno's overthrow two years later. Initially, his rights as president were curtailed and in 1967 General Suharto finally removed him from office and placed him under house arrest for life. Raden Ahmed Sukarno died on 21 June 1970 in Jakarta.

K'tut Tantri (1899–1997)

English artist, writer, broadcaster and Bali devotee

K'tut Tantri was born Vannine Walker on the Isle of Man in 1899. In various guises as writer, broadcaster, and painter she became known under a variety of names, including Muriel Walker, Miss Manx and Surabaya Sue, her broadcasting nom de plume. It was in the 1930s that Walker went to the US West Coast, where, one rainy afternoon in 1932, she saw the film that was to change her life: *Bali, the Last Paradise*. Inspired, she set sail alone for Bali with her paint brushes and easel to live the life of an artist there. She was to set down her adventures on the island in her book, *Revolt in Paradise*, in which, admittedly, the distinction between fact and fiction is somewhat blurred.

The story goes that on her arrival in Bali she was adopted by a Balinese raja and his family. Soon after, she had started one of the first hotels in Bali on the then »undiscovered« beach of Kuta. She mixed with such famous fellow artists as ▶ Walter Spies and Adrien le Mayeur, and developed a close relationship with the local Balinese, which upset »proper« Dutch colonial society.

When the Japanese invaded Bali in 1942, the Dutch and other Westerners were evacuated – but K'tut Tantri remained behind. Her book relates the privation, torture and hardship she suffered at the hands of the Japanese. After the Japanese surrender, she joined the resistance movement fighting for independence from the Dutch colonists. As Surabaya Sue she broadcast to the fledgling republic from clandestine radio stations. She thus became a confidante of many of Indonesia's revolutionary leaders, including President ▶Sukarno.

K'tut Tantri's long and eventful life was rather a tangled web, shrouded in mystery. Whatever the truth, she is regarded as a heroic figure in Bali. After her death in 27 July 1997, she was presented with a posthumous award by the Indonesian government in 2002. A major roadway in Bali is named after her, forever cementing her place in the island's history.

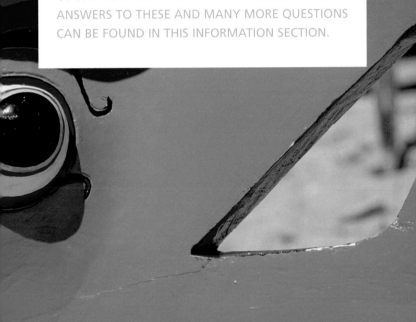

Practicalities

WHAT IS A JAMU? HOW SHOULD YOU
BEHAVE IN A TEMPLE? WHEN MIGHT YOU
ENCOUNTER AN OGOH-OGOH? WHAT IS SURPRIS-
ING ABOUT EATING A DURIAN? AND WHICH SIDE
OF THE ROAD DO THEY DRIVE ON IN BALI? THE
ANSWERS TO THESE AND MANY MORE QUESTIONS
CAN BE FOUND IN THIS INFORMATION SECTION.

Accommodation

Hotels

The hotel industry in Bali effortlessly reaches international standards. Along with countless accommodation facilities run by locals, many of the international hotel chains are represented (▶Baedeker Special p.168). But of course there are cheaper alternatives, namely the many small hotels that are perhaps relatively modest in the level of comfort they offer but make up for it by being all the more attentive to the needs of the guests.

Among the most inexpensive accommodation are the guesthouses known as homestays or losmen, which are found almost everywhere in Bali.

Situation on Lombok In the past, Lombok, Bali's neighbouring island to the east, was at best a destination for excursions and offered only modest accommodation. A few years ago, the tourist industry discovered Bali's neighbour and since then some comfortable hotel complexes have been built, primarily on Sengiggi Beach (north of the island's capital, Mataram).

Reservations Making reservations in advance is necessary, particularly during the main travel season (April–October). It is almost impossible to get a place to stay before and after the Islamic month of fasting, Ramadan, because so many visitors from neighbouring countries take their vacation here.

Inexpensive alternatives There are some inexpensive alternatives to hotels in Bali, especially for visitors on a tight budget. They are called »homestays«, »losmen« and »penginapan«. Be ready to accept limitations regarding quality and service at such places. The converted price for an overnight (usually two or more beds in a room, seldom a single room) is about £4–12/$8–24 (occasionally including a modest breakfast). Prior reservations are highly recommended, and not only during the peak season.

Camping There are no official camp sites. Backpackers are no longer welcomed in Bali. Even if it is not officially banned, camping anywhere in the open countryside is considered taboo.

Arrival · Before the Journey

Destination Bali

Flying is the most common way of travelling from the UK, USA and Australia to Bali. There are no direct flights from the UK and USA; travellers will need to change planes in either Singapore, Sydney, Hong Kong, Taipei, Tokyo, Bangkok or Doha.

Numerous airlines offer flights from London Heathrow and Gatwick to Ngurah Rai International Airport near Denpasar (code DPS); these include Malaysia Airlines, Qatar Airways, Singapore Airlines, Cathay Pacific, Thai Airways, Emirates and Qantas. The total distance from London to Denpasar by air is about 12,500km/7770mi, and the flight time (depending on stopovers) is about 16 hours. The stopovers can be **extended** if desired. The price for a scheduled economy class return flight from London to Bali is about 600/$1200.

Qantas flies direct from Sydney to Denspasar. Singapore Airlines, Qantas and Japan Airlines fly from the USA to Denpasar. Qantas also fly from Canada.

The carriers mentioned above operate numerous routes in the Asiatic region so that a flight to Bali is also possible from all major cities in East, South and Southeast Asia. Cheap deals can be found online.

By air from UK, USA and Australia

It is possible to travel to Bali (largely) by land from the Indonesian island of Java, but it is time consuming. Trains leave regularly from Jakarta and Yogyakarta to the ferry port of Ketapang (not far north of Banyuwangi) at the eastern end of Java (travel time approx. 16 hrs). There it is possible to transfer to one of the car ferries that cross regularly several times daily to Gilimanuk on the west tip of Bali (crossing takes approx. 30 to 45 min). As there is no railway in Bali, the rest of the trip is by bus.

By train and ferry from Java

On to Lombok

The trip to Lombok is best undertaken from Bali. The regional airline »Merpati« has planes flying several times daily between Ngurah Rai Airport, southwest of Denpasar in Bali and Lombok's airport northwest of Mataram. The flight time is only about 25 minutes and the price is very low. Lombok is also served by domestic flights from other Indonesian cities, as well as international flights from Singapore and Kuala Lumpur.

By air

A ferry travels three times a day between Padang Bai (in Bali; to the east of Klungkung) and the harbour of Lembar (in Lombok; south of Mataram). The crossing takes about four hours. The Mabua Express Jumbo ferries are faster and take only half the time.

By sea

Travel Documents

Passport Citizens of the UK, Republic of Ireland, USA, Canada, Australia and New Zealand wishing to enter Indonesia must have a passport that is valid for six months beyond the time of entry. It is recommended that travellers make photocopies of travel documents and store them separately. In case of loss, these copies greatly facilitate the issue of replacement documents.

Visa The rules regarding the issue of visas change frequently, so it is advisable to check up on current details before travelling. A visa is required before citizens of the UK, Republic of Ireland, USA, Canada, Australia and New Zealand can enter Indonesia. The 60-day visa is only issued to those applying in advance; the visa on arrival, stamped in the passport upon entry to the country on payment of £12.50/US$25, is valid for 30 days. Visitors are issued with a tourist card corresponding to the length of their visa; unless there is a special reason (such as illness or legal problems) it is not possible to get an extension. To get a new visa and tourist card, it is necessary to

Skilfully executed woodcarvings, along with shadow figures and ikat and batik textiles, are among the most popular souvenirs.

leave the country and then return. Indonesian authorities will demand proof of possession of a paid return or onward flight or passage by ship. They may wish to see evidence that travellers have access to sufficient funds for their trip.

At present, a certificate of vaccination is not required of travellers entering Indonesia directly from Western Europe. In case of a stopover in an area infected with yellow fever, namely various African countries as well as India, Nepal, Myanmar, Sri Lanka and others, it is best to consult the Indonesian embassy or consulate (▶ Information) about the current situation. Occasionally a smallpox vaccination is required that should not be older than three years – even after the World Health Organization has declared the earth to be free of smallpox. It is recommended to be vaccinated against cholera and to take medicines to prevent malaria when travelling outside the tourist areas (during tours), as well as during the rainy season.

Vaccination guidelines

Customs Regulations

The following are duty free: items for personal use in reasonable quantities, cigarettes (at most 200), 50 cigars, 100g/3.5oz tobacco, 2l/68fl oz wine or spirits, two cameras with film, and a film or video camera. The importing of drugs, Communist literature and pornographic materials is absolutely prohibited, as is bringing in hunting weapons and ammunition. It usually does not take a visitor to Bali long to get through customs.

Entry into Indonesia

Consumer goods purchased in Indonesia and souvenirs may be exported in any amount. The export of antiques is subject to special regulations (▶Shopping). The export of Indonesian currency is restricted (▶Money).

Departure from Indonesia

The importing of plants, animals or animal or plant products that are under protection according to the CITES agreement (also known as the »Endangered Species Act of Washington«) is prohibited. This includes – in reference to Bali and Indonesia – coral (particularly black coral), reptiles (especially geckos), turtles and tortoises (also tortoiseshells), birds and products from protected plants. Persons arriving in the European Union (EU) by air or ship from non-EU states may bring travel souvenirs and gifts up to a total value of £345/$630 without having to pay additional value added tax. In addition, persons over 15 years of age may import 500g/1.1lb coffee or 200g/7oz soluble coffee, 50g perfume and 0.25l eau de toilette; persons over 17 years of age may bring in 1l/34 fl oz spirits with more than 22 % alcohol content by volume or 2l/68fl oz spirits with a maximum of 22 % alcohol content by volume or 2l/68fl oz sparkling wine, 2l/68fl oz wine, and 200 cigarettes or 100 cigarillos or 50 cigars or 250g/8.8oz smoking tobacco.

Re-entry into the UK

Children in Bali

Bali is a virtual paradise for children. They are welcomed everywhere. Even so, issues such as vaccination, the long flight, the difference in times, and adequate sun protection should be considered beforehand. Besides the beaches, a suitable place for the whole family to visit on a daytrip is naturally the zoo. Elephant rides are among the highlights for the little ones. All manner of tips for activities with children in Bali can be found on the internet at **www.travelforkids. com**. And if for once a longer tour of a temple complex or a simple excursion without the children is planned, some of the larger hotels offer very good, supervised children's programmes, full of variety, that are also open to non-hotel residents (for a small charge).

● ATTRACTIONS FOR CHILDREN

▶ **Bali Zoo Park (formerly Bali Bird Park)**
Jl. Serma Cok Ngurah Gambir (2km/1.2miles north of Batubulan)
www.bali-bird-park.com
There are all kinds of strange birds to be discovered in the middle of an exotic landscape. Living right next door are snakes, crocodiles, turtles and some komodo dragons.

▶ **Elephant Safari Park**
Taro
(approx. 20min north of Ubud)
www.baliadventuretours.com
Here it is not only possible to pet and feed the pachyderms, but also to explore the area on the back of an elephant. In addition, the animals can be observed painting and there is an elephant museum to visit.

▶ **Waterbom Park**
Jl. Kartika Plaza
Tuban
www.waterbom.com
Children will be kept busy the whole day in Bali's favourite water adventure park. They have eight different pools and more than a dozen water slides to choose from. In addition, there is an extensive range of sport facilities and a spa in which to relax.

▶ **Pondok Pekak Library and Learning Center**
Monkey Forest Road
Ubud
Along with the courses for adults offered in this cultural centre, there are also activities (dance, gamelan) for children, plus a well-organized children's library.

▶ **Water Playground**
Jl. Pantai Kuta, Kuta
Along with bridges, canals and waterfalls, the Hard Rock Hotel's huge pool also boasts two waterslides and a small island with a volleyball court. Lifeguards provide for safety.

Electricity

The mains supply in Bali is 220 volts alternating current (50 Hertz). Fluctuations in current should be expected. Plug sockets conform to the European standard; visitors from the UK or USA should bring an adapter with them.

Emergency

 USEFUL TELEPHONE NUMBERS

► **Police**
Tel. 110

► **Fire Department**
Tel. 113

► **Ambulance**
Tel. 118

► **Indonesian Red Cross**
Tel. (03 61) 22 64 65

Etiquette and Customs

Primarily in the places frequented by tourists, children and some-times also sick or disabled people do beg in Bali. Especially in the case of children (who are increasingly being abused by adults who send them out to beg or sell grossly over-priced merchandise), tourists should refrain from giving money so as not to support their social neglect. Children are also pleased with little things like a bar of soap or a ballpoint pen.

Begging

As in almost all Asian states, the consumption of drugs and especially drug dealing is punished with severe penalties in Indonesia – and thus also in Bali. The importing or exporting of any and all controlled substances is strictly forbidden; possession of illegal drugs is also punishable by law.
As a rule, the long-term prison sentences resulting from violations against the narcotics laws apply to foreigners as well; in very serious cases the death penalty is applied. No help can be expected from homeland consulates in cases of drug offences.
Under no circumstances agree to transport anything home as a favour for someone. This has often been attempted in the past to exploit travellers as drug couriers.

Drugs

THIS IS A RELIGIOUS EVENT

PLEASE WEAR THE FULL

TRADITIONAL BALINESE COSTUMES

USE NO FLASH PLEA...

The dress code for Bali's temple festivals apply to tourists as well.

Photography and film cameras

The Indonesian archipelago offers a wealth of delightful subjects to photograph, so be sure and take ample amounts of film (in Bali expensive and often improperly stored).

Generally, the Balinese are happy to be photographed, but it is always best to ask permission first (a simple motion with the camera is usually enough) and if the response is a declining gesture, simply accept it. Those who do not want to be photographed will not do it for money either; strict Hindus are occasionally camera-shy. There can be moments during temple festivals when photographing with a flash can cause great annoyance among the believers. It is difficult to recommend the correct behaviour in such instances because it could vary from village to village and temple to temple. For this reason it is always best to ask permission before pressing the shutter. It should absolutely go without saying that tourists should not offend people by photographing them while they are practising their religion.

The X-ray equipment at the Indonesian airports is not always safe for film. Checked-in baggage is also X-rayed, so keep exposed as well as unexposed **film in your hand luggage**. When in doubt (especially in the case of extremely sensitive film), request a luggage inspection without X-ray.

Information for women

Unfortunately, in Bali as elsewhere, women travelling alone must reckon on being an object of interest for male tourists and be prepared to deal with their advances. There is hardly any danger of this from the local male population. Despite that, single women should not undertake walks alone, especially at night, and not into uncertain terrain.

Light, air-permeable clothing is recommended all year round. However, warmer pieces of clothing (such as sweaters and cardigans) should be taken along for the »cooler« months and for trips into the hilly regions. Clothing that covers bare arms and legs is recommended for evenings on the beach to protect against annoying insects. Respect for the religion of the Balinese **forbids entering their sacred sites dressed in things like shorts or T-shirt**. Women should definitely cover their shoulders and men wear long trousers. Before entering a temple site, wrap a temple sash, called a selendang, about the hips. The wearing of a sarong is obligatory when attending a temple festival – for all tourists, male and female alike! Selendangs and sarongs can either be purchased right at the start of your stay in Bali or hired out for a small sum at the temple entrance.

Clothing

The left hand is considered unclean. Do not proffer or take anything with the left hand. The exchange of intimacies in public is improper. Nude bathing is banned and considered as showing a disregard of Balinese sensitivities. Climbing on the temple walls or, even worse, temple figures, is strictly forbidden and punishable with stiff fines. This is an offence that confronts the local population with a nigh to unsolvable problem; a temple that has been desecrated in this manner has, to a large extent, lost its spiritual character. A temple visit (see dress code above) by people with open wounds (this includes menstruating women!) is strictly forbidden: violations are considered sacrilege and to desecrate the temple. Restoring it to its original, sacred condition requires highly elaborate rituals.

Taboos and sacrilege

> ! **Baedeker** TIP
>
> **Understanding Indonesia**
> Duncan Graham's book *The People Next Door: Understanding Indonesia* (University of Western Australia Press, 2004) is an exploration of the way real Indonesian people live. The Australian journalist's interviews with and observations of his homeland's close neighbours has resulted in a book that aims to cross the cultural divide and increase understanding between the two countries. Something to add to the reading list (see also ▶Literature).

»French« toilets can still be found, mostly in rural areas, whose use requires a certain amount of skill. Toilet paper is only seldom provided for wiping (with the left hand, which is why it is considered »unclean«); usually there is a container full of water and a ladle. Public toilets, if available, can be recognized by the sign »Kamar Kecil«; »Laki« for gentlemen, »Perempuan« for the ladies.

Toilets

Although the bill in the most restaurants and hotels already provides for a service charge of between 5 and 10 percent, it is customary

Tipping

when satisfied with the service to give an additional tip or round off the bill upwards. Giving a small gratuity to porters and chambermaids at the beginning of the stay is a good idea, and if satisfied with the service at the end of the holiday, another tip is in order. Taxi, bus and bemo drivers are not normally tipped.

Rules of behaviour

As tolerant as the Asians are toward the visitors from the West, there are some forms of behaviour that bring even the legendary composure of the Balinese to boiling point. Even if the offending tourist does not notice it, he has lost face and the Balinese consider him to be a person of little account.

When conversing, exercise **elegant reserve**. Wild gesticulating or pointing at other people with the finger is considered improper. Intimate subjects are not customary conversation, even among friends. Questions about income or personal financial status, for instance, are answered evasively. And never forget that important part of every conversation: the smile. The rule is, the more non-committal the answer, the friendlier the smile. If invited to a Balinese home, it is customary to bring along a **small gift**. The lady of the house is always pleased with a bouquet of flowers, and if there are children, remember to bring sweets. Shoes are removed before entering the home.

Festivals, Holidays and Events

Every day a holiday

It is almost impossible to spend any time in Bali and not experience one of the numerous festivals. Somewhere on the island a temple anniversary (odalan) festival is sure to be taking place. They are easy to recognize when travelling in the interior by the colourfully decorated, open temples or by the fair held there prior to the festival.

Celebrations of a religious nature are held all year round in Bali. The believers are tolerant toward other religions and open to foreigners. After all, the festivals and holidays of other faiths also provide an opportunity for exuberant celebration, as well as a cause for inner reflection. Eventually, a long-term visitor to the island can end up celebrating the New Year three times, according to Western, Chinese and Balinese customs.

Events programme

According to an unofficial count, there are well **over a thousand** festivals and celebrations in Bali throughout the year. The festivals in

Young dancers on Melasti Day, which is always observed shortly before New Year's with cleansing ceremonies and offerings on the beach or on the shore of a body of water.

Bali and Lombok are held according to three customary but differing calendars, causing the dates to shift from year to year so it is practically impossible to name a fixed date in advance. The tourist information offices in Denpasar and in Mataram (▶ Information) can provide annually published brochures (in English) with the current calendar dates for the festivals. Questions relating to this can also be answered by the people working at the hotel receptions. In addition, the *Bali Echo*, a tourist magazine (in English), is published regularly with a current events calendar.

Calendar

Apart from the everyday Gregorian calendar, there are three other calendar systems in Bali that play an important role in determining the dates for religious festivals: the uku calendar and the saka calendar. Their structure and use are so complicated, however, that only Brahman and special astrologers are capable of interpreting the calendars, which can hardly be compared to Western systematics and logic. Added to that is the Islamic calendar, which is less important in Bali.

Four calendar systems

THE OGOH-OGOH OF NYEPI

In Western countries, the turn of the year is celebrated with colourful rockets, exploding firecrackers, sparkling wine or champagne and the old year is seen off in a boisterous, jovial way. Not so in Bali.

And there is undoubtedly no other place on the face of the earth that celebrates the transition from one year to the next as it is marked on the island of gods, spirits and demons. The Balinese observe their new year's festival (Nyepi) in spring, at the time of the solstice or equinox, to be precise. But they begin with the preparations weeks ahead. The major preparations actually take the form of a competition among the Balinese boys to conjure up a more ugly and frightening ogoh-ogoh, an oversized monster made of a bamboo frame, papier mâché, paste and paint, than the youths in the neighbouring village. Spirits are used to frightening things, so the demon made by human hand naturally has to look wilder and more shockingly scary than even the very worst of the spirits.

Traditions surrounding the New Year

Three days before the festival celebrating the beginning of a new year, on saka day, thousands of festively dressed Balinese march to the island's coasts and lay down offerings to gain the favour of the spirits and demons dwelling in the sea for the coming year. This festival is especially beautiful to watch on the beach of Sanur. It is appropriate to wear a sarong for the occasion.

On the day of pengerupuk, the last day of the year, the islanders make

offerings in their temples to thoroughly cleanse Bali. Bamboo poles decorated with yellow and white ribbons, set up along the roadsides days beforehand, are intended to show the gods that they are welcome. Above all, it is the designers of the monster figures that most feverishly look forward to the parades planned all over the island for the night of New Year's Eve. The parades in Kuta and Denpasar, where masses of people line the roads, are the largest and most colourful. Those in the villages in the interior of the island are no less worth seeing though, and perhaps even a little more primal.

The Nyepi festival reaches its climax during the night on the eve of the New Year. After nightfall, in a manner somewhat similar to the carnival processions elsewhere in the world, the rickety ogoh-ogoh figures are paraded about, carried by their makers and preceded by musicians creating deafening sounds on their instruments. Any evil spirit not awakened, frightened and inspired to make a hasty exit to parts unknown would have as tough as old boots!

Yet it cannot be counted out that the odd, particularly stubborn spirit ignores this exorcism. So, the next day, the Balinese, an extremely mistrustful people, pretend that Bali is completely uninhabited.

This is the reason that no fire can be lit or light turned on anywhere on the whole island, any visible human movement must be stopped, and all work is held in abeyance. By the way, even tourists are not allowed to leave the hotel on »Nyepi«! It is a good chance to relax and enjoy the peace and quiet on this otherwise busy and bustling island.

Javanese-Balinese calendar

Almost everything that is of importance to the Balinese is calculated according to the Javanese-Balinese **uku** calendar, above all »birthdays«. Birthdays are not only celebrated for people, but also for farming equipment, weapons, cars and machines. Even the individual occupational groups celebrate their birthdays – rice farmers as well as artists, craftsmen and intellectuals. These events are moved to dates promising blessings, which are still of fundamental importance for the traditional farming population; essential dates such as the day on which the rice harvest can begin and the day on which it must be finished. Naturally, the most auspicious days for the temple anniversary or »birthday« festivals are calculated. The large festival for the state temple is the most important. The birthdays can only be determined by lengthy calculations and observations, which may then be on a completely different day the following year.

Hindu-Balinese calendar

The Hindu-Balinese calendar – **saka** – is more similar to the Gregorian calendar than the others, but is orientated on the lunar cycle; the year (caka) has twelve months each with 29 or 30 days. As this method of calculating the year diverges from the astronomical year, an intercalary month is added every 30 months. The Hindu faith knows no numbering for the years because, to the Hindu, everything that happens is continuous and bound in an eternally repeating cycle. So there is no »year zero«.

Islamic calendar

The Islamic calendar also has a part to play, though it only has a secondary role in Bali (it is more important in Lombok). It is based on the Arab calendar, which is also lunar oriented. The Islamic calendar has 354 days arranged into twelve months, each with 29 or 30 days. Again, the variance to the astronomical year is evened out with the inclusion of an intercalary month. The Islamic calendar begins with the year of the Prophet Mohammed's flight from Mecca (»Hejra« or »Hijra«; AD 622 = year 1).

Western calendar

The Western calendar, along with central Indonesian time, is quite customary in Indonesian public life – this applies equally to Bali and Lombok.

 CALENDAR OF EVENTS

FIXED HOLIDAY DATES

▸ **1 January**
New Year's Day
(as in the West)

▸ **21 April**
Kartin Day
(comparable to Mother's Day)

▸ **17 August**
Indonesian national holiday
(Proklamasi Kemerdekaan =
declaration of independence
1945). Local festivals are celebrated on this day on the whole island.

► **1 October**
Panca Sila Day (Day of the Five Principles). Commemoration of the address delivered by state founder Sukarno (►Famous People), which forms the preamble to the Indonesian constitution.

► **5 October**
Indonesian Armed Forces Day (military parades, etc.).

► **25–26 December**
First and second days of Christmas (as in the West)

MOVABLE HOLIDAY DATES

► **January / February**
Chinese New Year (first day of the first Chinese lunar-month).

► **March**
Nyepi
(►Baedeker Special, p.90)

► **March / April**
Ascension Day
(Christians)
Major temple anniversary (odalan festival) in Pura Besakih and in Pura Batu in Kintamani

Worshippers during Bhatara Turum Kabek in Besakih; it is said that the gods of all Balinese temples gather together here.

▶ **July**
Kite Festival: kite-flying competition in Padang Galak near Denpasar

▶ **September / October**
Odalan festival in Pura Kehen in Bangli

▶ **October / November**
Odalan festival in Pura Jagat Natha in Denpasar

In contrast to Bali, the number of festivals on the neighbouring island of Lombok is quite low. This is because the Islamic faith dominating there offers less occasion for exuberant celebrations than Hinduism does in Bali.

▶ **Christmas and New Year**
Christmas (25 December) and New Year's Eve (31 December) are celebrated according to Western tradition.

▶ **National holiday**
The Indonesian national holiday is celebrated on 17 August (cf. Bali).

▶ **Movable festivals**
The Islamic festivals are on Mohammed's birthday and the end of Ramadan, the month of fasting. Once a year, the islanders (Sasak) gather in Kuta (in Lombok) for a ceremony involving the collection of the legendary Nyale sea worms from the ocean. In addition, there are some celebrations in Lombok that take place only on a modest scale, such as within the family or village community. Such a celebration is called for when, for example, a young girl has her first menstruation or a boy is to be circumcised. The children are then carried on wooden animals through the village with the necessary background sounds being provided by drums, pipes and other noise-makers.

▶ **Cock fights**
Despite the cruelty to the animals, cock fights (with betting) are very popular in Lombok. The specially-trained cocks have razor-sharp blades attached to their legs, and frequently fight to the death.

Food and Drink

Indonesian Cuisine
Indonesian Cuisineis quite varied; indeed, it is **full of surprises**. Although the area achieved culinary independence some time ago, the Chinese, Malayan and Indian influences united within Indonesian dishes are quite clearly discernable. A **wide range of spices** (chilli, coriander, cumin, curry, ginger, and garlic) is used in the preparation of food here, with flavours ranging from mild and sweet and sour to extremely hot. A type of spicy paste (**sambal**) consisting of dried and crushed red peppers, tomatoes, chillies, onions, garlic and salt with cooking oil as a binder is a popular condiment.

Along with the Indonesian cooking offered in countless restaurants  Restaurants (»rumah makan«), international cuisine has become established especially in places frequented by tourists in Bali and Lombok. Whether a Balinese Wiener schnitzel really tastes like it does in the Austrian capital is debatable. Indonesian cooking, however, is so varied and good that visitors can readily do without European dishes. Reservations are recommended for

> ### *i* Price categories restaurants
>
> ■ Expensive: from £12/$22
> ■ Moderate: from £5.50/$11 to £12/$24
> ■ Inexpensive: from £2.40/$6 to £5.50/$11
>   (3 courses, without drinks)

high-quality restaurants; it is customary, upon entering a restaurant, to wait for the waiter to show you to a seat. The **snack bars** typical of many Asian countries are called »warung« in Bali. A »warung makan« is a simple eatery, open towards the street, where small dishes are served, primarily soups. Hygiene, however, is not always a priority in such establishments.

The delicious grilled satay meats are usually served in a spicy peanut sauce.

Food

Rice, vegetables, fish and meat

The most important part of the main meal is rice (cooked: nasi putih; fried: nasi goreng), always served with fresh vegetables prepared in a variety of ways, fish, seafood and/or fried meat (beef, pork, poultry). Sometimes there are noodles, while potatoes are rather rare – and actually unknown in Indonesian cuisine – only occurring in so-called international dishes.

The **Indonesian rice table** is famous: it is a collection of several dishes served in family circles only on high holidays. The meal always begins with a vegetable soup. The basis of the rice table is, of course, rice, and it is served with variously prepared meats, vegetables, fish, seafood and eggs, sauces ranging from hot to sweet and sour, as well as nuts, fruit, coconut meat, krupuk (prawn crackers) and much more.

Soups

Baso is a soup consisting of a spicy broth with rice noodles, vegetables and pieces of meat added. **Bubur ayam** is a thick rice soup with chicken; **bakmi kuah** is a simple (usually spicy) broth with vegetables and noodles. **Soto babad** is a soup with beef and vegetables. When the temperature is high, often just a portion of **capcay kuah** (cabbage soup) is sufficient.

Skewered meat

The meats (beef, lamb and pork, occasionally also offal) on a wooden skewer known as **satay** (sate) are grilled over a charcoal fire and enjoyed as a small snack as well as an essential part of the Indonesian rice table. When the meat is cooked, it is dipped for a moment in a sauce to which ground peanuts have been added.

Main dishes

The preparation of the good, nourishing main dish called **nasi goreng** is simpler than its exotic name might suggest. Cooked rice is fried with vegetables, onions sautéed in oil and strips of beef or pork. It is seasoned with finely chopped peppers and chillies. A version of nasi goreng goes by the name of bami goreng in Java; there, noodles are used instead of rice.

Fried chicken (**ayam goreng**), pork (**kolo bak**) and sucking pig meat (**babi kecap**) in a sweet and sour sauce is popular. **Babi guling**, a Balinese speciality, is very tasty: it consists of sucking pig grilled over an open fire with rice added as a side dish. **Bebek betutu** (duck meat cooked in banana leaves) and **bebek panggang** (grilled duck meat) are quite delicious. **Cap cai**, inspired by Chinese cooking, is actually a version of the world famous chop suey: meat and vegetables cut into bit-size pieces are fried in a pan and served with rice.

Crepes and prawn crackers

Martabak is a kind of crepe filled with lamb, onions and spices, folded together and fried briefly on each side. Krupuk is a speciality of Indonesian cooking: crisp crackers made from tapioca flour and dried shrimp or fish are cooked in oil.

Bananas deep-fried in batter (pisang goreng) and rice pudding are popularly served for dessert. Acar is a savoury dessert of gherkins, small onions, sweet and sour pickled ginger and roasted peanuts.

Fruits

The **art of fruit and vegetable carving** is widespread in Bali. There are specialized employees in the kitchens of the large hotels who are true masters in creating designs from fruit and vegetables.

Pineapples (nanas) are fresh from April to July. Some varieties are consumed locally customarily in a fermented state, which can have a laxative effect. **Bananas** (pisang), available all year round, are soaked in coconut milk and grilled. Tip: the smaller the banana, the sweeter they taste.

Even if Europeans find it takes some getting used to, the somewhat mealy meat of the **durian fruit** – also called stinky fruit because of its overpowering smell – is considered a delicacy by Asians (ripe from April to June).

On the other hand, **jackfruit** (nangka), a roundish fruit weighing several kilos, is sweet and aromatic. It is cut into slices and served on ice cream (August to September). The yellow-green to dark blue, oval **passion fruit** (up to 20cm/8in long) is also widespread. Its juicy, jelly-like flesh is scooped out by spoon and has a sweet-sour taste.

The meat of the hard-husked **coconut** (kelapa) is extracted with a narrow spoon after the coconut milk has been poured out (see drinks: fruit juices). **Limes** are the local alternative to lemons and available all year round. The larger, yellow lemons must be imported and are therefore quite expensive. **Lychees** are cultivated more in other parts of Indonesia than in Bali. When ripe, the light-coloured flesh of the fruit with the reddish skin tastes sweet and fresh (May to August). **Mangos** (mangga), along with pineapples, are probably the tourists' favourite. This fruit is sweet, juicy and aromatic only when it is fully ripe (yellow skin; does not keep well). Mangos are cut in half and the flesh is either spooned out or sucked out (March to June).

Oranges have a thin, green skin in Indonesia; those with a yellow colouring are particularly sweet. **Grapefruit**, usually with the pleasant-tasting pink flesh, are fresh all year round and are popularly eaten with a pinch of salt. **Papaya**, native to the American tropics, is the cheapest of all Asian fruits and available at any time of year at every market stand. In hotel breakfasts, it is served in halves with a lemon. Some caution is advised: enjoyed in larger amounts, papaya is sure laxative. The small, red, hairy-skinned **rambutan fruit** that grows on a variety of the soapberry tree tastes similar to a grape. The **malabar plum** has the form of a pear with a rust-coloured, waxy skin and a porous, light-coloured flesh; both skin and flesh are edible. As the fruit has a somewhat sour taste, it is preferably eaten with sugar and a pinch of salt (January to March).

Drinks

Given the high temperatures in Bali, doctors specializing in tropical medicine recommend drinking **at least two to three litres (three to five pints) of liquids daily**. In which form the moisture lost through perspiration is replaced in the body is left up to the individual, but the absolutely wrong way to go about it is to drink alcoholic beverages. Indeed, the tropical heat increases the unpleasant side-effects of alcohol. Good thirst-quenchers are mineral water, tea or fruit juices. Pineapple (air jeruk) and coconut (es kelapa muda) juices are especially refreshing.

The national drink of Indonesia is tea. It is served warm at meals (teh panas) and ice cold (teh es) as a refresher. Some caution is necessary: tea is sometimes chilled with ice cubes and if there are doubts about hygiene, it would be better to go without. Coffee is prepared Turkish-style and served as mocha, complete with the grounds. *Tea and coffee*

Beer (bir) is brewed in Indonesia under license to foreign companies: these include German, Dutch and Danish beers bearing their internationally known brand names. A large beer in a bar is called »bir besar«, a small one »bir kecil«; beer is sold in large and small bottles in the supermarkets. Compared to prices at home, beer is – as are the following alcoholic beverages – relatively expensive. *Beer*

Arak, high-proof brandy typical of Indonesia, is more suited as part of a mixed drink, for example mixed with rice wine or lime juice and honey in long drinks. All the usual international spirits are available in hotels, but are often very pricey. *Spirits*

The rural population of Bali drinks rice wine (brem) or the slightly tart palm wine (tuak) made from fermented coconut palm flowers. While both are called wine, they are made in a brewing process is similar to that of beer. *Wine*

Health

Health Care

A holiday in the tropics demands some preparation before leaving and a certain amount of caution once there to ensure that the trip is a positive experience. As a rule, consult your family doctor before departure: he or she will advise you on avoiding health risks.

← *Aromatic fruits*

Traveller's first aid kit

Because the risk of infection is greater in the tropics, a first aid kit plays a much greater role when on holiday in Asia than when travelling within Europe. It should contain scissors, tweezers, cotton wool, two gauze bandages, a package of bandaging materials, two first aid dressings, sticking plasters, disinfectant and medicines against fever, pain, diarrhoea, constipation, travel sickness, circulatory trouble and infection. Along with sun lotion, an insect repellent that can be applied to the skin is very important.

Vaccinations

The Indonesian authorities do not require that European visitors have any specific vaccinations as long as they have not passed through areas infected with certain diseases. However, protection against tetanus and poliomyelitis (polio) is recommended. It is best always to carry a medical certificate listing possible allergies and intolerances as well as your blood group. Furthermore, an inoculation against hepatitis A, whose pathogens are transmitted through the un-

Sun protection Bali-style

IMPORTANT CONTACT DETAILS

INTERNATIONAL AIR AMBULANCE SERVICES

► **Cega Air Ambulance (worldwide service)**
Tel. +44(0)1243 621097
Fax +44(0)1243 773169
www.cega-aviation.co.uk

► **US Air Ambulance**
Tel. 800/948-1214
(US; toll-free)
Tel. 001-941-926-2490
(international; collect)
www.usairambulance.net

DENTISTS

► **Nusa Dua Dental Clinic**
Jalan Pratama 81A
Nusa Dua
Tel. (03 61) 77 13 24

HOSPITALS IN BALI

Emergency medical care is available in the following hospitals:

► **Bali International Medical Center**
Jalan Bypass Ngurah Rai, Kuta
Tel. (03 61) 76 12 63

► **Dharma Ushada Hospital**
Jl. Panglima Sudirman, Denpasar
Tel. (03 61) 22 75 60

► **Kuta Clinic**
Jl. Raya Kuta 100, Kuta
Tel. (03 61) 75 32 68

► **Ubud Clinic**
Jalan Ubud 36, Campuhan
(24 hour ambulance service)
Tel. (03 61) 97 49 11

---

hygienic preparation of food and drink (particularly ice!), is advisable. Sensitive tourists should have themselves immunized with gamma globulin before departure. The National Travel Health Network and Centre in London (www.netdoctor.co.uk), funded by the Department of Health, promotes clinical standards in travel medicine. Information on recommended vaccines country by counry is available at www.tmb.ie. Cases of malaria have recently been on the rise again in Southeast Asia. The use of medication offering protection against malaria, especially when travelling outside the tourist centres, is recommended. ◄ Malaria prophylaxis

It takes time for the body to adjust to the tropical climate. It is best to avoid physical exertion the first couple of days, and to minimize exposure to the intense rays of the sun. It is essential to take a sun lotion with a high sunscreen factor: Bali is after all located not far from the equator. Treat air conditioning with caution. Even if the artificially produced cool air feels initially pleasant in contrast to the tropical temperatures outside, there is an acute danger of catching a cold for those that remain in air conditioned – which often means chilly – rooms for longer periods of time. When sleeping at night, the air conditioning should be turned down. Adjusting to the climate

Bali fever The mysterious »Bali fever« is notorious among Bali tourists. It begins abruptly and the body temperature rises to over 39°C/102°F, normally in the absence of other complaints. Antipyretics and two days in bed have proven to be a helpful way of treating the disease. If the fever does not subside, consult a doctor.

AIDS The danger of becoming infected with HIV/AIDS in Indonesia is relatively great for those who engage in those activities known to carry a risk of infection. Only the well-known precautionary measures can help protect against the transmission of the virus. The use of condoms reduces the risk during heterosexual and homosexual intercourse, and disposable syringes should be used only once for injections.

Food Food from snack bars is generally also safe for tourists to eat, but do pay attention to cleanliness. Fruit must always be thoroughly washed before eating. Avoid, as a matter of principle, the consumption of raw foods, unpeeled fruits, ice cream, and beverages served in glasses with a lot of ice. Caution is advised in the consumption of alcohol in the tropics. Heat can intensify its well-known unpleasant side effects.

In Case of Illness

Pharmacies There are numerous pharmacies in Bali, above all in places frequented by tourists, recognizable by the signs »Apotik« or »Toko Obat«. They stock a selection of the usual medicines, although some with names only customary in Asia. Those dependent on certain medicines (or requiring contraceptives) should bring an ample supply from home or ensure by comparison with an original packaging that the preparation available in Indonesia is identical to the one needed. If in doubt, go and see a doctor. Medicines are – as everywhere in Asia – significantly cheaper than in Europe.

Doctors and hospitals Particularly in the tourist centres, medical care is well provided for in both Bali and Lombok. There are free-practicing doctors in the cities and villages, though very few of them speak a lot of English. English-speaking physicians in the employ of large hotels can be summoned to reception when needed. In an emergency, the local tour organizer's representatives are also ready to arrange for a suitable doctor or dentist.

There are no hospitals in Bali capable of handling very severe injuries or life-threatening illnesses. It is therefore advisable in such cases to consider being transported to Jakarta or Singapore. In cases of serious illness, your consulate or embassy (▶ Information) should be notified without fail.

Ambulance Service The ambulance service in Bali and Lombok is, according to Western standards, barely operational. Expect to wait for a longer period of

Never sample unwashed or unpeeled fruits.

time in cases of accidents outside of the tourist centres, although generally you can depend on the local Balinese who are anxious to help. Should there be a need for an early return flight for medical reasons, a rescue aircraft must be requested from home. Return transport can be very expensive, so it would be advisable to take out travel health insurance that covers the possibility of return transport for medical reasons.

Information

There is currently no Indonesian tourist office in the UK. Information can be obtained from the Indonesian Embassy in London. The Garuda Indonesia Office in Sydney Australia promotes tourism in Indonesia, as does the Indonesian Tourist Office in Los Angeles. All addresses are listed below. In addition, a wealth of information about Bali and Indonesia, as well as hotel directories and personal travel reports, can be found on the internet.

ADDRESSES FOR INFORMATION

▶ **Bali Tourism Board**
Jl. Raya Puputan 41
Renon, Bali 80235
Tel. (03 61) 23 56 00
Fax 23 92 00
www.bali-tourism-board.com

▶ **Bali Government
Tourism Office**
Jl. S. Parman 1, Niti Mandala
Renon, Denpasar 80235
Tel. (03 61) 22 23 87, fax 22 63 13

▶ **Lombok Regional
Tourism Office Jalan**
Langko 70, Mataram
Tel. (03 70) 63 17 30
Fax 63 18 66
Opening hours: Mon–Sat
8am–3pm

▶ **Garuda Indonesia Office**
4, Bligh Street, PO Box 3836
Sydney 2000
Tel. 232-6044, fax: 2332828

▶ **Indonesian Tourist Office**
3457 Wilshire Boulevard
Los Angeles, CA 90010
Tel. 213 387 2078

▶ **In the UK**
38 Grosvenor Square
London W1K 2HW
Tel. 020 7499 7661
Fax 020 7491 4993
www.indonesianembassy.org.uk

▶ **In the Republic of Ireland**
Honorary Consul
25 Kilvere Rathfarnham
Dublin
Tel. 353 852 491

▶ **In the USA**
2020 Massachusetts Ave NW
Washington DC 20036
Tel. 202 775 5200
www.embassyofindonesia.org

▶ **In Canada**
55 Parkdale Ave
Ottawa, Ontario K1Y 1E5
Tel. 613 724 1100
www.indonesia-ottawa.org

▶ **In Australia**
8 Darwin Ave
Yarralumla, ACT 2600
Tel. 02 6250 8600
www.kbri-canberra.org.au

▶ **In New Zealand**
70 Glen Road
Kelburn, Wellington
Tel. 04 4758 697
www.indonesianembassy.org.nz

▶ **Diplomatic Representation
in Bali**
Foreign embassies are based in
Jakarta. In Bali, the following
consulates can provide assistance
in the case of an emergency:

UK
Jl. Tirtanadi 20
Sanur
Tel. 270601

USA
Jl. Hayam Wuruk 188
Renon, Denpasar
Tel. 233605

Australia
Jl. Hayam Wuruk 88B
Renon, Denpasar
Tel. 241118
www.dfat.gov.au/bali

The Australian consulate shares responsibility for Canadian citizens, and can also offer assistance to citizens of the Republic of Ireland and New Zealand.

Language

In contrast to many other Asian languages, the local language »Bahasa Indonesia« (Bahasa for short), which is closely related to Malaysian, is relatively easy for Europeans to learn.

Malaysian grammar **grammar** is quite simple. For example, plurals are expressed by simply doubling the singular (»bulan« = month; »bulan-bulan« = months) – although under certain circumstances a doubled word can also take on a completely different meaning. Bahasa Indonesia has no articles. »How much does the room cost?« is in Bahasa »Berapa harga kamar kosong ini?« (= »How much cost room?«). Verbs are not conjugated; the context of the sentence indicates what the inflected form would be. Possessive pronouns are postpositional: »my room« is »Kamarku« (end syllable »ku« = »my«).

Bahasa Indonesia demonstrates some peculiarities regarding **pronunciation**. A »c« is always pronounced as »cha« (»candi« is thus »chandi«); a »z« is always devoiced (= »s«).

A formal **salutation** is not customary in Indonesia. There is also no corresponding expression for it. A favourite way of opening a conversation is to ask the other person's name (»Siapa namayana?«) or place of origin. Sometimes a question concerning general well-being is asked (»Apa khabar?«), which can be answered either with »Bagus, bagus« (= »good, good«) or with »Khabar baik« (= »I feel fine«).

Indonesia is largely an Islamic country, and this has resulted in several Arabic words entering the language. For example, the word »selamat!« (= »May your deeds be blessed!«), which is always linked to a time of day or a request.

Bahasa Indonesia

INDONESIAN PHRASES

At a Glance

Yes	Ya.
No	Tidak.
Perhaps	Mungkin. / Bis jada. / Barangkali.

Please	Silankan (offering, inviting).
	Tolong (ask for help).
	Kembali (you're welcome/think nothing of it).
Thank you	Terima kasih.
Many thanks.	Terima kasih banyak.
You're welcome	Sama-sama.
Sorry!	Maaf! / Sorry!
Pardon?	Maaf, bagaimana?
I don't understand you.	Saya tidak mengerti.
I speak only a little ...	Saya hanya bisa berbicara sedikit ....
Do you speak ...	Apa Bapak / Ibu / kamu berbicara bahasa ....
English?	Inggris?
French?	Perancis?
German?	Jerman?
Would you please help me?	Apa Basak / Ibu bisa menolong saya?

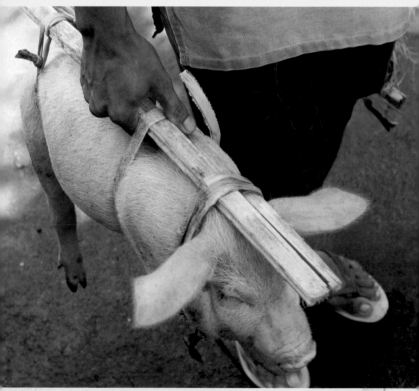

Off to market

I would like ...	Saya mau ...
I (do not) like that.	Saya (kurang) menyukainya.
Do you have ...?	Apa di sini ada ...?
How much does it cost?	Berapa harganya?
What time is it?	Jam berapa sekarang?

Becoming Acquainted

Good morning!	Selamat pagi!
Good day!	Selamat siang!
	(11am to 3pm)
	Selamat sore! (3pm to 6pm)
Good evening!	Selamat malam!
Hello! / Hi!	Halo!
My name is ...	Nama saya ...
What is your name (please)? (informal)	Siapa nama Bapak / Ibu?
How are you?	Apa kabar Pak / Ibu?
Very well, thank you.	Terima kasih.
And yourself? (infomal)	Dan Bapak. / Ibu / kamu?
Goodbye	Sampai jumpa lagi!
Good night	Selamat tidurr!
Cheerio!	Permisi! / Ayo! / Bye! / Daag! / Mari!
See you later	Sampai nanti!
See you tomorrow	Sampai besok!

Getting Around

left / right	kiri / kanan
straight ahead	terus, lurus
near / far	dekat / jauh
Please, where is ...?	Maaf, di mana ...?
How far is it to ...?	Berapa jauhnya ke ...?
Which bus goes to ...?	Bus mana pergi ke ...?
Where can I buy a ticket?	Di mana saya bisa membeli karcis?
Where is the next taxi stand?	Di mana pangkalan taksi terdekat?
to the train station / ... hotel	Ke stasiun / hotel.
to ... (please)	Ke ...

petrol station

Where is the next petrol station (please)?	Di man pompa bensin terdekat?

It is usually no problem making contact with children.

I would like ... litres	Saya mau ... litre
... two-star petrol / regular	... premium.
... super	... premix.
... diesel	... solar.
... mixture	... bensin campur.
Fill it up, please.	Isi penuh.

Emergency

Help!	Tolong!
Watch out!	Awas!
Careful!	Hati-hati!
Please quickly call	Tolong cepat panggil
... an ambulance	... ambulans.
... the police	... polisi.
... the fire department	... pemadam kebakaran.
It was my / your fault.	Ini kesalahan saya / Bapak / Ibu.
Please give me your name and address!	Tolong berikan saya nama dan alamat Bapak / Ibu.

Dining / Shopping

Where do I find	Di mana ada
... a good restaurant?	... restoran yang baik?
... a typical restaurant?	... restoran yang khas?
Please reserve (for us) a table for tonight for a party of four.	Saya mau memesan meja untuk vier orang untuk malam ini.

Do you have vegetarian dishes/diet-low calorie food?	Apa ada hidangan tanpa daging / untuk diet?
Could we have a little more rice / water?	Apa bisa mendapat nasi / ar lagi?
Cheers!	Cheers! / Prost!
Enjoy your meal!	Selamat makan!
Not too spicy, please!	Tolong jangan terlalu pedas!
Can we have the bill, please.	Saya mau bayar.
The meal was excellent.	Makanannya enak sekali.
That is for you.	Ini untuk Bapak. / Ibu.
Where are the toilets?	Di man kamar kecil?
Where do I find	Di mana saya bisa membeli
... a chemist's shop?	... apotik?
... a bakery?	... toko roti?
... a batik shop?	... toko batik?
... a camera shop?	... toko alat-alat foto?
... a department store?	... pasar swalayan?
... a travel agent?	... biro perjalanan?

Accommodation

I reserved a room with you.	Saya telah memesan kamar die sini.
Do you still have a vacancy	Apa di sini masih ada kamar kosong
... for one night?	... untuk satu malam?
... for a week?	... untuk satu minggu?
... with bath?	... denang kamar mandi?
How much does a room cost with ...	Berapa harga kamar dengan ...
... breakfast?	... makan pagi?
... half-board?	... makan pagi dan malam saja?
... full-board?	... tiga kali makan?

Doctor

Could you recommend a good doctor?	Apa Bapak / Ibu tahu seorang dokter yang baik?
I have an upset stomach.	Perut saya tidak enak.
I have diarrhoea.	Saya diare.
I have a fever.	Saya demam.
I have pains here.	Saya sakit di sini.
I cannot tolerate the heat / food.	Saya tidak tahan makanan itu / panas.

Bank

Where is a bank (please) / a bureau de change/money changer?	Di mana ada bank / money changer di sini?
I would like to exchange ... euros into rupiahs.	Saya mau menukar ... Euro dalam Rupiah.

Numbers

0	nol	19	sembilan belas
1	satu	20	dua puluh
2	dua	21	dua puluh satu
3	tiga	30	tiga puluh
4	empat	40	empat puluh
5	lima	50	lima puluh
6	enam	60	enam puluh
7	tujuh	70	tujuh puluh
8	delapan	80	delapan puluh
9	sembilan	90	sembilan puluh
10	sepuluh	100	seratus
11	sebelas	200	dua ratus
12	dua belas	1000	seribu
13	tiga belas	2000	dua ribu
14	empat belas	1000	sepulu ribu
15	lima belas		
16	enam belas	1/2	seperdua, setengah
17	tujuh belas	1/3	sepertiga
18	delapan belas	1/4	seperempat

Literature

Illustrated Books **Joyce Jue:** *Savouring Southeast Asia.* Time Life UK (2000). A successful example of a new generation of cookery books that offer information about the country and its people with large format photographs along with the recipes. Because the culinary traditions of other Southeast Asian countries are greatly valued in Bali, the similarities in the recipes are not restricted to the typical use of ingredients such as rice, coconut milk, fresh herbs and spices; rather numerous dishes exist that have an »international« character. This book presents a collection of 130 recipes together with a wealth of information about eating traditions and related cultural history. Local products and customs are described, as well as selected restaurants. The glossary introduces the basic preparation and special ingredients of Southeast Asian cuisine.

Angelika Taschen (Ed.): *Inside Asia* (2 vol.). Taschen (2005). For leafing through, reading, obtaining information, planning, and dreaming. The renowned Swiss photographer, Reto Guntli, Asia expert and enthusiast since his childhood, travelled for months through the region searching for subjects to photograph that express the essence of what constitutes life and living in Asia, namely the calmness and harmony with all sentient and feeling beings. Bali captivated him once more through the warm-heartedness of its people, its tropical nature and the spirituality possessed by everything on the island. These two magnificent volumes will provide lasting enjoyment for anyone interested in Asian culture.

! *Baedeker* TIP

Travel reading

Almost every destination frequented by tourists has a book shop offering a large selection of second-hand books, mostly in English. If you have read a book, you can exchange it for another used book for a pittance or at no cost at all.

Angelika Taschen (Ed.): *Living in Bali.* Taschen (2005).
»When it comes to Balinese houses, walls are not compulsory, wood is everywhere, earth tones are dominant, and thatched roofs abound«, report the authors of this opulent volume that portrays 19 magnificent houses, villas and hotels. Inspiring photographs of private living spheres allow the viewers to immerse themselves into the diversity of Balinese living. Concise commentaries in three languages provide explanations of each interior. Along with famous hotels such as Begawan Giri Estate, smaller, delightful guesthouses are also highlighted, as well as the houses of local and foreign artists who have lived in Bali for years.

Vicki Baum: *A Tale of Bali.* Tuttle Publishing, US (2000). Vicki Baum **Novel** (▶Famous Persons) spent several months in Bali in 1935; she delved into the history of the island, observed life there and intensely studied its history and culture. With this novel, published in 1937, she helped a European reading public gain an insight into the exotic island for the first time.

Media

There are a number of radio stations in Bali that normally broadcast **Radio** the news in English on the hour. Those with a shortwave radio should be able to receive the BBC World Service and Voice of America. As the frequencies change, check the transmission schedule online before leaving home: www.bbc.co.uk/wordservice and www.voa.gov respectively.

Television Most of the larger hotels in Bali and numerous others offer satellite television with programmes in English. Furthermore, English-language films shown on Indonesian television channels are not dubbed, instead having subtitles. The news in English is broadcast daily at 6.30pm by RCTI, a private TV station.

Newspapers and magazines Among the more than 70 dailies published in Indonesia, three are in English and available throughout the land. Although no direct censorship exists, a myriad of press laws are meant to prevent reports critical to the system.

The *Jakarta Post* is in the main newspaper available in Bali, though usually not until around noon. International newspapers and magazines are only available at the newsagents of the larger hotels, and are very expensive. Several monthly or bimonthly magazines, containing features, travel articles and what's-on guides, are targeted specifically at tourists. These include *Bali and Beyond*, *Bali Echo*, *Hello Bali*, *Bali Tribune* and *Bali Travel News*.

Money

Currency The Indonesian currency is called the rupiah (Rp.). The coins come in denominations of 5, 10, 25, 50, 100 and 500 rupiahs. The Indonesian banknotes have values of 100, 500, 1000, 5000, 10,000, 20,000 and 50,000 rupiahs.

Exchange rate The exchange rate for banks is officially set by the authorities. This rate is used by Bank Negara Indonesia's (BNI) official bureau de change at the airports as well as in the bank's branches in the island's interior. On the other hand, it is quite possible that other money changers may offer a somewhat better exchange rate. The variation becomes obvious after arriving at Ngurah Rai airport, where the money changers inside the airport itself sometimes offer a distinctly worse rate than those outside the arrival hall. Only exchange money in hotels in emergencies because the rate there is generally less favourable. By the way, it is only possible to sell back rupiahs by presenting a receipt for a previous exchange.

> ### *i* Exchange rates
>
> - 1000 rupiahs = £0.05
>   £1 = 18,000 rupiahs
> - 1000 rupiahs = €0.07
>   €1 = 14,400 rupiahs
> - 1000 rupiahs = US$0.11
>   US$1 = 9,090 rupiahs

Foreign currencies can be brought into the country in unlimited amounts. Without authorization, the amount of local currency that can be brought into and taken out of the country should not exceed 50,000 rupiahs per person.

It is recommended bringing **rupiahs in cash** from home to cover the first expenses incurred upon arrival (taxi, bus, tips, etc.). Pay special attention to the quality of the banknotes, at home as well as in Indonesia. They must be in perfect condition, as damaged or heavily soiled notes of any currency will not be accepted.

Taking along **traveller's cheques** is also recommended. The built-in insurance helps quickly in case of loss or theft – though only when the instructions have been followed with care (above all, keep cheques and purchase receipts separate).

Cash can be withdrawn from automatic teller machines (ATMs) all over Bali with a **debit card** bearing a Maestro symbol. The usual **credit cards** such as American Express, BankAmericard/Visa, MasterCard/Eurocard and Diners Club are accepted mainly in the areas frequented by tourists in Bali and Lombok. In case of the loss of a credit card, contact the card issuer at home or the respective representative without delay.

i **Lost or stolen card**

■ There is a number on the back of every credit card which should be called in the case of the card being lost or stolen – it is a good idea to make a note of this number as well as those given by the bank. Some emergency contact numbers are listed below:
■ HSBC: tel. +44 (0) 1442 422 929
■ Lloyds TSB Bank: tel. +44 (0) 1702 278 270
■ Barclays Bank: tel. +44 (0)1904 544 666
■ NatWest Bank: tel. +44 (0) 142 370 0545
■ Citibank: tel. +44 (0) 207 500 5500
■ MasterCard: tel. 0800 96 4767 (UK) or 001 63 67 22 71 11 (USA)
■ American Express: tel. +44 (0)1273 696 933
■ Visa: tel. 0800 89 1725 (UK) or 800-8-11-824 (US)
■ Contact details in Bali
  – American Express: Jl. Legian Kuta 80, Kuta tel. (03 61) 75 87 81
  – Mastercard: Bank Central Asia, Jl. Raya Kuta 55, Kuta, tel. (03 61) 76 22 47
  – Diners: Jl. Diponegoro 45, Denpasar, tel. (03 61) 23 55 59

Banks
The recommended banks to deal with all the usual monetary transactions in Bali and Lombok are Bank Negara Indonesia (BNI), Niaga Bank and Dagang Negara Bank. There are branches in the larger towns on the islands.

◄ Telegraphic money transfers
It is possible to transfer money by telegraph between Europe and Indonesia, but it takes at least two days. A passport must be presented when collecting the money.

Personal Safety

Don't flaunt luxury
Bali is no »island paradise« as far as security is concerned. Still, the rate of crime is no higher here than in other places in the world frequented by tourists. The visitor should not fail to take necessary precautions, remembering the motto »opportunity makes a thief«. After all, a holidaymaker often carries more cash on him than a simple ho-

tel worker can earn in a month (or longer). Do not flaunt your superior standard of living and leave your valuables in the hotel safe. Also, it is best to carry only as much money around with you as you expect to spend. Always leave your room keys at the hotel reception.

Precautionary measures

For security purposes, travel documents should be photocopied before leaving home and the copies taken along and kept separate from the originals. In case of loss, this greatly facilitates their replacement. When using traveller's cheques, remember to store the purchase receipt apart from the cheque forms; only then is the insurance coverage guaranteed. It is useful to note down important telephone numbers for emergencies, such as that of your bank, credit card company or traveller's cheque issuer.

Most of the large hotels offer **free safe-deposit boxes** or even room safes, although they accept no liability at all for any theft occurring in the rooms. Neck pouches or special belts next to the body to hold money and other valuables, invisible from outside, provide security from pickpockets, who are certain to be active at all the marketplaces and anywhere that large crowds of people gather. There are no official lost property offices in Bali; even bus companies do not offer this service. Lost articles, if turned in, can be picked up at the nearest police station (► Emergency).

i **Tourist police hotline**

■ Tel. (03 61) 22 41 11

Security advice from the Foreign Office

There has been some success in the investigation into the 2002 terror attack in Bali resulting in numerous arrests and convictions, although some of the extremists identified as the masterminds are still at large. The attacks in Bali confirm that there are groups in Indonesia who have the capability and motivation to carry out (suicide) attacks. Such acts of terrorism will most likely continue in the future. Areas considered to be at particular risk are Jakarta and, in Bali, the places frequented by foreigners or identified with Western countries such as hotels, embassies, shopping centres and tourist facilities.

Post and Communications

Post office

As a rule, the Indonesian post office in Bali and Lombok operates dependably. It normally takes seven to ten days for postcards and letters to reach Europe. Indonesian letter boxes are red, and collection times are listed on a sign on the front. It is also possible to give letters to the hotel reception for posting. The main post office in Denpasar is located in Jl. Raya Puputan; there are more post offices in Sanur (Br. Taman), in Kuta (Jl. Raya Kuta Gung Selamat) and in Ubud (Jl. Payangan). Business hours are usually Mon–Thu 8am–2pm, Fri 8am–11am, Sat 8am–12.30pm.

INFORMATION AND AREA CODES

AREA CODES

► From the UK and Republic of Ireland

... to Indonesia:
  tel. 00 62
... to South Bali:
  tel. 00 62 361
... to North Bali:
  tel. 00 62 362
... to West Bali:
  tel. 00 62 03 65
... To East Bali:
  tel. 00 62 03 63
... to Klungkung:
  tel. 00 62 03 66
... to Lombok:
  tel. 00 62 370

► From the USA, Canada and Australia

As above, but replace the 00 with 0011

► From Bali and Lombok

... to the UK: tel. 001 44
... to the Republic of Ireland:
  Tel. 001 353
... to the USA and Canada:
  Tel. 001 1
... to Australia: tel. 001 61

TELEPHONE INFORMATION

► National
Tel. 100

► International
Tel. 101

Telephoning in Bali and Lombok can occasionally be quite arduous because the lines are often overloaded. There are **card telephones** almost everywhere across Bali and Lombok. Telephone cards can be purchased in post offices and call shops, as well as in hotels and supermarkets. A personal **mobile phone** is more handy but also quite expensive. Information about roaming tarifs can be obtained from the mobile companies at home.

There is **no specific local area code** for Bali, but a distinction is made between the five regions when calling from abroad.

◄ Telephoning

Many large hotels offer an (expensive!) direct dial service from Bali to Europe by IDD (International Direct Dialling). It is also possible to make calls abroad in all post offices on the island, although there are often long waiting times. Normal overseas calls are decidedly cheaper, as is the sending of faxes via the state-sponsored Wartel Telecommunications Service.

◄ Calls abroad

A three minute call to Europe costs about 30,000 rupiahs; a local call from a public telephone costs 50 rupiahs (more expensive in hotels). **Reverse-charge calls** are somewhat problematic. A hefty connection fee will be charged in a public telephone office, or wartel, if they allow such calls at all. It is best to use a public telephone and ask to make a reverse-charge call either via the Indonesian operator (dial 101) or by using the Home Country Direct Service to talk directly

◄ Home Country Direct Service

with an operator from your home country. The Home Country Direct Service can be accessed from any phone capable of IDD. Dial 001 801 and then the country code (44 for the UK).

Fax and internet Faxes can be sent from the wartel offices located in the larger towns, recognizable by their white signs with black lettering and a blue logo. Fax machines can be found in almost every hotel. They are available to hotel guests and sometimes also to non-residents. A minimum charge is frequently demanded for sending a fax (for example, the price of a three-minute phone call). Larger hotels offer an office service in a so-called business centre, where business travellers will find all the modern means of communication. There are also numerous internet cafés offering cheap communications, telephone and fax services.

Prices

▶ WHAT DOES IT COST?

One-course meal
from £1.20–1.60/
$2.40–3.20

Glass of beer
from £0.65–1.60/
$1.60–4.00

Taxi
from £0.08/$0.16

1l petrol
from £0.08–0.12/$0.16–0.24

Shopping

Mainly arts and crafts Bali is certainly no shopping paradise like Singapore, Bangkok or Hong Kong, for instance; but the islanders are known for their artistic skills and they use them to good effect to produce attractive items. All the larger hotels have their own souvenir shops and there are countless souvenir dealers in the places frequented by tourists, but the prices are cheaper in the interior of the island. Except in established shops and hotels, it is quite possible to bargain over the price; in fact, **haggling is almost a national sport** for Asians. The following selection lists some typical souvenirs and the places where they are best purchased.

Antiques

Authentic antiques have become rare in Bali. Really old items worth the price demanded are found only rarely. The Balinese are experts, however, at producing reproductions of old objects that are often very difficult to differentiate from the original. The export of antiques – in Indonesia, art objects more than 50 years old – requires official approval; the Bali Government Tourism Office in Denpasar (▶Information) can provide more information.

Bamboo furniture

Rattan and bamboo furniture is produced in Mas. Ordering is carried out by catalogue, and worldwide delivery by (expensive) shipping freight. Make sure that the material is impregnated and treated against insect attack.

Batik

Batik textiles are sold in Bali, but be aware that not all are authentic. Many cloths are simply printed using a simplified batik stamp pro-

The Balinese shadow figures used in the plays are cut from buffalo leather and painted colourfully.

! *Baedeker* TIP

Design your own jewellery

Those in the know in Bali have rings, necklaces and even belts produced according to their own specifications. Working from a sketch or a photo provided by the customer, silversmiths create made-to-measure objects. There is just one drawback: it takes about 1–2 weeks to complete an order.

cess. Expect to pay high prices resulting from the elaborate handiwork involved (see p.61) for authentic ikat fabrics. Double ikat cloth can only be found in Tenganan.

The small **woodcarving** village of Mas near Ubud is one of the largest centres of woodcarving art (dance masks, figures, etc.); here, shopping is done at the »factory outlet«, as it were, and the prices are correspondingly advantageous. There are also good woodcarvers in the neighbouring village of Nyuhkuning.

Painting
Ubud is the island's centre of art, and countless artists have set up their shops there. Balinese painting can also be found in Pengosekan, a good 3km/1.9mi south of Ubud.

Shadow theatre figures
Firm favourites amongst souvenir hunters are the shadow figures, usually produced from buffalo leather. Some caution is advised: sometimes purportedly old figures are offered at excessive prices. Most of the figures, however, are not at all as old as the seller maintains – instead they have been put through an aging process. That hardly diminishes their exotic charm, but it does not justify the high price.

Jewellery
Gold worked into jewellery in Bali – almost exclusively 14 karat gold – has a strong yellow cast. Balinese silverwork is also of high quality and can be found, among other places, in Celuk and Kamasan (near Klungkung).

Textiles
A whole industry in Bali has specialized in the wants and needs of tourists. Sport and leisure clothing, T-shirts and other articles of clothing and accessories are offered here at noticeably lower prices than in Europe; but make sure you check the quality.

Pottery
Along with the weaving industry, some potter's workshops on Bali's neighbouring island, Lombok, produce attractive pottery.

Sport and Entertainment

Sport

Seaside holiday
Bali is not necessarily a paradise for a seaside holiday. Visitors will look in vain for beaches with white coral sand, because the sand on

⊙ SPORT AND OUTDOORS

HORSE RIDING

► **P.T. Bali Jaran
Jaran Kencana**
Loji Gardens Hotel, Legian
Tel. (0361) 751672 and 751746
Offers half or all-day tours on
horseback, including those head-
ing inwards from the coast of the
island.

SIGHTSEEING FLIGHTS

► **Bali Avia**
Jl. Bypass 04, Tuban 8036, Kuta
Tel. (0361) 751257, fax 720620

DIVING

► **Bali Marine Sports**
Jl. Bypass Ngurah Rai 490
Belanjong-Sanur, Denpasar
Tel. (0361) 289308
www.bmsdivebali.com

► **Baruna Water Sports**
Puri Bagun, Lovina
Tel. (0362) 753820
Baruna Water Sports maintains

offices for reservations in some of
the larger hotels in Bali and in the
large hotels at Senggigi Beach in
Lombok.

► **Golden Hawk Cruises**
Jl. Danau Poso 20 A, Sanur
Tel. (0361) 287431, 289508
Golden Hawk Cruises offers one-
day or several-day diving cruises
with the two-masted barque
Golden Hawk (only for experi-
enced divers).

WHITEWATER TOURS

► **P.T. Bali Adventure Tours**
By Pass Ngurah Rai,
Pesanggaran
Tel. (0361) 721480
www.baliadventuretours.com

► **Sobek Expeditions**
Jl. Bypass Ngurah Rai
Jl. Tirta Ening 9, Sanur
Tel. (0361) 287059

the island is mixed with volcanic ash. Those who can live with this
will be happy at the seaside resorts of Kuta, Legian and Nusa Dua
(South Bali), Candi Dasa (East Bali) and Lovina Beach (North Bali).
There are very beautiful beaches in Lombok and on the islands just
off Bali: Gili Air, Gili Meno and Gili Terawangan. Be sure to use a
sun cream with a high sunscreen factor when swimming and
snorkelling. Beaches suitable for bathing and swimming are
marked. It can be extremely dangerous to swim at other spots becau-   ◄ Warning!
se waves can occasionally tower up several metres high and dangerous underwater **rip tides**, not obvious at first glance, can pose a serious threat to even the most practised swimmer. Bali's beaches are
not infrequently dirty, so beach sandals are recommended.

There are particularly delightful sailing areas around Bali. The num-   Charter boats
ber of places that charter boats is limited, however. Usually, a crew
familiar with the area must also be chartered.

Bali is a dream destination for many surfers, but the high waves and dangerous underwater currents should not be underestimated.

Golf

See Baedeker recommends p.156 ▶

The famous 18-hole **Bali Handara Golf Course** (Desa Pancasari, tel. 03 62 / 226 46, www. balihandarakosaido.com) in the highlands of Bedugul is uniquely laid-out with lush and colourful vegetation in the middle of the crater of an extinct volcano. The course lies at an elevation of 1142m/3747ft. This means pleasant and constant temperatures ranging from 16°C/61°F to 20°C/68°F. The green fee for the 6321m/6913yd-long course is about US$90. Along with a clubhouse, there is a pro shop, a fitness centre and a restaurant.

Located among the hotel complexes of Nusa Dua, only a few steps away from the Indian Ocean, is the **Bali Golf & Country Club's** 18-hole, par 72 course (tel. 03 61 / 77 17 91), easy to reach by bicycle for holidaymakers living in one of the nearby up-market resorts. The green fee for this 6263m/6849yd-long course is US$125. From November to March, it is advisable to reserve tee-off times in the cooler morning and evening hours. Cooling ocean breezes also make playing pleasant around noon.

There are **other 18-hole courses** belong to the Ritz Carlton Hotel in Jimbaran (tel. 03 61 / 60 22 22) and Le Meridien Nirvana Golf & Spa Resort (tel. 03 61 / 81 59 00) near the Hindu shrine of Tanah Lot. The 18-hole course in Lombok, Lombok Golf Kosaido, has been exquisitely designed in harmony with the surrounding landscape. The course, just 40 minutes away by car from Senggigi, offers a view of the Gili Islands and Mount Rinjani. The green fee is about US$60.

Surfing

Surfing the waves off the Balinese coast can be enticing, especially if you have the necessary skills. Beginners do well to stay between Kuta and Seminyak. More demanding surf can be found south of the airport and in Canggu, 20min northwest of Legian. Expert surfers, though, are drawn to the high waves on Bukit Badung near to Pura Luhur Ulu Watu, on Nusa Lembongan or on Padang Padang.

Many international hotels have **tennis courts** (some with flood-lighting, trainers and ball boys).

Diving: Bali is not a particularly favoured destination for divers, but it nevertheless unquestionably has a couple of beautiful spots for both beginners and advanced divers. Several hotels in Nusa Dua, Sanur and Kuta as well as at Senggigi Beach in Lombok have diving centres offering the necessary equipment for hire. While staying in Bali, it is also possible to qualify for »PADI certification«, a type of basic training for divers recognized worldwide.

The best time for diving trips around Bali is from April to October.

There are beautiful places to dive at Sanur, Nusa Dua, Padang Bai, Tulamben, Gili Toapekong, Amed, Singaraja-Lovina and around the islands of Menjangan and Penida. With a little luck, you might be able to observe an anglerfish: it is said that there are some very beautiful specimens in the waters around Bali. This solitary fish often lives on coral or rock reefs, reaches a maximum body-length of about 30cm/12in and is capable of completely adapting its colouring and appearance to blend in with its surroundings.

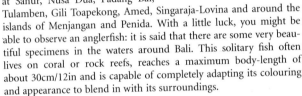

Whitewater trips can be taken in Bali on the Ayung River. The starting point, about 11km/7mi to the north of Ubud, is near the small village of Kedewatan (below Bedugul). Rubber rafts are available, steered by guides who know the waters. Those interested in taking part in this rather expensive adventure should get in touch with one of the organizers.

Whitewater trips

There are fitness centres in some of the larger hotels offering an extensive range of sport and leisure facilities (including table tennis, volleyball, football, gymnastics, sauna, steam bath).

Other sports

Entertainment

A work of batik you made yourself is certainly a unique souvenir to take home from Bali. A number of organizers offer courses to learn traditional and modern batik techniques. One-day and occasionally several-day courses are available. A large number of batik studios can also be found outside the tourist areas, in Ubud, for example. Here, too, it is possible to combine a holiday in Bali with artistic endeavour under professional instruction.

Batik courses

A feeling of well-being for body and soul; the beguiling fragrance of flowers, finest incenses, beneficial massages and baths

BALINESE SPAS

The art of enjoyable health and beauty care is alive and well in Bali. Even the newly-born are gently massaged with fragrant herbal oils, school children receive a light head massage for headaches, and a variety of packs, compresses and the like are used to regain a slim figure after pregnancy.

Tourists can also enjoy the extremely beneficial treatments on the island. Almost every hotel has its own spa or at least a designated area where guests can be massaged with fragrant oils by trained personnel. It is assumed in Bali that for good health to be possible, body and soul, or to be precise, »inside« and »out«, must be in a state of harmony.

The inhabitants of Bali, like almost all Indonesians, are adherents of the traditional jamu medicine. These remedies, produced from dozens of medicinal herbs, are administered in the form of beverages, tablets, ointments and compresses. Jamu can, it is said in Bali, cure or at least alleviate a number of illnesses, make inflammations disappear and stimulate the circulation and metabolism. Jamu medicines, freshly mixed by saleswomen (jamu gendong) specifically trained in the art of healing, are sold in small, open stalls at the roadside as well as in elegantly-designed herbal shops in Ubud and Denpasar. On request, spas also offer invigorating jamu drinks that improve the texture of the skin or hair.

Entering another world

Flickering candlelight, the delicate fragrance of exotic flowers and grasses, glass and ceramic flacons wrapped in bast and filled with medicinal

herbal oils; just visiting a Balinese spa is an experience in itself and a blissful relief for the stressed visitor. The treatments offered are many and varied, but various baths (mandi), including flower pedals or yogurt-milk-based therapies are always on the list. Mandi lulur treatments provide a long-lasting relaxing effect. As a rule, these consist of a massage, followed by a peeling and a flower bath. Balinese massages are extremely gentle and pleasant. Oils are worked into the skin with caressing movements. The massage covers all parts of the body, from head to toe. A peeling consists of a creamy paste being applied to the skin and, after it has dried, being removed by circular rubbing motions. This removes older, dead skin cells, revealing radiant-looking skin.

Most Balinese spas are ambitious enough to do without finished products and prepare their own distinctive recipes from natural ingredients, including, for example, rice flour, sandalwood and fragrant herbal and floral oils.

Traditional boreh is attributed with healing powers. This paste, prepared from herbs, spices and rice flour, stimulates the flow of blood in the skin, relieves muscle and joint pains and has a relaxing effect.

Book tip: *Spa Style Asia: Therapies, Cuisines, Spas* by Ginger Lee, published by Weatherhill Inc (2008).

Sightseeing flights

Getting a bird's-eye view of Bali from a helicopter is an exciting if expensive adventure. Interested parties should contact Bali Avia.

Museums

There are a number of museums in Bali that are worth a visit. The reference arrows in front of the places named in the following paragraph refer to an entry in »Sights from A to Z« in the main red section of this guide.

A **visit to the National Museum** of Bali in ▶Denpasar is an absolute must. The collection provides a vivid insight into Balinese history, and includes displays of cultural and religious items (such as costumes, weapons and cult objects). Dioramas document the important events in the life of a Balinese; for example, the tooth filing ceremony or the cremation of the dead. Equipment used to cultivate rice fields can be found in a small museum, located in ▶Tabanan, dedicated to the history of rice cultivation in Bali. There is an archaeological museum in ▶Bedulu.

Balinese painting is famous all over the world. ▶Ubud, the »city of the arts«, offers two museums or art galleries at once, the Neka Museum and the Antonio Blanco House, with important collections of various painters. Another painting collection, the gallery of Agung Rai, is located in ▶Peliatan. A permanent exhibit in the Werdi Budaya Art Center in ▶Denpasar also displays Balinese painting. At that very place, the home of the Belgian painter, Le Mayeur, has been turned into a small museum. When in ▶Singaraja, tourists interested in Balinese history will not want to miss visiting the Gedong Kirtya Library with its valuable lontar (palm) leaf manuscripts. The small village of Penglipuran in the vicinity of ▶Bangli almost has the character of an open-air museum. There is also an interesting museum in Mataram, the capital of the neighbouring island of ▶Lombok, whose particular focus is the history of the Sasak, the island's original and main inhabitants.

In Lombok ▶

Nightlife

Nightlife in the Western sense has only existed in Bali since foreigners started coming to the island; even today it is restricted to areas most visited by tourists. The biggest centre of nocturnal entertainment with bars, discos and other night time haunts is Kuta Beach, which has since merged together with the neighbouring town of Legian. All of the large hotels in Nusa Dua on the southern peninsula of Bukit Badung have their own places of entertainment. The nightlife in Sanur is relatively modest and is found mostly in the vicinity of the hotels.

Focal point Kuta / Legian ▶

The centre of nightlife in Kuta/Legian is the district between Jl. Pantai Kuta and Jl. Legian. There are many popular spots here, where mainly the younger visitors to Bali gather. Many bars such as the »Jaya Pub« in the Jl. Raya Seminyak offer live music. Discos are also to be found everywhere, some charging an entrance fee or imposing a set drink minimum. The »Double Six« disco in Seminyak has become a popular place to go.

Time

Indonesia has three time zones from west to east. Bali and Lombok are on Central Indonesian Time (= GMT + 8 hours). There is no daylight saving time.

Central Indonesian Time

Transport

By Ferry

Car ferries and jetfoils ply regularly (several times daily) between Bali and Java and between Bali and Lombok. The terminals in Bali for ferries to Java (Ketapang, most eastern port) are in Gilimanuk on the western tip of the island. The ferries to Lombok are in the port of Benoa (south of Denpasar). Boats to Bali's smaller islands of Lembongan and Penida leave from Benoa, Sanur, Kusamba and Padang Bai. The terminal in Lombok is in Lembar (south of the island's capital, Mataram), on Lembongan near Jungutbatu and on Penida near Toyapakeh.

Ferry terminal

Reservations can be made in all travel agencies, in the terminal in the port, or directly with the ferry companies themselves.

By Air

Garuda Indonesia, the state airline, maintains a dense network of routes that includes the airport in Denpasar in Bali. Along with numerous intercontinental connections (including London, Sydney and

 FERRY SERVICES

BALI – LOMBOK ·

▶ **P.T. Mabua Intan Express**
Benoa Harbour (Bali)
Tel. (03 01) 77 25 21
Fax 26 12 12

Mataram (Lombok)
Tel. (03 70) 258 95
Fax 372 24

BALI – PENIDA

▶Sights from A to Z: Penida ·
Nuda Penida, Arrival by water

BALI – LEMBONGAN

▶Sights from A to Z: Penida · Nusa Penida, smaller island of Lembongan. The 34m/111ft-long Luxury katamaran *Bali Hai* regularly sails between Benoa Harbour and Nusa Lembongan; make reservations for day trips or evening »dinner cruises« (2.5hr) with Bali Hai Cruises, Benoa Harbour (tel. 03 01 / 720 331, www.bali haicruises.com).

Los Angeles), there are regular flights to Indonesian airports such as Jakarta, Palembang, Surabaya and Yogyakarta, as well as neighbouring Malaysia, the city-state of Singapore, Bangkok, Manila, Hong Kong and Tokyo. The smaller airlines providing air travel within the Indonesian archipelago besides Garuda Indonesia are Merpati, Sempati, Bouraq and Air India. As a rule, the **price of a ticket** in Asia is cheaper than in Europe. However, count on the flights being booked up, if not over-booked, before and after a national holiday. As air travel within Indonesia is often the only possible way to cover longer stretches within a short time, the aeroplane has also assumed a certain social function in the lives of the islanders (visiting relatives, etc.).

At the airport Ngurah Rai Airport is named after a Balinese freedom fighter. It is located about 12km/7.5mi south of **Denpasar** and around 3km/2mi south of Kuta. Flights within Indonesia are handled in the left part of the airport building (Domestic Airport) and international flights in the right (International Airport). The centre is reserved for arrivals, and the arrival hall has a counter for inquiring about and reserving hotel rooms. Upon request, transportation to the hotel can also be arranged. There are also several money changers in the arrival hall, but before exchanging larger amounts, check the exchange rates offered (for more information see ▶ Money). It is advisable to exchange only a small amount here.

Normally, the hotel or the tour operator provides the **transfer** from or to the airport. Otherwise there is a »Koperasi Taxi Service« counter in the airport building. This is a cooperative of taxi drivers that has organized the transfer between the airport and destinations in Bali at set prices. The price for each ride can be found on a notice displayed at the counter, where it is also paid. The taxi driver is then only given the receipt.

Mataram Airport on Bali's neighbouring island to the east, Lombok, is located just a few miles north of the capital Mataram, on the way to the hotel resort of Senggigi Beach. A sufficient number of taxis are available for getting to the desired hotel upon arrival. The local representatives of tour organizers will be waiting outside the arrival hall for travellers with package hotel arrangements. There is a counter in the arrival hall to provide independent travellers with information about vacant hotel rooms. **Porters** offer assistance in both airports; the charge is determined by the number of bags to be carried.

Even if the airline ticket has »OK« printed on it, the flight must be confirmed with the airline by telephone or in person at least two days before the **return flight** or the seat reservation can be deleted. Check-in time for international flights is two hours before departure; one hour is normally enough for flights within Indonesia. An airport tax must be paid in cash before flying, which is at present about 100,000 rupiahs for international flights and 30,000 rupiahs for domestic flights.

⏵ TRANSPORT INFORMATION

AIRLINES

▶ Garuda Indonesia (in the UK)
Flighthouse
Fernhill Road, Horley
Surrey RH6 9SY
Tel. 01293 874963
Email:
web@garudaindonesia.co.uk

▶ Garuda Indonesia (in Bali)
61, Jl. Melati, Denpasar
Tel. (03 61) 28 80 11

In Kuta:
Kuta Beach Hotel
Tel. (03 6 1) 75 11 79

In Sanur:
Grand Bali Beach Hotel Arcade
Tel. (03 61) 28 79 15

▶ Bouraq
Jl. Sudirman, Denpasar
Tel. (03 61) 24 13 97

▶ Cathay Pacific
Wisthi Sabha Building
Ngurah Rai International Airport
Denpasar 80361
Tel. (03 61) 76 69 31

▶ China Airlines
Wisthi Sabha Building
Ngurah Rai International Airport
Denpasar 80361
Tel. (03 61) 75 48 56

▶ Merpati Nusantara Airlines
1, Jl. Melati
Denpasar
Tel. (03 61) 23 53 58

▶ Thai Airways
Grand Bali Beach Hotel (main lobby)
Tel. (03 61) 28 81 41; fax 28 80 63

▶ Qantas
Grand Bali Beach Hotel, Sanur
Tel. (03 61) 288 33 31

CAR RENTAL

▶ Denpasar Airport (International Arrival Hall)
Golden Bird Bali
Tel. (03 61) 70 11 11, 70 17 91
fax 71 16 28
www.bluebirdgroup.com
Hertz
Tel. (03 61) 76 83 75
fax 76 83 73
hertzlhnbali@yahoo.com
Indorent
Tel. (03 61) 744 11 41
fax 744 11 43
www.indorent.co.id

BICYCLE HIRE

▶ Sobek Expeditions
Jl. Bypass Ngurah Rai 56 X, Jl. Tirta Ening, Sanur
Tel. (03 61) 28 75 09

By Car

It is possible to explore Bali as well as Lombok by hire car. Particu-   Hire cars
larly in Bali there are a large number of car rental companies. The
cars for hire are usually Japanese (mostly Suzuki) four-wheel drive

vehicles (Jeeps). The car rental agencies are less interested in seeing an international driving licence than the Balinese police, who will impose fines if the necessary papers are not in order. The driver must be at least 21 years of age. Drivers should be prepared for unaccustomed driving conditions and for the islanders' driving style that occasionally borders on the anarchic.

Defensive driving is highly recommended. Avoid driving at night. In fact, many consider it sensible when hiring a car to hire a local driver as well. They do not cost much, know their way around and, most important, possess the Balinese driving mentality.

When hiring a car, check the vehicle's roadworthiness (above all, brakes, condition of tyres, lamps) and be sure to look for signs of previous accidents. It goes without saying that the vehicle should be adequately covered with third party liability insurance. If in doubt, rely on vehicles from well-known car rental companies.

Automotive services
There are no breakdown services in Bali as there are in Western countries; you will also search in vain for emergency telephones along the roads. Instead, stranded drivers are dependent on the help of other road users. In case of a breakdown, it is best to try to get attention by waving. Towing to the next garage is allowed. The situation can become more difficult at night, especially outside the tourist areas or inland, where it often takes a long time before someone will agree to help. This is one good reason to avoid driving at night. Be sure to ask the car rental agency for a directory of reliable garages. If none is available, find out what to do in case of a breakdown.

Motorcycles
Renting a motorcycle is only recommended to people with a lot of driving experience. But even so, the best driver can often find him or herself in a tricky situation. The miserable condition of many roads,

especially in the interior, holds great potential danger (potholes, sudden changes in road surface, lack of traction after a rain shower, etc.). Another risk factor is the driving style of the natives. Innumerable accidents occur annually, often resulting in prolonged hospital stays or even death. Incidentally, **helmets are mandatory**!

Many of Bali's roads are flooded during the monsoon season.

The island of Bali is just made for exploring by **bicycle**, which would explain why the number of bicycle rental shops continues to increase, particularly in the tourist centres of Sanur, Kuta and Legian, as well as in Denpasar. Some hotels also

A drive through lava fields; the road to Lake Batur

offer bicycles for hire (sometimes even mountain bikes). Naturally, when hiring a bicycle, check it for safety (brakes, lamp). Sobek Expeditions organizes bicycle tours with mountain bikes (for example, on the »Batur Trail«).

Asians have a fundamentally different relationship to their car and traffic than central and northern Europeans, and it is no different in Bali (and Lombok). To put it somewhat crudely, behaviour in traffic here is based on the relatively simple principle that the five drivers in front of your car, the five behind and the seventeen bicyclists or motorcyclists or pedestrians to the right and left are supposed to act just as you expect and do nothing silly. Traffic regulations are there to be broken more than followed; speed limits appear to be understood as more of a challenge to coax the last bit out of just barely roadworthy vehicles. Incidentally, **driving on the left** is the rule in Indonesia.

Behaviour in traffic

With the exception of the four-lane »Jalan Bypass« between Denpasar and Nusa Dua, there are no expressways or highways in Bali. Particularly in rural regions, the condition of even vital overland roads is precarious. Hazards such as potholes, ruts and soft shoulders are often recognized too late, which is why it is advisable to drive cautiously. The islanders make abundant use of their horns, especially when passing through villages – a habit that even visitors quickly adopt.

Traffic signs, for the most part, follow the customary international regulation. The roads in Bali are not systematically numbered, not even on the roadmaps available everywhere. Even if only a few locals keep to it, the **speed limit** in built-up areas is 25mph/40kmh. Out of town, 50mph/80kmh for passenger vehicles and 31mph/50kmh for buses and lorries is allowed.

Various forms of transport There are ample **taxis** in Denpasar equipped with taxi meters (recognizable by their blue and white paint job). In addition, there are a great number of unofficial taxis. In these, the price for the trip must be settled on beforehand by bargaining with the driver. The meter is usually turned on during the day and in the early evening hours; but in the late evening and at weekends, when there are not many taxis, the driver will often just name a price that can either be accepted or rejected in the hope of getting a better price from the next driver. Taxi drivers are more inclined to agree on a set price for longer trips.

A trip on a **bus** in Bali can be a special kind of experience. For the islanders, the bus is the cheapest form of transportation for covering both shorter and longer distances. Taking the bus is extremely popular and the price quite cheap; moreover, it is set and does not have to be bargained over. On the other hand, there are no time schedules. The bus driver usually waits in the bus terminal, which are in every town, until he has collected enough passengers to make the trip worth his while.

Minibuses are sometimes called »**colts**«. A widespread form of passenger transport is the minibus called a »**bemo**«, which is a converted delivery truck fitted out with benches on the truck bed. They tend to become uncomfortable on longer trips, which is why buses should be given preference.

A ride on a »**dokar**« (called a »cidomo« on Lombok), a two-wheeled, horse-drawn carriage, can be comfortable and peaceful – if you don't happen to take it in Denpasar. This is the islanders' favourite form of transport for short distances. The (modest) fare must be negotiated before the start of the trip.

A modicum of courage is required to entrust your life to one of the ever increasing number of motorcycle taxis (»**ojek**«). Although the drivers usually possess the expertise necessary to deal with the prevailing chaotic traffic conditions, a large number of ojek drivers confuse Bali's streets with (poorly) groomed racetracks. In any case, demand a helmet; once again, a price must be agreed upon beforehand.

Travellers with Disabilities

Large tour operators provide information about travel possibilities for the disabled. Public transport adapted to meet the needs of disabled travellers is the exception rather than the rule in Bali, but the friendly assistance of the locals can be counted on. Most of the sights, especially the temple grounds, can be viewed from a wheelchair.

The major hotels in particular are equipped for the needs of disabled guests. However there is no list of accommodation that specifically caters for disabled visitors.

UNITED KINGDOM

► **RADAR**
12 City Forum, 250 City Road,
London EC1V 8AF
Tel. (020) 72 50 32 22
www.radar.org.uk

USA

► **SATH (Society for the Advancement of Travel for the Handicapped)**
347 5th Ave., no. 610
New York, NY 10016:
Tel. (21) 4 47 72 84
www.sath.org

When to Go

For those used to a central or northern European climate, the most High season
pleasant time to travel to Bali is from May through to September.
The lowest rainfall is recorded in this period: there are six rainy days
on average. The reason for these conditions is the southeast monsoon blowing in from Australia, bringing daily highs of about 30°C/
86°F. The Balinese consider the months of June and July to be
»cool«; the thermometer then climbs on average up to »only« 26°C/
79°F during the day. Hot days are best spent in the cooler hilly
country, where pleasant winds make the temperatures tolerable. Peak
season in Bali is considered to be the period from June to the beginning of September. Many tourists also come to Bali over the Christmas holidays (especially from neighbouring countries).

The west monsoon blows from October through April/May, Low season
bringing, to some extent, abundant rainfall with it, although the customary term for these months, the »rainy season«, is often falsely
understood. It does not rain all day but mostly in the night or in the
early morning, and then really heavily. Afterwards the clouds withdraw quickly, revealing blue skies again. The considerably quieter off
season also means that there are sufficient vacancies in the hotels of
Bali and Lombok; it is sometimes possible to obtain a price reduction by asking at the hotel reception.

►Climate p.20   Weather

Tours

A TROPICAL WORLD FULL OF GREEN RICE FIELDS, HINDU TEMPLES, BEAUTIFUL BEACHES AND FRIENDLY PEOPLE AWAITS YOU ON AN ISLAND CHARACTERIZED BY A CHEERFULNESS AND A SENSE OF TRANQUILITY.

TOURS THROUGH BALI

Are you interested in temples and culture? Do you want to journey through enchanting landscapes? A little of both perhaps? Our suggestions may provide inspiration when planning excursions of your own ....

— TOUR 1 **In the Centre of Bali**
This is the most beautiful tour Bali has to offer – through fascinating landscapes, past some of the island's major sights.
► **page 137**

— TOUR 2 **The Southeast**
A day trip to Kerta Gosa with its wonderful Wayang paintings, the bat caves of Goa Lawah and on to Amlapura's princely palace. Lovers of the decorative arts will find plenty to discover on this tour.
► **page 139**

— TOUR 3 **The Island Tour**
This tour provides an overall impression of Bali and introduces the charms of its culture and landscape
► **page 140**

The sowing, tending and harvesting of the rice fields – a permanent cycle

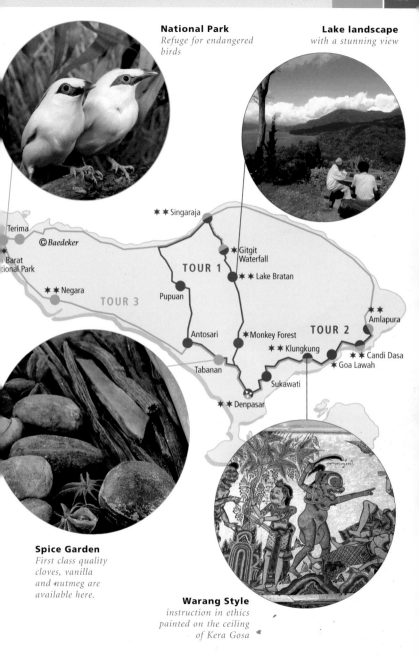

National Park
Refuge for endangered birds

Lake landscape
with a stunning view

Terima

© Baedeker

Barat
ional Park

** Singaraja

** Gitgit
Waterfall

TOUR 1

** Lake Bratan

** Negara

TOUR 3

Pupuan

Antosari

** Monkey Forest

TOUR 2

** Amlapura

** Klungkung

Tabanan

** Candi Dasa

* Goa Lawah

Sukawati

*** Denpasar

Spice Garden
First class quality cloves, vanilla and nutmeg are available here.

Warang Style
instruction in ethics painted on the ceiling of Kera Gosa

The faithful bring their artistically arranged offerings to the temple.

Travelling in Bali

The following tour suggestions are intended to provide ideas for exploring the island of Bali in a rented car without taking away the freedom of planning your own routes. If you plan to use public transport (bus, bemo), count on the tour lasting longer due to the varying quality of the connections. As Bali is a relatively small island, **all of the destinations can be reached on one-day tours** – assuming you start early in the morning and are willing to return late in the evening. Only a round-trip tour of the whole island takes longer: allow for two to three days. The roads on Bali are not systematically numbered, posing a problem; but there are kilometre stones placed along the roads in the direction of the capital Denpasar marking the distance from it, and in the other direction is the distance to the next town or village. The distances given in kilometres/miles in parentheses behind the route heading correspond to the total distance of the most direct route. The suggested routes can be followed on the map of the island included with this guide.

Tour 1 In the Centre of Bali

Distance:: approx. 220km/137mi (round trip)   **Duration::** 1 day

This day trip is probably the most beautiful tour that can be taken on Bali. It leads you through a fascinating landscape with living villages and hospitable inhabitants; moreover, it touches some of the greatest sights on the island. Get an early start!

From **❶ ✶ ✶ Denpasar,** first take the road to Gilimanuk, turning right after about 40km/25mi at the small village of Antosari and heading for Serjrit or Singaraja.

Enchanting landscape

Leaving **❷ Antosari**, the road runs through a landscape of extraordinary charm. On many places along the way, the winding mountain road opens up to surprising vistas of artistically arranged rice terraces. The villages in which the rice farmers live are lined up only a few miles apart. **❸ Pupuan**, the next largest town, is known as the centre of vegetable cultivation. Besides its beautiful setting, it has no special tourist sights so it is best to continue on to the northern edge of the island and Seririt.

Turning off here in the direction of **❹ ✶ ✶ Singaraja** will bring you – at around noon – to the island's second largest city with the well-known Gedong Kirtya Library. A couple of restaurants in the city centre are to be recommended. About halfway to the next major destination, it is possible to take a side trip to see the beautiful **❺ ✶ Gitgit Waterfall**. **❻ ✶ ✶ Lake Bra-**

> ## *i* Along the way
>
> - Krambitan: a few miles west of Tabanan are some traditional Balinese palaces that have been converted into hotels offering an interesting cultural programme.
> - Banjar: a short time after reaching the coastal road, a stop can be made at a Buddhist monastery and Air Panas Hot Springs.
> - There are wonderful areas for walks around Tambligan Lake and Bayan Lake, south of Gitgit Falls.
> - Blayu, south of Sangeh, is a particularly picturesque village. There is a monkey forest here as well, and the small temple of Pura Alas Kedaton.

tan nestles in a gorgeous setting in the midst of an unspoilt tropical landscape. **Pura Ulu Danu** temple, appearing on its western shore, can be reached by boats available there. If there is still time, **Bedugul** is worth a visit. After taking a look at the wonderfully laid-out botanical garden head off again, driving south. The rest of the route depends on how much time is left. If you leave Bedugul around 3pm, it is still early enough to choose the route described next before heading back to Denpasar. Or, as an alternative, why not close the day with a visit to the **❼ ✶ monkey forest** of Sangeh Natural Tourism Park (►Mengwi) by taking the road from Pacung to Mengwi. If you decide in favour of the more time-consuming alternative with the side trip to the temple complex of **Pura Luhur Batukau** at the foot of

Alternative

the mountain of the same name, take the road from Pacung to ❽ **Tabanan**, which runs almost parallel to the road to Mengwi. The stretch from Badjera to Tabanan leads through a breathtakingly beautiful landscape. Tabanan itself is known for having one of the best gamelan orchestras on Bali. From here, the 23km/14.3mi back to ❶ ✷✷ **Denpasar** are covered quickly.

❹ ✷✷ Singaraja

34 km/ 21 miles

15 km/ 9 miles

❺ ✷ Gitgit-Waterfall

15 km/ 9 miles

❸
Pupuan

✷✷ Lake Bratan ❻

22 km/ 14 miles

28 km/ 17 miles

Lovina
*offers black-sandy beaches
and pristine coral reefs.*

Monkey Love
*The animals are
considered sacred,
but should be
approached only
with caution*

❷
Antosari

18 km/ 11 miles

✷ Monkey forest

❼

❽
Tabanan

19 km/ 12 miles

21 km/ 13 miles

Rice Basket
*Cultivation on terraces pro-
tects the land from erosion.*

✷✷ Denpasar ❶

Tour 2 The Southeast

Distance: 180km/112mi
(there and back)

Duration: 1 day

**The day trip described below leads into the eastern part of Bali.
Along the way are some major sights and places to shop.**

Set out from ❶ ✶ ✶ **Denpasar** on the road heading east in the direction of Celuk and Sukawati. Enticing gold and silversmith shops line the main road passing through **Celuk**. The village of ❷ **Sukawati** is reached after about 17km/10.5mi. There are numerous shops here offering arts and crafts, but the village itself offers little for the photograph album. There is an »art market« in the village centre, though, where the prices are mostly lower than in the tourist centres around Denpasar.

Shopping and bathing

The route continues through a varied landscape before coming to **Cianyar** and, after another 13km/8mi, to the city of ❸ ✶ ✶ **Klungkung**. Here, the court hall, Kerta Gosa, is certainly worth taking a look at. After Klungkung, the road turns again toward the sea and follows the coastline after Kusamba. The ❹ ✶ **Goa Lawah** (►Candi Dasa) shrine cave is located right next to the road. There are thousands upon thousands of bats at the cave's entrance. It is only a few miles

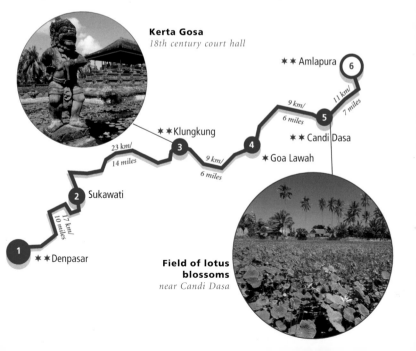

Kerta Gosa
18th century court hall

✶ ✶ Amlapura ⑥

9 km/
6 miles

11 km/
7 miles

⑤

✶ ✶ Klungkung
③

23 km/
14 miles

9 km/
6 miles

④

✶ ✶ Candi Dasa

✶ Goa Lawah

9 km/
6 miles

② Sukawati

17 km/
10 miles

① ✶ ✶ Denpasar

Field of lotus blossoms
near Candi Dasa

from here to ❺ ✳✳ **Candi Dasa**, the tourist centre of the eastern part of the island, which you should reach about lunchtime. The route continues from Candi Dasa through small villages to ❻✳✳ **Amlapura**. At first, the road runs along the ocean shore, but then it turns inland, in places winding over hills and occasionally offering nice views. There is a major sight in Amlapura, formerly Karangasem: in the centre of the village stands the princely palace of Puri Agung Kanginan, whose beautiful buildings are set in a marvellous park.

Only a few miles outside of Amlapura are the princely baths of **Tirthagangga**, an inviting place to take a refreshing swim. In clear weather the volcano, Gunung Agung, Bali's highest mountain at 3142m/10,308ft, can be seen rising upwards in the island's interior.

ℹ️ **Nice side trips**

- Celuk, Batuan and Mas near Sukawati are noted for arts and crafts, in particular the production of jewellery, painting and wood-carving.
- It is only a few miles from Amlapura to the fishing village of Ujung with its impressive, newly-restored water palace set in the middle of a beautiful park. A tour to the east point of the island is wonderful, but before attempting the drive it is advisable to inquire about the current condition of the road.

Tour 3 The Island Tour

Distance: approx. 450km/280mi   **Duration:** 2–3 days

A tour of the whole island is only recommended for people interested in seeing the less exciting western part of the island. The »only« sight worth seeing in this area is the Bali Barat National Park. The difficulty here is that there are no roads passable for vehicles inside the park's grounds.

First Day

Between the ocean and the National Park

Leave ❶ ✳✳ **Denpasar** in a northwesterly direction heading for Gilimanuk. About 15km/9.3mi beyond the two villages of Sempidi and Lukluk, where there are a couple of brightly painted and richly decorated temples to be seen, you will arrive at the village of **Kapal** with the two temples of Pura Desa and Pura Puseh. There are some shops along the main road offering cement sacral figures made from moulds. It is only 7km/4.4mi from Kapal to ❷ **Tabanan**, the capital of the district of the same name. The road leads through a varied landscape that gradually climbs to the north of the island. The town itself offers no sights to speak of, though there are more to be seen in the surrounding area. A worthwhile side trip is to the small village

Water buffalo races
*Only two teams race
at a time.*

Ceremony
*in honour of the
sea gods*

★★ Singaraja   **6**

Terima
*8 km/
5 miles*   **5**

★
li-Barat-
tional Park

*28 km/
17 miles*   **3**

★★ Negara

7 ★ Gitgit-
Waterfall

*78 km/
48,5 miles*

*15 km/
9 miles*

*112 km/
70 miles*

★★ Amlapura   **8**

*74 km/
46 miles*

Tabanan

2

*21 km/
13 miles*

1

*40 km/
25 miles*

10

★★ Klungkung

*18 km/
11 miles*

9

*11 km/
7 miles*

★★
Candi Dasa

★★ Denpasar

Art Center
*with an art museum, theatres,
dance and music performances*

of **Krambitan**, located in the direction of the sea, with the former
princely residences of Puri Gede and Puri Anyur. There is an unusually beautiful hotel in Puri Gede that is almost always fully booked
because of its limited number of rooms. The road now leads further
westward along the coast to ❸ ★★ **Negara**, on the way passing the
little town of Pulukan, where beautiful beaches are inviting places to
take a short (bathing) break. Negara is known less for its sights than
for the water buffalo races that take place here annually in November. If you just happen to visit the village at that time, it is naturally
worth staying a little longer. During the drive, the ocean is almost a

constant companion on the left-hand side, while ❹✱✱ **Bali Barat National Park** stretches out to the right. The main office of the park administration, which issues visiting permits for the park and collects the entrance fees, is located just outside of Gilimanuk near Cecik. **Gilimanuk** has next to no sights of note. It is worth a short stop though to observe the bustling activity in the harbour, where the ferries to and from Java dock. The road between Gilimanuk and ❺**Terima** is the only passable road through the Bali Barat National Park. It is worth driving slowly through this short stretch, taking time to take in the extraordinarily beautiful landscape. Providing there is time, take the approximately half-hour boat ride from Terima to the island of Manjangan (good beach, nice spots for snorkelling and diving). The stretch of road hugging the shore from Terima eastward past Seritit is relatively monotonous. The route leads through the well-developed tourist area of **Lovina Beach** just outside Singaraja. There are rows and rows of hotels, restaurants and shops here. ❻✱✱ **Singaraja** was the seat of the colonial government during the Dutch occupation and as such was once the capital of Bali. Today it is the island's second largest city. In order to have enough time to see all the sights (Pura Dalem, Gedong Kirtya Library) as well as the city itself, it is worthwhile finding accommodation in Singaraja. Alternatively, stay at Lovina Beach and drive into the city from there.

Second Day

Highlights in and around Amlapura

Providing you spent the night in Singaraja or at Lovina Beach, get an early start on the second day. There are two reasons for this: firstly, to watch the island come to life along the road; and secondly to have enough time to see all the sights in and around Amlapura. A nice side trip inland to the south of Singaraja along the road in the direction of Bedugul will lead through charming countryside to ❼✱ **Gitgit Waterfall**. Once back on the coastal road to Amlapura, continue through the agricultural land that includes the largest coffee plantations on Bali. After a good three-hour drive, the road leaves the coast and reaches ❽✱✱ **Amlapura** in a little less than a half hour. Amlapura (formerly Karangasem) was heavily damaged during the last eruption of the Gunung Agung on 17 March 1963. New, modern and functional buildings were constructed on the ruins of the old town. In some places, old soot-blackened walls and houses that have not been rebuilt can be discovered, silent witnesses of the devastating natural catastrophe. The princely palace of Puri Agung Kanginan survived, however: do not miss touring the palace as well as visiting **Tirthagangga**, the former princely baths. Although the distance between Amlapura and Klungkung is only about 40km/25mi, it is rather a shame just to drive through this part of Bali's landscape as it is particularly worth seeing. The road leads through partly hilly country and at some spots opens up to reveal fantastic vistas of

ocean and landscape. Just along the road on the far side of
❾ ✳✳ **Candi Dasa** is the cave temple of **Goah Lawah**, one of the
most important shrines in Bali. The tourist buses that head daily to

this temple can be recognized from
a distance. The main attraction is
the entrance to the cave itself.
Thousands upon thousands of bats
cling to the naked rock here. It is
only about 10km/6mi from Goah
Lawah to Klungkung. ❿ ✳✳
Klungkung is mainly famous for
the Kerta Gosa court hall, which in
turn is known for its unique wayang style paintings. The last leg of
the tour of the island passes
through some villages and smaller
built-up areas. If you have planned
the recommended two days for this
tour and wish to reach Denpasar
by nightfall, there is hardly any
time left for visiting further sights.
The villages of **Gianyar**, **Sukawati**

Don't miss

- Makam Jayaprana hill near Terima offers a fantastic view of Java, the Menjangan islands and Gilimanuk.
- Plan to take a break on the way to Singaraja on the tranquil, exquisite, white sandy beach of Pantai Gondol.
- Visit the little mountain village of Sembiran, located south of Pacung. It boasts about 20 temples!
- Further along, the coastal road passes the unconventional seaside shrine of Pura Ponjok Batu and the Chinese-influenced Tejakula, famous for its silver decoration and wayang wang dance.

and **Celuk**, each with some temples that are definitely worth taking a   ◄ Tips for half-day
look at, can be reached from Denpasar in a short time and are rec-   excursions
ommended destinations for half-day excursions.

Sights from A to Z

TROPICAL LANDSCAPES, TURQUOISE WATERS, MULTI-COLOURED CORAL REEFS, IMPOSING VOLCANIC CRATERS, ARTFULLY ARRANGED RICE TERRACES, IMPRESSIVE HINDU TEMPLE COMPLEXES, TRADITIONAL VILLAGES AND A VIBRANT ARTS AND CRAFTS SCENE!

✶✶ Amlapura (Karangasem)

Q 6

Capital of the administrative district of Karangasem	**Region:** East Bali
Distance: 80km/50mi northeast of Denpasar	**Altitude:** 2–90m/6.5–295ft
	Population: approx. 30,000

Amlapura (formerly Karangasem), the administrative seat of the district of Karangasem, is Bali's easternmost city and lies at the foot of the Gunung Agung volcano.

History   Amlapura, known prior to 1964 as Karangasem, the same name as the administrative district, played an important role during the years in which the Dutch were attempting to gain a foothold in Bali. While the rulers of the principalities of central Baliresisted the impending occupation, the rajas of Karangasem agreed terms with the occupying forces, leaving an exposed flank on the eastern part of the island. The Dutch were then able to sail as far as Sanur on the south coast and attack the defiant princes of Gianyar and Badun near their capitals. Karangasem did not go unrewarded: it became one of the wealthiest towns in Bali and the raja retained his power.

Almost all of the city's structures were destroyed during the **eruption of Gunung Agun volcano in 1963**. The buildings as well as the main roads linking the city to the rest of the island have since been restored.

▶ VISITING AMLAPURA

INFORMATION

Karangasem
Tourist Office
Jl. Diponegoro
Tel. (03 63) 211 96
Fax 219 54

GETTING AROUND

Take the road from Denpasar to Sakah, and after making a right turn there in the direction of Blahbatuh, continue on to Klungkung, travelling along the coast past Candi Dasa. There is a bus connection from Denpasar-Kerenang with several buses daily.

WHERE TO EAT

▶ **Inexpensive**
There are some simple eateries in the vicinity of the bus terminal; in addition there are snack stalls in the car park of Hardy's new supermarket (Jl. Diponegoro).

WHERE TO STAY

▶ **Budget**
Losmen Lahar Mas
Jl. Gatot Subroto 1
Tel. (03 63) 213 45
20 inexpensive and simple rooms, some with views of the rice fields.

The palace complex of Amlapura

What to See in and around Amlapura

Although it was partially destroyed by the earthquake accompanying the eruption of the volcano in 1963, the 19th-century royal palace of Puri Agung Kanginan on the road to Ujung is still well worth seeing. The palace consists of three parts. The traditional festivals were held in the first part, the bencingah; in the second is the garden, while in the third and innermost section are the residential buildings of the royal family. The palace is entered through a gate on a square foundation, guarded by two lions. A second gate to the right of where the entrance fee is paid leads into the garden and then to the actual palace precinct. On the right is an artificial pond with a pavilion (Bale Kambang) and to the left of it is a bale decorated with numerous **scenes from the *Ramayana***. There are some notable buildings in the main palace precinct. The Bale London not only has richly carved doors and well preserved or restored paintings on the outer walls and inside (a leaflet about the paintings is available at the ticket office), but it also contains the instruments of a gamelan orchestra, which were allowed to be played only in the presence of the raja. Standing next to the Bale London is the Bale Pemandesan, in which the ritual tooth-filing was performed on the raja's children. The Puri

Madura, the royal audience hall, also known as the »**Maskerdam**«, can accommodate 150 people. It has been closed since the death (in 1966) of the last occupant, Prince A. A. Angurah Ketut Karangasem. It is possible, however, to look in through the windows. There are several other buildings outside the palace complex and across the main road, which either belong to Puri Agung or were part of two old palaces (Puri Gede and Puri Kertasura). Some of these structures were also destroyed by earthquakes.

✳
Tirthagangga

🕐
Opening hours:
daily 9am–6pm

About 5km/3mi west of Amlapura are the former royal baths of Tirta Gangga (Water of the Ganges). They have been converted into an outdoor swimming-pool, which is open to the public. Have a look at the **beautiful water spouts in the ponds** laid out around 1947 by the last Raja of Amlapura, as well as the figures and mythical creatures. The baths were severely damaged during the volcanic eruption of 1963. Great care was taken in restoring everything to its original form during reconstruction work.

Ujung

The remains of the **Puri Taman Ujung** water palace, largely destroyed by an earthquake, are located near Ujung, about 5km/3mi along the coast south of Amlapura. The original water palace was commissioned by the last Raja of Amlapura.

✳✳
Landscape

The road between Candi Dasa and Amlapura leads through exceedingly charming, tropical, hilly countryside. The area surrounding Amlapura is intensely cultivated, with **rice** growing on numerous terraces.

✳✳ Bali Barat National Park (West Bali NP)

C 2

Region: West Bali	**Administrative district:** Buleleng
Altitude: sea level	**Area:** approx. 77,000ha/300 sq mi

Almost the whole of the western part of the island of Bali was declared the Bali Barat National Park (West Bali National Park or Taman Nasional Bali Barat) in 1983. A more modestly sized national park had been previously established in the same region by the Dutch.

Wild Animal Refuge

The last tigers in Bali lived in the area that is now the Bali Barat National Park up until about a half century ago. Even today, the huge park is still a refuge for quite a few species including the indigenous **banteng cattle, red deer and monkeys**. Among the many species of bird is the Bali Starling, which nests mainly in the northern part of the national park. Having become very rare, it is now a protected species. There are only about 200 individuals left, and the species is

VISITING BALI BARAT NATIONAL PARK

GETTING AROUND

Bali Barat National Park can be reached from Denpasar by driving west along the coast. There are good bus and bemo connections from Gilimanuk and Singaraja. The park entrance can be reached either from the little village of Terima or from Gilimanuk or Singaraja. The headquarters of the national park administration is in Cecek (4km/2.5mi south of Gilimanuk), with additional offices in Labuhan Lalang and Telik Terima; there is a small admission charge to enter the park.

WHERE TO EAT / WHERE TO STAY

There are homestays and losmen in Gilimanuk. Modest accommodation is located not far from the national park administration headquarters. For further information contact the Bali Recreation and Parks Organization (PUTRI), Jl. Nusa Indah, Denpasar, Tel. (03 61) 23 66 19.

► Luxury
Matahari Beach Resort & Spa
P.O. Box 194 – Pemuteran, Singaraja
Tel. (03 62) 923 12
Fax (03 62) 923 13
www.matahari-beach-resort.com
40 bungalows with every conceivable amenity. Balinese, Indonesian, Eurasian and international cuisine served in the gourmet restaurant; plus a beach bistro and cocktail bar. There is also a wellness centre, beauty salon, fitness studio, library, PADI resort diving school, swimming pool and a wading pool for children.

► Mid-range
Pondok Sari
Pemutaran
Tel. (03 62) 947 38
Fax (03 62) 923 37
www.pondoksari.com
Very nice bungalow complex on the ocean, surrounded by tropical greenery. Diving school.

in grave danger of extinction within the foreseeable future because, despite all appeals, it is still being caught and offered for sale at markets. The great variety of other tropical birds, however, will thrill those with an interest in ornithology.

Those who appreciate an almost unspoilt landscape can undertake walking tours along the (few) trails and paths through this unique wilderness. Most of these are in the northwest part of the national park; the south and east have hardly been developed.

Hiking trails

Lying just off the coast in the extreme northwest of Bali Barat National Park is the uninhabited island (pulau) of Menjangan. It can be reached by boat in about half an hour from **Labuhan Lalang** in the bay of Teluk Terima, where plain lodgings are available. Divers will find a fascinating underwater world here, which even those equipped only with a snorkel and a diving mask can explore.

Island of Menjangan

The white Bali Mynah is an endangered species.

Pemutaran   The fishing village of Pemutaran is a fast-growing holiday resort Pemutaran with a beautiful beach, coral reef and tropical fish. There are good spots for scuba-diving and snorkelling. Visitors to Menganan Island like to spend the night here. In addition, there is a nature reserve for turtles.

✴✴ Bangli

Capital of the administrative district of Bangli
Distance: 39km/24mi north of Denpasar

Region: Central Bali
Altitude: 392m/1,286ft

Bangli, the capital of one of a total of nine administrative districts in Bali, was once an independent principality. The lower reaches of the Gunung Agung volcano begin not far to the north of the city, but Bangli itself lies at the upper end of the well-irrigated central hill country, making possible productive agriculture. Lake Batur, Bali's largest lake, is also in the district.

History   The first documentary evidence of the city of Bangli, today **one of Bali's cultural centres**, dates back to 1204 when a huge religious festival was celebrated here. Later, Bangli became the capital of an independent principality, whose rulers, however, never exercised any great political influence. They sought – when the situation demanded – protection and council from neighbouring regions, namely from the powerful lords of Klungkung.

⏵ VISITING BANGLI

INFORMATION
Bangli Tourist Office
Jl. Sriwijaya 23
Tel. (03 66) 915 37

GETTING AROUND
Travel northeastward from Denpasar through Sukawati to Sakah, take a right turn there in the direction of Blahbatuh and continue on past Gianyar to Bangli. There are regular bus connections from Denpasar-Kerenang. Bemos travel from Denpasar to Gianyar; you need to change to get from there to Bangl.

WHERE TO EAT
► Inexpensive
① Pasar Malam
Some good warungs (snackbars, simple restaurants) can be found at the Pasar Malam (night market) near the bemo station; during the day there are also some food stands in the vicinity of the market.

WHERE TO STAY
► Mid-range
① Artha Sastra Inn
Jl. Merdeka 5
Tel. (03 66) 911 79
The rooms here vary quite a bit – some in the old palace, some in simple bungalows. The hotel is located directly across from the bus station.

② Bangli Inn
Jl. Rambutan 1
Tel. (03 66) 914 19
Simple but clean lodgings.

What to See in Bangli

Bangli is dominated by the **magnificent backdrop** of Mount Batur, especially impressive in the morning hours. Later in the day, the volcano almost always disappears behind a cloud cap. There are a number of temples in Bangli worth taking a look at, including five dedicated to the powers of the underworld. A large **market**, where farmers from all over the surrounding area sell their produce, is held every third day in the centre of Bangli in front of the palace of the raja, Puri Artha Sastra.

The former residence of the princes of Bangli, Puri Artha Sastra, was converted a few years ago into a small hotel; the young prince himself is the owner. The bales are decorated with traditional Balinese as well as Chinese paintings. There are a number of statues and figures from Hindu mythology on the attractive grounds. Take a look at the large gate leading into the interior of the palace and the ornate reliefs to the right and left of it.

★
Puri Artha Sastra

The Pura Kehen (Temple of the Treasury), about 2.5km/1.5mi north of the city centre, is considered to be **one of the most beautiful and**

★ ★
Pura Kehen

Pura Kehen *Plan*

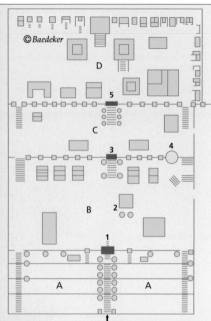

© Baedeker

A	four terraces	1	covered gate (candi korung)
B	outer forecourt (jaba sisi)	2	sacred stone (batu kermat)
C	inner forecourt (jaba tengah)	3	split gate (candi bentar)
D	temple interior (jeroan)	4	Waringin tree (kulkul base)
		5	split gate (candi bentar)

Opening hours:
daily 8am–5pm,
donations requested

is, at the same time, the largest shrine in Bali. Preserved inside are valuable bronze tablets said to date back to the year 1204 when Bangli was founded. The temple complex itself, built on seven terraces below Bukit Bangli, was founded even earlier, in the 11th century, by the royal priest, Sri Brahma Kemute Ketu.

The actual temple is only reached after passing through the first four terraces and a covered gate (candi korung), guarded over by a kala demon, a lion-like mask. To the right is a bale for the musicians of the gamelan orchestra to sit; to the left another bale serves as a gathering place for the temple visitors.

A sacred stone (batu keramat) can be seen on the way to the second courtyard, which stretches out across yet another terrace. Beyond a split gate (candi bentar) stand two buildings to the right and the left in which shadow plays are presented during temple festivals.

Before entering the third courtyard, the most holy precinct of the temple, pieces of faience of Chinese origin can be seen set in the separating wall. On the front side of the inner courtyard, the side nearest the hill, are a number of merus with varying numbers of tumpangs (the tallest, with eleven tiers, is dedicated to Shiva), as well as shrines for deities and tugus (stone lanterns which are the abode of gods of lower rank).

There is a **good view of the whole temple complex** and the mountain scenery from the uppermost terrace of the inner courtyard.

Pura Nataran

The beautiful Pura Nataran temple on Bangli's main road is almost always closed. It belongs to the royal family and is their ancestral temple.

Pura Dalem Cungkub

On the road running east past Bangli's bemo station is Pura Dalem Cungkub, one of the five underworld temples in Bangli. This temple is also arranged on a number of terraces.

Bangli *Map*

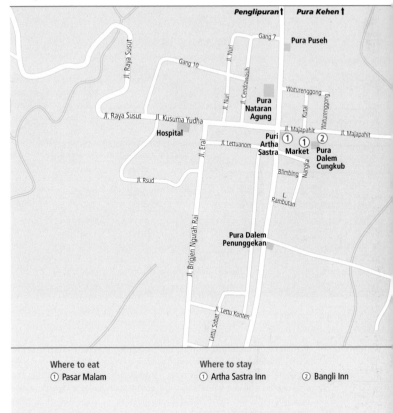

Where to eat
① Pasar Malam

Where to stay
① Artha Sastra Inn   ② Bangli Inn

Pura Dalem Penunggekan is on the road in the south of the city leading to Gianyar. It is worth paying it a visit to see its particularly finely worked reliefs. Do not miss the **figures of the witches** on the so-called Flame Gate. The place of cremation and a Chinese cemetery are outside the temple.

★
Pura Dalem
Penunggekan

Around Bangli

The little village of Penglipuran now has a place on every tour organizer's itinerary. What effect this will have on the fascinating charm of the village and its some 750 inhabitants remains to be seen. At any rate, children and teenagers now stand on the access roads waiting to guide the tourists through the village once they have paid the obligatory donation and signed the visitors' book.

★ ★
Penglipuran

Pura Kehen is one of the most important shrines in Bali.

Penglipuran lies a little way off the road from Bangli to Kintamani in a breathtaking, almost unspoilt landscape. About 5km/3mi north of Bangli there is a sign that says **»Traditional Village«** pointing the way. Penglipuran's kampongs, the traditional Balinese family compounds, line the right and left hand sides of the road that runs through the village, which is laid out in a series of terraces. A narrow canal running between the road and the houses serves for waste disposal. The family temples that are a part of each kampong face toward Gunung Agung. At the upper end of the paved road stands the village temple, Pura Desa, an exact copy of a temple in Bayung Gede (near Kintamani).

The older inhabitants of the village in fact claim that their ancestors originally came from Bayung Gede. This suggests that Penglipuran is not an older settlement but of more recent origin. At the lower end of the road, to the right on the edge of the forest, is another shrine with elaborately worked figures on its base.

Letting one of the local children or teenagers act as a guide through Penglipuran usually results in an invitation into one of the family compounds. The villagers are glad to see visitors and give them a friendly greeting everywhere. The inhabitants of Penglipuran live primarily from farming and forestry; some also work as artists.

✶ ✶ Bedugul

L 4

Region: Central Bali
Altitude: 1,224m/4,016ft

Administrative district: Tabanan
Distance: 30km/18.6mi south of Singaraja

Lying high in the hills, Bedugul is set in a uniquely stunning and primitive landscape and is the starting point for visiting some special attractions in the surrounding area. Although there is nothing exceptional in Bedugul itself apart from a major vegetable and flower market, a visit to Lake Bratan or an extended stroll through the charmingly arranged botanic gardens are worth the trip.

Around Bedugul

Lake Bratan was formed in an extinct volcano and is **surrounded by a superb landscape** dominated by the 2020m/6627ft-high Gunung

✶ ✶
Lake Bratan

Pura Ulun Danu lies in an extraordinarily picturesque setting on the western shore of Lake Bratan.

▶ VISITING BEDUGUL

GETTING AROUND

Take the road north from Denpasar in the direction of Singaraja (49km/30mi); from there, it is only about another 30km/19mi to Bedugul. There are good bus connections several times a day from Denpasar-Ubung and from Singaraja. Bemos leave from Denpasar-Ubung.

WHERE TO EAT

▶ Moderate

Warung Bali Restaurant
Pacung Asri Mountain Resort
Jl. Raya Pacung Baturiti
Ambitious Indonesian cooking, stylishly presented on an open terrace with a view of the Balinese hill country.

WHERE TO STAY

▶ Mid-range

Enjung Beji Resort
North shore of Lake Bratan
Tel. (03 61) 73 15 20
Fax 73 43 79
The small cottage-style resort (22 rooms) lies amidst blossoming tropical shrubbery and has direct access to the lake temple; spacious rooms and a beautiful, open restaurant.

Pacung Asri Mountain Resort
Jl. Raya Pacung Baturiti
Tel. (03 61) 73 15 20, fax 73 43 79
www.asia-hotel.net/
pacung-asri-hotel/
Hotel complex (40 rooms) wonderfully integrated into the landscape between rice fields and forests in a valley shimmering in every imaginable shade of green; regular meditation courses, pool and library, fishing in the surrounding area, coffee shop and restaurant.

RECREATION / GOLF

Baedeker recommendation

Bali Handara Country Club
Lying in the crater of an extinct volcano enclosed by tropical rainforest, this 18-hole golf course offers unforgettable views of idyllic Lake Bunyan and its magnificent scenery.

Bratan. The area and the lake are well developed for tourism; besides swimming, visitors can take out motor boats and go waterskiing. The restaurant can also be recommended.

★★
Pura Ulun Danu
🕐
Opening hours:
daily 8am–10pm

A small island is situated near to the village of Candi Kuning on the western shore of Lake Bratan. On it stands the charming Pura Ulun Danu lake temple, which has anunusual feature: to the left of the entrance into the first temple courtyard is a Buddhist **stupa with figures of a meditating Buddha** set in niches in the square base. The stupa is evidence of the adoption of principles of the Buddhist faith by the Hindus. The Hindu shrine itself (best viewed in the morning when its scenery is at its most impressive) has a three-tiered meru dedicated to Dewi Danu, the goddess of the sea and of lakes. Another meru with eleven tumpangs is probably dedicated to Dewa Pucak Manu.

Spread out over an area of some 130ha/325ac above Lake Bratan are the **Eka Karya Botanic Gardens** (Kebun Raya). Paths and hiking trails through the gardens are especially enticing for visitors with an interest in botany. Growing within the gardens are trees, shrubs and plants from various regions of Asia. There is also a herbarium with some specimens of tropical flowers. Several spots in the park offer excellent views of Lake Bratan and the surrounding hills.

★★
Botanic gardens

Leave Bedugul heading north and drive through the little mountain village of Wanagiri. About 11km/7mi past **Lake Buyan** is a turning to the village of Asah Munduk on the shores of Lake Tamblingan, situated in the midst of a fascinating tropical landscape. The shrine of Pura Gubug Tamblingan on its shores, the ancestral temple of the rajas of Buleleng, should not be missed.

★
Lake Tamblingan

Bedulu

★★

M 7

Region: Central Bali
Altitude: 280m/919ft

Administrative district: Badung
Distance: 6km/3.8mi south of Ubud

Bedulu was the centre of the oldest principality on the island of Bali. It lies in the middle of an agricultural area that gradually ascends to the hill country of central Bali. Over the course of time, Bedulu has grown and merged with the neighbouring town of Pejeng.

There are no sights of particular interest in Bedulu itself. There is more to see in the near vicinity and in neighbouring Pejeng (see p.160). A four-headed figure of a deity can be seen on the main intersection when passing through.

Around Bedulu

About 1km/0.6mi south of Bedulu is the spring sanctuary of Yeh Pulu with a 27m/89ft-long and up to 2m/6ft-high **relief**, believed to be the oldest in Bali, showing scenes of everyday life; archaeologists, however, are divided as to the purpose and meaning of this relief. Some pictures could possibly represent the god Krishna or relate to the legends woven around his many manifestations. The life-size figures with a three-dimensional appearance probably date back to the 14th or 15th century (opening hours: daily 7am–7pm).

★★
Yeh Pulu

 BEDULU

GETTING AROUND

Coming from Denpasar past Sukawati and Sakah, make a right turn at Teges just before Ubud. There are good, regular bus and bemo connections from Denpasar-Kerenang.

★ ★
Goa Gajah
(Elephant Cave)
🕐
Opening hours:
daily 9am–6pm

It is only about 2km/1.2mi from Bedulu to the famous Goa Gajah Elephant Cave, which has been venerated by Hindus since the first millennium (and possibly before then by Buddhists). The cave was discovered in 1923 and the bathing area in front of it was first excavated only in 1954. Actually, it is a **spring shrine** that gained its name from the cave's entrance, which resembles the head of an elephant (legend has it that there have never been elephants in Bali), although the cave does contain a 1m/3.3ft-high figure with four arms representing the elephant god Ganesha, one of Shiva's sons, which is venerated. Rising up to the right of it on a stone base are three lingams symbolizing Shiva in three of his manifestations as Brahma, Vishnu and as Shiva himself. Grouped around each lingam are eight smaller phallic symbols representing the eight guardians of the world. One of the bathing basins in front of the cave was for men and the other for women; the purpose of the middle one is unknown (it was possibly intended for use by members of the priestly caste for ritual ablutions). The waterspouts set into the walls are particularly elaborate. Be sure to **take a torch** along when touring the Elephant Cave (they are not available at the site).

No far from the Goa Gajah cave is the temple of **Pura Samuan Tiga**, dedicated to the Hindu trinity, Brahma, Vishnu and Shiva. Inside are several holy shrines holding figures that are highly venerated.

At the eastern end of Bedulu on the road to Pejeng is the wellstocked Gedong Arca Purbakala Archaeological Museum. A total of **53 tuff sarcophagi** of varying sizes, thought to date from around 300 BC, are kept in the inner courtyard. They were found at 37 different locations in Bali in the early 1970s and collected in Bedulu. Some of them show signs of damage, possibly caused by grave robbers or

Goa Gajah *Map*

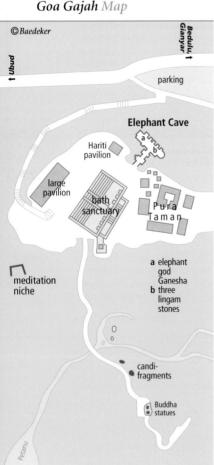

© Baedeker

↑ Ubud

Bedulu,↑ Gianyar

parking

Elephant Cave

a
b

Hariti pavilion

large pavilion

bath sanctuary

Pura Taman

meditation niche

a elephant god Ganesha
b three lingam stones

candi- fragments

Buddha statues

Petanu

★ ★
Archaeological
museum

The entrance to Goa Gajah depicts an elephant or a demon.

unprofessional excavators. The dead were not laid to rest in the sarcophagi in the traditional Western manner, but in a crouching position. Perhaps this is a symbolic representation of the eternal cycle of birth, death and rebirth, whereby the deceased is then reborn from a pre-natal position. The sarcophagus found at Taman Bali (near Bangli), fashioned in the **form of two turtles on top of each other** (a symbol of the underworld), is particularly impressive. Amazingly, the head of the lower turtle bears human facial features.

On display inside the museum are a number of pieces of jewellery, implements and tools dating from both the Stone Age and the Bronze Age. The finds are for the most part not the result of elaborate excavations; instead, they were found by chance. Do not miss the miniature stupas discovered in the vicinity of Bedulu and Pejeng, thought to date from the Buddhist period in Bali (8th–10th century).

On the left-hand side of the road about 200m/656ft further on down is Pura Kebo Edan, the »Temple of the Crazy Water Buffalo«. In its centre is a **colossal 3.6m/12ft-high figure**, possibly representing the giant Bhairava, standing on the back of a figure that probably represents the god of death, Yama. A bull and a giant demon were added to the right and left of the. On the bales are numerous figures and fragments, some displaying terrifying grimacing faces. It is possible

★
Pura Kebo Edan

that the religious rites of the Tantric cult were celebrated here, which were excessive, orgiastic events.

The big attraction in the temple of Pura Panataran Sasih, located on the road between Bedulu and Pejeng, is **the biggest kettledrum in the world**, also called the »Moon of Pejeng«. Strictly speaking, it is less a drum and more a gong, because a bronze disc is struck by the beater.

The instrument has a diameter of about 125cm/49in, though it must be admitted that determining the size of the extremely elaborately decorated gong, with its spiralling bands of ornamentation, stylized faces and Hindu symbols, is difficult because it is hung high up in a bale and is partially hidden from view. While the age of the gong is well established (Dongsong culture, *c*300 BC), in spite of intensive research it has not been possible to date to determine its place of origin or the meaning of the decoration. The local population is of the opinion, however, that the »Moon of Pejeng« was originally one of thirteen moons in the sky that fell down and landed precisely at the spot where the temple stands today. What's more, the gong is allegedly a threat to life and limb, and the following dreadful story is told in an attempt to substantiate this. The night the moon fell to earth, it landed in the branches of a tree and its bright moonlight disturbed a band of thieves. When one of the thieves climbed up the tree and urinated on it to extinguish its light, the moon exploded, killing the unfortunate thief. The moon then fell to the ground as the »Moon of Pejeng«.

** ** Besakih

Region: Central Bali	**Administrative district:** Karangasem
Altitude: 980–1011m/3215–3317ft	**Distance:** 40km/25mi northwest of Candi Dasa

The expansive, terraced temple complex, its structures built mostly of dark lava stone, may not seem that impressive – unless it happens to be the time of the annual temple festival when tens of thousands of the faithful flock here from all parts of the island. Bali may have more colourful and more elaborately decorated temple sites but, for the Hindus, Pura Besakih is the »mother of all temples«.

** ** Pura Besakih (the Mother Temple)

Guides ► In the car park at the entrance to Pura Besakih, Balinese of all ages offer their services as guides. Usually they speak very little English and their knowledge of the temple is limited to only the main facts. If you do want to use a guide, agree on a price in advance (about 10,000 rupiahs).

History

Pura Besakih was probably founded as early as the 8th century, **possibly as a Buddhist shrine** since at the time Bali had not yet been converted to Hinduism. Legend tells of a Shiva priest named Sri Markhadeya who is said to have erected a shrine here. The main parts of today's temple were most likely built by the ruler Kesari Warmadewa in the 10th century.

◀ Tip

Some areas of the temple are normally not open to non-believing visitors (particularly during preparations for a festival). However, a well signposted path, from which visitors are asked not to stray, runs through the grounds.

 ## VISITING BESAKIH

GETTING AROUND

From Denpasar, head northeastwards to Klungkung, then take the road branching off to the north as far as Rendang and then continue on to Besakih (approx. 63km/39mi). There are regular bus connections from Denpasar-Kereneng as far as Klungkung; bemos then continue the journey. Taking a bemo from Denpasar is not recommended, but there are good connections from Klungkung or Rendang (in part only with chartered bemos).

FESTIVALS

Bhatara Turun Kabeh festival
Legend has it that once a year all the Balinese gods descend from the heights of Gunung Agung and abide in the temple of Besakih. The Balinese celebrate this event with a festival, the Bhatara Turun Kabeh (March–April).

Eka Dasa Rudra festival
In addition to the annual temple anniversary (Odalan festival, ▶Baedeker Special p.90), every hundred years the Eka Dasa Rudra, the premier Balinese temple festival, is held in Pura Besakih. It was last celebrated in 1979, which was a departure from the normal cycle. There was a good reason for this: during the preparations for the scheduled date in 1963, the Gunung Agung volcano – which had been considered extinct – erupted. Severe eruptions lasted for days, destroying a number of villages in the surrounding area and claiming the lives of more than 2,500 people. The festival was finally celebrated a decade and a half later.

WHERE TO EAT / WHERE TO STAY

Inexpensive and basic (shared) lodgings for travellers, so-called losmen, can be found outside Besakih on the road to Menang. Losmen place little value on amenities and comfort. There are even some near the temple entrance, close to the souvenir stands. There are also several simple warungs there offering inexpensive but tasty Indonesian dishes.

PURA BESAKIH (Pura Penataran Agung)

✱ ✱ On the southwest flank of Gunung Agung, the sacred volcano regarded
as the abode of the gods and the symbolic centre of the universe, lies the Pura
Besakih temple complex, honoured as the »mother of all temples« on Bali. It is
not in fact a single temple, but rather a huge array of more than 30 separate
complexes with over 200 different structures spread over a series of terraces.
Illustrated here is the heart of the Besakih complex, Pura Penataran Agung.

🕐 Opening hours:
Daily 8am–7pm

① Split Gate

The first of the five temple precincts is reached by
way of an expansive stairway and a split gate
(candi bentar). The precincts are separated by
lava rock walls of differing heights. A bell tower
(kulkul) stands on either side of the gate. From
here there is a view of the inner courtyard, which
cannot be entered by non-Hindus.

② Main courtyard

A covered gate leads into the second temple
precinct with a throne and various bales, where
the village elders gather, gamelan orchestras play
during festivals and offerings are prepared.
Towering above it all are two merus, one nine
storeys and the other eleven storeys high.

③ Lotus throne

The most important shrine of the whole complex is
a triple lotus throne (sanggar agung) dedicated to
Sangyang Widi Wasa in his manifestation as the
Hindu-Trinity: Brahma – Vishnu – Shiva. It serves
as a seat of honour during Bhatara Turun Kabeh.

④ Inner Courtyards

On the next terrace above are various bales
reserved for priestly rituals and some three to
eleven stepped merus – shrines for gods,
ancestors and spirits.

⑤ Temple Treasure

The temple treasures, for the most part old,
wooden inscriptions, are kept in the so-called
kehen.

*A great many worshippers visit the temple grounds once a year during Bhatara
Turun Kabeh when all of the Balinese gods are gathered here.*

Meres are towering structures with pagoda-like roofs. They symbolize Mount Meru, where all Hindu gods dwell.

The climb up the steep stairs leading to the split gate is rewarded by a superb view of the surrounding countryside.

© Baedeker

The profusely decorated throne serves as the seat of honour for the gods during temple festivals.

Decorated stone figures flanking the steep steps at the entrance

Temple site Cars can use the wide road leading uphill to the temple site except during religious celebrations. Shops selling religious items and souvenirs line either side of the road up until the first of the **smaller family temples** on the left-hand side. It is not only the old royal houses which maintain a temple here; clans, guilds and village communities have also set up their shrines and altars here to strengthen their bonds with this sacred site, establishing Besakih as the **symbol of the Hindu-Dharma religion**, which was created out of the fusion of the old beliefs of the original inhabitants of Bali and Hinduism. The number of shrines will probably increase in the future: when a family achieves a certain amount of importance it erects its own family or ancestral temple within Pura Besakih.

! *Baedeker* TIP

Etiquette and customs when visiting a temple

Visiting a temple in a miniskirt or shorts is considered inappropriate. The solution is available on site: the temple guardians hand out cloths (selendang) to visitors that are wrapped around the hips. It is, however, preferable to carry your own clean selendang with you.

Each of the three main shrines into which the temple complex is divided has smaller satellite temples grouped around it. They stand for the Hindu triad; the creator of the world, Brahma, Vishnu as life-giver and preserver, and Shiva, the destroyer and bringer of death. The spiritual centre is the **Pura Penataran Agung** in which Sangyang Widi Wasa, an incarnation of Shiva, is venerated. It stands at the end of a 1km/3000ft long processional road. A steep flight of steps guarded by figures from the Mahabharata leads to a split gate opening into the interior of the temple complex through which only Hindus may enter. Inside is the most important shrine of this site, the three-seated lotus throne. It is possible to take a look into the first temple precinct where there are a number of secular buildings in adjoining walled courtyards in which offerings are prepared for the great temple festival. If a temple festival is scheduled to take place in a few days, it is possible to observe these preparations. Otherwise, **non-Hindus** only have the possibility of viewing the shrine from the outside, which is **quiet easy because of the low surrounding wall**. The royal families or their descendants are responsible for the maintenance of the shrines in the Pura Panataran Agung: the rajas of Bangli for the place of offering for Vishnu, those of Karangasem (Amlapura) for the place of offering for Brahma and the rajas of Klungkung for the place of offering for Shiva.

The other two main shrines on either side of the Pura Penataran Agung are, to the west, the **Pura Batu Madeg**, dedicated to Vishnu, and, to the east, the **Pura Dangin Kreteg**, in which Brahma is venerated. On special holidays the shrines are decorated in the symbolic colours of the gods; red for Brahma, white for Shiva and black for Vishnu.

✳ ✳ The Ascent of Gunung Agung

Gunung Agung, **the island's highest mountain** and the abode of Shiva, can be climbed from several sides, e.g. from Besakih, from Amlapura (about 6 hours) and from Sebudi (near Selat; about 7 hours). The following is a description of the southwestern route from Besakih. Participants need to be in good physical condition because there are no mountain huts in which to spend the night, meaning the ascent and descent must be made in one day (it can get quite cold during the night and early morning). Sturdy footwear, weatherproof clothing, sufficient food and water are essential. It can be extremely dangerous to wander off the designated paths in this volcanic area; even experienced mountain climbers should take along a guide who knows the terrain. Get as early a start as possible for the ascent of Gunung Agung, preferably around 2am. A practiced mountain hiker needs between six and nine hours for the ascent and at least another five for the descent. The trail begins at the main temple of Pura Besakih and leads through a dense forest, relatively level at first but becoming much steeper later. After about five hours, a rock face is reached. It is known as the Kori Agung and is considered to be the **gateway to the summit region**. It is about two to three hours from this point to the crater's rim, from whose inner wall there are abrupt drops of up to 100m/328ft. Having taken the more strenuous route, the **fascinating views** of large parts of the island are now all the more rewarding.

Strenuous mountain tour

◄ *Route*

✳ ✳ Bukit Badung

K/L 10/11

Region: Southern Bali
Altitude: 0–200m/656ft

Administrative district: Badung
Distance: 15km/9.3mi south of Denpasar

Bukit Badung is the name of the peninsula at the southernmost point of Bali. It is joined to the main island by an isthmus only 1.7km/1mi across at its widest point. Bukit Badung has only become known since the 1970s through the development of Nusa Dua as a tourist centre.

What to See on Bukit Badung Peninsula

The small fishing village of Jimbaran lies on the narrow isthmus linking the Bukit Badung peninsula with Bali. For years there was no tourism here to speak of, despite the beautiful beach of white sand. In recent years, however, some of the most luxurious hotel complexes on the island have been built in the surrounding area, among them the Four Seasons Resort. The **Bulgari Hotel Bali**, with a beach

Jimbaran

▶ VISITING BUKIT BADUNG

INFORMATION

Badung Government Tourism Office
Jl. Raya Kuta 2, Kuta
Tel. (03 61) 75 61 75, fax 75 61 76
www.badung.go.id

GETTING AROUND

Take the Jalan Bypass (approx. 21km/
13mi) from Denpasar; it is about
15km/9.3mi from Kuta and Legian,
and about 23km/14.3mi from Sanur.
There are regular bus services from
Denpasar-Tegal; bemos can be found
along the road between Denpasar and
Nusa Dua. Registered taxis drive
between Denpasar, Kuta, Legian and
Sanur. Taxi drivers often offer to
switch off their meters (particularly in
the evening and at night) and name a
»fixed« price – presenting a great
opportunity for a little haggling.

SHOPPING

Baedeker recommendation

Galeria Nusa Dua
Shoppers can get brand names like Prada,
Armani and Versace at quite low prices in
the Nusa Dua Tourist Complex. Free shuttle
buses ply between the hotels and the shopping complex in the midst of a large park
with 150 boutiques, including a good variety
of supermarkets, department stores and
handicraft shops such as the popular batik
shop, Galeri Keris. In addition, dozens of
restaurants, cafés and bistros are open late
into the night. After sunset, music and
Chinese lanterns radiate a truly magical
atmosphere.

Only real experts should attempt to negotiate the waves off Bukit Badung.

WHERE TO EAT
► Expensive
Lotus Garden
Nusa Dua, Jl. Ngurah Rai
Tel. (0361) 77 33 78
Although situated on the town's main road, it is quiet and comfortable here; tables are surrounded by pools of water and fountains; mainly Mediterranean cuisine.

► Moderate
Balangan
Jimbaran
Br. Cenggiling 88
Tel. (0361) 70 80 80
Popular but small, so arrive early; the crab and corn balls are delicious.

► Inexpensive
Kakul Café
Jimbaran
Jl. Bukit Permai 5C
Tel. (0361) 70 28 14
Live music is served up with the hamburgers, pizzas and pasta at the weekend.

WHERE TO STAY
► Luxury
Four Seasons Resort at Jimbaran
Kawasan Bukit Permai
Tel. (0361) 70 10 10, fax 70 10 20
www.fourseasons.com
One of the most exclusive establishments in Bali; only 15 minutes away from the airport in the south of the island on the Bukit peninsula, situated in a 1.5ha/3.7ac tropical garden with a private, 3km/1.9mi-long, white sand beach. There are 147 villas available, the smallest (with a mere 200 sq m/ 2,153 sq ft living space!) consists of three thatched pavilions and its own 12 sq m/129 sq ft pool with a view of Jimbaran Bay and Gunung Agung, Bali's sacred mountain; breakfast, served in the Taman Wantilan restaurant overlooking the sea, fulfils even the most extravagant expectations; in addition, there are other restaurants, a library and an excellent art gallery, as well as a renowned spa; and right next door are two popular golf courses.

Ritz Carlton
Jimbaran
Jl. Karang Mas, Sejahtera
Tel. (0361) 70 22 22
Fax 70 15 55
www.ritzcarlton.com
The resort, a 375 room estate, boasts a location set on cliffs overlooking the Indian Ocean. Guests value the ambience traditional of this luxury chain: fabulously designed rooms and suites, an atmosphere typical of the country, set in gardens designed by leading Balinese gardeners, with its own golf course and splendid spa.

Baedeker recommendation

Nusa Dua Beach Hotel & Spa
Nusa Dua, Kawasan, Pariwisata, Lot North 4,
Tel. (0361) 77 12 10
Fax 77 26 17
www.lhw.com/nusadua
This hotel, owned by the Sultan of Brunei and one of most prestigious leading hotels in the world, has an enchanting and seemingly intimate atmosphere despite its size (381 rooms). Contributing to this are the 9ha/22ac tropically landscaped gardens, as well as the employees, who bring their offerings to the hotel altar, and the ducks waddling around the pond. The decor of the Balinese spa, designed for meditation, is also excellent. The rooms in the Palace Club are highly recommended, with direct access to the park and lounge (private breakfast, afternoon tea, and evening cocktails included) as well as the library.

This will really do you good: luxurious furnishings and scores of wellness offers

FIVE-STAR ACCOMODATIONS IN HARMONY WITH NATURE

This is far more than your usual luxury accommodation. A stay in Bali's most beautiful hotels is a special experience that appeals to the senses. The harmonious integration of buildings into their surroundings is an art form well understood in Bali. On the island of the gods, hotels are built that have a peaceful, beneficial influence on their residents.

Segawan Gin is a legend among travellers. It is a place that bodes happiness: Begawan, »The Valley of the Wise Man«, a primeval tropical forest valley near the artists' city of Ubud, is named after three Hindus, the Begawanthas, who once meditated here and soon attracted many believers to the valley. A British business couple purchased eight hectares of land here in the 1980s, which also included a river and a spring regarded by the local population as sacred and whose water, according to an investigation carried out by European scientists, is among the finest on the island. The villagers were assured that they would continue to have access to the spring and so hotel guests can now watch as processions of festively-dressed Balinese mindfully descend the mossy stone steps through the jungle to reach the water. A responsible attitude toward the neighbourhood was also demonstrated by the building of a road, a health care facility and an art academy for the children of the village.

The hotel was constructed with the same consideration. Jeffrey Bauer, an architect from Sri Lanka, designed five residences, each around one of the five elements and each subdivided into four or five suites. From Wanakasa, symbolizing the earth, there is a direct view into the green leaves of the forest. Tirta Ening, in turn, embodies water; a rock weighing several tonnes taken from the vicinity of a volcano was hewn out for use as an exotic bathtub in the villa of »Clear Waters«. Several tonnes of rock from the island of Sumba and antique wooden masts were imported to impart an elegant yet archaic appearance to the »Sound of Fire« villa (Tejasura). The interior impresses even the most discriminating visitor, from the polished teak floors, the massive gleaming black bamboo bed, the bath of limestone and warm tropical woods, Victorian shower fittings and the marvellous

flower arrangements. Guests in other residences are seen only if desired. A butler and his assistant look after all the guests' needs with charming Balinese composure, from breakfast on serving whatever the guest desires, wherever he or she desires it.

Other Feel-Good Oases

It is only a couple of miles from Begawan Giri to another real gem of the Balinese hotel industry. Although the **Four Seasons** has a totally different architectural design, the guest lives here too in a magnificent, spectacular manner within and with the surrounding tropical scenery. Modern, innovative and extravagant are the attributes that come to mind when approaching the entrance across a contemporary interpretation of a drawbridge. Immediately upon entering the lobby, a view of palm trees and vegetation opens up far below. The hotel has been built on a steep escarpment and the entrance is located on the uppermost floor. The other floors are located beneath. In the morning, swathes of mist from the steaming jungle pass by on the

horizon and, come evening, the golden light of the setting sun sets the valley aglow.

A round swimming pool appears to float over the precipice; beneath it, supported by massive pillars, is the lobby with an open café and a restaurant. Waking up in the large rooms and suites is a very special experience as the tropical greenery is close enough to touch and the screams of the monkeys and calls of the birds penetrate up from out of the valley. Nature, merged with modern design, and pervaded with Balinese elements.

Equally extraordinary, yet in still another way, is the **Bali at Jimbaran**, owned by a Balinese and also managed by the Four Seasons. There are almost four employees per guest here and a so-called Village Chief looks after the guests. The 147 villas are joined together in seven villages. It is almost like being in an exotic kingdom, for even in the most modest room category (the so-called One Bedroom Villas) there is 200 sq m/ 2153 sq ft of living space and an individual 12 sq m/129 sq ft pool for a

Friendliness and attentive service included

private dip. Wealthy guests book the Royal Villas (600 sq m/6460 sq ft), furnished with antiques and including the services of a butler and nanny.

Enhancing an already unique natural environment with architecture

Baths perfumed with jasmine oil and lemongrass tea instead of golden water facets; electric fans and the sweet air of the tropics instead of air conditioning; subdued furnishings instead of pompous ornateness: this is the ethos of the **Aman hotels**. Their name has come to stand for the finest in small hotels; architectural enhancement of an already unique natural environment. Aman means »peaceful« in Sanskrit and the secret of their success probably lies in this small word. The hotels that the Indonesian Adrian Zecha founded are jewels in a world of hotels marked by standardization and optimization; they are private paradises that not only pamper the traveller with luxurious, harmonious surroundings, but offer a total lifestyle experience. There are not one but three Aman resorts in Bali. The magic of the island can be especially felt in **Amandari**, near to the artist's town of Ubud. The guest accommodation, with a minimum size of 100 sq m/1076 sq ft, radiate peace, beauty and inner retreat. The jungle, with its plants, many feet tall, stretching out directly in front of the huge windows, seems to be growing right into the room. The Japanese style sliding doors open up to the secluded, private patio. Here, couples enjoy exotic drinks in the lotus blossom decorated plunge pool.

The bungalows and the main building of **Amankila** (»Peaceful Harbour«), situated on the east coast near Candi Dasa, are spread out over a steep hill that drops down into the Indian Ocean. It is a brilliant architectural achievement: three huge terrace-shaped swimming pools merge into one another, bounded by open pavilions. The guests convene here in the afternoon for the tea ceremony.

The **Amanusa** (»Peaceful Island») is located in Nusa Dua overlooking the »Bali Golf and Country Club«. Guests enter their own villa through a carved wooden gate that leads to a terrace. Inside is a bath that fascinates all the guests. It has a sunken bathtub that looks out through glass panes onto a small pond with water-lilies and goldfish. Aman resorts, according to some, represent a special form of spirituality. One thing is certain in Bali; the staff plays a key role. With inimitable grace and composure, they respond to the guests, determine their wishes and fulfil them without fuss.

Amanusa Nusa Dua
Nusa Dua
Jl. Pura Batu Pageh Ungasan
Tel. (03 61) 77 23 33
Fax 77 23 35
www.amanresorts.com
Adrian Zecha, the founder of Aman, has managed once again to repeat the miracle of creating the perfect hotel. The rooms with their appealing, simple styling create a tranquil mood that extends into the park-like atmosphere of the Nusa Dua complex and the adjoining golf course.

Grand Mirage
Nusa Dua
Tel. (03 61) 77 18 88
Fax 77 21 48
www.grandmirage.com
This spacious hotel is a favourite with Australian guests. It offers a large variety of room categories, several restaurants, cafés and bars, and a diverse cultural programme.

The Balé
Jl. Raya Nusa Dua Selatan
Tel. (03 61) 77 51 11, fax 77 52 22

www.slh.com/thebale
Small (only 20 rooms) but superb; the accommodation consists of spacious, palm leaf covered pavilions with their own pools, veranda and open bathroom in a dramatic setting on a hill overlooking the Indian Ocean.

► Mid-range
Keraton Cottage Resort
Jl. Mrajapati, Jimbaran
Tel. (06 31) 70 19 61
Fax 70 19 91
99 large rooms with balcony or terrace in an expansive park. Swimming pool, tennis courts and facilities for water sports.

Inna Putri Bali
Nusa Dua
Tel. (03 61) 77 10 20
Fax 77 11 39
www.innabali.com
Large, four-storey hotel (384 rooms) with an impressive open-air lobby and a tropical garden. Various room categories including some decorated in Balinese style. Facilities for a large variety of water sports.

cable car for the guests in its 59 private villas, opened at the end of 2006 on a plateau on the southern tip of the Jimbaran Peninsula. More changes are coming: bulldozers are already levelling land for a golf course behind the region's most beautiful beach, the fantastic Dreamland Beach.

Ungasan Garuda Wisnu Kencana Cultural Park in Ungasan is a large scale cultural project that showcases Bali's art and culture against the dramatic backdrop of the region's breathtaking landscape. All sorts of cultural events can be staged here; the venues include the

! Baedeker TIP

Fresh from the sea

Freshly caught fish and seafood are prepared in each of the countless beach restaurants in Jimbaran. The delicious meals here are enjoyed in either regal or rustic surroundings in open huts covered with palm leaves. It is especially pleasant here at dinner time, with candles and Chinese lanterns creating an enchanting mood. Reservations are not necessary; just take a seat wherever you like.

With its unique position on the western tip of Bukit Badung, Pura Luthur Ulu Watu is regarded as a bastion against the demons of the sea and darkness.

gigantic Lotus Pond area, which has a capacity of 7500 people, an 800-seat amphitheatre, the Street Theatre, suitable for processions and fashion shows, the intimate Plaza Kura Kura and the 200 sq m/ 240 sq yd Exhibition Gallery. Numerous cafés and restaurants serve Indonesian, Oriental and international cuisine. The GWK is dominated by the world's largest statue, an almost 150m/492ft-high representation of Vishnu riding on the mythical bird deity, Garuda.

★ ★
**Pura Luhur
Ulu Watu**
(mostly inacces-
sible) ▶

The **sea temple** of Pura Luhur Ulu Watu, near the small village of Pecatu, sits high atop a cliff that drops abruptly into the sea. The temple can be reached via the road branching off in a southwesterly direction from the Jalan Bypass (around Denpasar); it is only 4km/ 2.5mi from Pecatu. Pura Luhur Ulu Watu is considered to be one of the most important temples in Bali. It enjoys the status of a state temple (sadkahyangan). The shrine is dedicated to the goddess Rudra (a manifestation of Shivas), and the temple site faces the sea. The richly decorated gates made of coral stone are particularly notable. There is a **magnificent view of the sea** from the entrance of the temple, the powerful surf at high tide battering the strongly eroded, over 80m/262ft-high cliffs.

Pura Luhur Ulu Watu

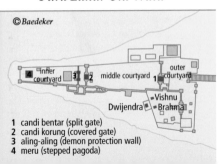

© Baedeker

inner courtyard • middle courtyard • outer courtyard • Vishnu • Dwijendra • Brahma

1 candi bentar (split gate)
2 candi korung (covered gate)
3 aling-aling (demon protection wall)
4 meru (stepped pagoda)

The east coast of the peninsula has seen the construction of luxury **Nusa Dua** hotels set in beautiful tropical gardens in the tourist centre of Nusa Dua. After the construction of the Nusa Dua Beach Hotel, the condition was made that no new hotel building may be higher than the tallest palm tree in its vicinity. It is through the strict observance of this condition and the efforts of architects to follow the traditional Balinese building style that Nusa Dua, with its spacious areas of lawns and parks, appears so elegant and harmonious today. By the way, on the road between Denpasar and the Bukit Badung peninsula, at about the point where the tourist

! Baedeker TIP

Oasis for cyclists

The traffic is heavy in Bali, and for foreigners the way the locals drive takes some getting used to – and can even be dangerous. Nusa Dua, however, is an oasis for cyclists. Here it is possible to get around on a bike on well-developed paths that lead through park-like areas, past hotels and even to the occasional small Balinese village. A very relaxing way to travel.

area begins, stands a huge, modern candi bentar (split gate). Does it perhaps to symbolize the invisible line separating the Balinese from the tourist? Is it the portal from one world into the other?

The narrow neck of land called Tanjung Benoa extends out into the sea on the northeast edge of the peninsula. The harbour of the same name lies opposite. **Boats head out to »Turtle Island«**, Pulau Serangan, from here.   **Tanjung Benoa and Benoa Harbour**

✷ ✷ Candi Dasa

P 7

Region: East Bali
Altitude: sea level

Administrative district: Karangasem
Distance: 20km/12mi south of Amlapura

Candi Dasa was first developed for tourism some years ago. Although the beach here is quite narrow, the pleasant and inexpensive accommodation and the good restaurants make the place an ideal base for exploring the east of Bali.

What to See in and around Candi Dasa

Once upon a time Candi Dasa, at the eastern end of Labuhan Amu Bay, was considered to be an insider's tip among backpackers. But that was then; now the small fishing village is a largely unspoilt **holiday centre** with a lively atmosphere. Although there are no top class hotels as in Nusa Dua, the infrastructure has been brought up to an acceptable standard. Tourists who prefer peace and quiet and seek lodgings away from the hustle and bustle of the big city of Denpasar would do well to look in Candi Dasa.

▶ VISITING CANDI DASA

INFORMATION

Karangasem Tourist Office
Jl. Diponegoro
Amlapura
Tel. (03 63) 211 96, fax 219 54

Klungkung Tourist Office
Jl. Untung Surapati 2
Semarapura
Tel. (03 66) 214 48, fax 228 48

GETTING AROUND

Travel from Denpasar to Sakah, turn right there and head in the direction of Blahbatuh, continuing on to Klung-kung; then follow the coast via Padang Bai. There is a bus service that runs several times daily from Denpasar-Kereneng. Bemos can be found along the road.

WHERE TO EAT

▶ Expensive
The Restaurant
Amankila, Manggis
Tel. (03 63) 807 01
Spend an unforgettable evening in one of the best restaurants on the island. Fantastic Indonesian cooking in charming surroundings accompanied by Balinese music; reservations necessary.

▶ Moderate
Vincent's
Jl. Raya Candidasa
Tel. (03 63) 413 68
For fans of tropical design. The light, exotic cuisine in the café and restaurant includes such delights as chicken satee, red snapper and Balinese fish dishes.

▶ Inexpensive
TJ's
Jl. Raya Candidasa
Tel. (03 63) 415 40
A young-at-heart clientele gather here for an early breakfast of muesli, pancakes and scrambled eggs; later diners enjoy the Indonesian special-ities and Australian steaks.

WHERE TO STAY

▶ Luxury
Amankila
Tel. (03 63) 413 33
Fax 415 55
www.amankila.com
This hotel (35 bungalows), part of the legendary Aman hotel chain, combines purist interiors with a touch of Asia and offers perfect service to boot. It is breathtakingly situated on a cliff to the west of Candi Dasa with a view of Lombok. The restaurant is excellent. A tour programme is tailor-made for each individual guest.

▶ Mid-range
Puri Bagus
Tel. (03 63) 411 31
Fax 412 90
www.puribagus.net
47 Balinese-style guest villas with open bathrooms situated in spacious grounds. Yoga classes and spa facilities await the guest, plus an open restau-rant, which can also arrange private candlelit dinners on the beach; nice snack-bar.

▶ Budget
Balina Beach
Tel. (03 63) 913 68
Fax 925 79
This hotel with only 20 bungalows is in a quiet cove a short distance from Candi Dasa and is thus also a little removed from the tourist bustle. Bi-cycle hire service.

One drawback of this resort, which has grown at an unnatural rate, is its beach. Since the relatively unprotected shoreline is occasionally directly subjected to very strong waves, the sand has simply been washed away. This was largely the result of the destruction of the offshore coral banks through uncontrolled quarrying (used in the production of lime). A government ban on quarrying came too late, and today the beach is quite narrow. The hotel owners had no other option but to protect their beaches by building very expensive stonewall barriers.

About 10km/6mi along the road from Klungkung to Candi Dasa, about halfway between the two and not far from the town of Kusambe, is the seaside cave shrine of Goa Lawah, one of the six sadkahyangans (state or royal temples) in Bali. It is highly venerated by the Balinese, not least of all because of the belief in the existence of an underground passage connecting the cave (which has yet to be explored to its end) with the island's holiest temple, Pura Besakih, believed to be the **point of contact between the upper world and the underworld**. Goa Lawah is in fact where Sangyang Basuki lives, one of the two snakes of the underworld. Approximately in the centre of the cave entrance stands a lotus throne (padmasana) reserved for the snake god.

★ ★
Goa Lawah
(Bat Cave)

Small bats live inside the cave, even right at the cave's entrance, and can be seen crowded tightly together hanging on the cave's rock walls. A small temple has been erected to the right of the mouth of the cave with several wooden merus. Every 15 days, worshippers bring offerings here and in return receive holy water necessary for use in various ceremonies, for example on the rice fields of the surrounding area. Numerous peddlers offering incense sticks, batik textiles and arts and crafts can be found at the entrance and in the area

Lotus blossom field near Candi Dasa

! *Baedeker* TIP

Diving in Gili Tepekong

Gili Tepekong, Gili Biaha and Gili Mimpan may be unknown in Europe, but the three tiny rock islands off the coast are known to every schoolchild in Candi Dasa. Many of the local fishermen in Candi Dasa are quite willing to take the experienced and adventurous diver over to the rocks. The area is considered to be excellent for diving, but some caution is in order; only seasoned campaigners should venture into its depths.

in front of the temple. Occasionally it is possible to attend Hindu ceremonies in the temple; entering the cave is **taboo**.

A new tourist centre with a large number of mid-range hotels has grown up not far from Candi Dasa (approx. 4km/2.5mi in the direction of Klungkung). It is called **Balina Beach**. The sand is lighter in colour there than in Candi Dasa.

The **Padang Bai** ferry terminal at the western end of Labuhan Amuk Bay has ferries serving the offshore island of ►Penida and ►Lombok. The large cruise ships that include a stopover in Bali on their itinerary also anchor in the bay. Thanks to the heavy ferry traffic there is a great number of around-the-clock bus and bemo services in the town. There are several nice beaches outside Padang Bai.

Celuk

M 8

Region: Central Bali	**Administrative district:** Gianyar
Altitude: approx. 100m/328ft	**Distance:** 12km/7.5mi north of Denpasar

There are several places in Bali with the name Celuk. The Celuk described here is the village near Sukawati known for its skilled craftsmen.

Gold and silver shops

Gold and silversmith shops are scattered along the main thoroughfare running through the village of Celuk, which itself stretches for some distance along the road. Some have adjoining workshops in

► VISITING CELUK

GETTING AROUND

Celuk is located about 12km/7.5mi from Denpasar along the road to Sukawati. Buses travel daily from Denpasar to Kerenang; bemos leave from Denpasar, Ubud and Mas, as well as from points along the road to Sukawati.

WHERE TO EAT / WHERE TO STAY

The village is almost exclusively visited by day-trippers who head for the many gold and silversmith shops. Fruit, beverages and small snacks can be purchased at a variety of open stalls.

which tours are possible. The prices are comparable to those in the main tourist centres. Organized bus tours make scheduled stops in Celuk.

Celuk is also known for its woodcarvers, particularly those that specialize in wayang figures and wooden topeng masks. Most of the work is original to Celuk, passed down by tradition; but also produced here are wayang figures that are copies of those produced on the neighbouring island of Java. Quite often the masks on offer are mass-produced for tourists. There are some more craftsmen's shops in the villages around Celuk, for example in Guang, Batuan and Sukawati. With a little luck, you can find craftsmen in these villages who sell properly produced masks and figures.

Woodcarvers

A former bird park and reptile farm near Singapadu, not far from Celuk and Batubalan, were combined to form the new 3.5ha/8.6ac **Bali Zoo Park**. A tour leads wends its way through the tropical vegetation past monitor lizards, crocodiles, iguanas and snakes, tigers, monkeys and flying foxes. 350 species of bird, including some magnificent-looking parrots, also call Bali Zoo Park home.

★
Bali Zoo Park
🕐
Opening hours:
daily 9am–6pm

★ ★ # Denpasar

L 8

| Capital of Bali and the administrative district of Badung | **Region:** South Bali
Population: approx. 550,000 |

Denpasar, or more precisely Ngurah Rai airport located to the south of it, is usually the first that holidaymakers see of Bali. Since the completion of the four-lane Jalan Bypass however, they will notice hardly anything of the hustle and bustle of the capital, heading as they now do directly for one of the tourist resorts.

Denpasar is definitely worth a visit though. The city boasts a number of attractions, such as temples and the well-stocked Provincial State Museum. Because of the density of traffic, using your own vehicle is not recommended.

Denpasar has been the island's capital and the seat of the governor of the Indonesian province of Bali and all governmental offices since 1946, a distinction formerly held by ► Singaraja in the north of the island. In the same year it was given the name Denpasar (new market); prior to this it had been called Badung, like the administrative district (kabupaten) in which it is located. The locals still prefer using the name **Badung** for their capital. The city lies in the south of the island and has experienced an enormous boom since the 1960s. One of the consequences of this has been the resulting population explo-

Capital of the island

▶ VISITING DENPASAR

INFORMATION

Denpasar Tourist Office
Jl. Surapati 7, Denpasar
Tel. (03 61) 22 36 02, fax 23 45 69

GETTING AROUND

By air
Arrival at Ngurah Rai
International Airport, located south of
Kuta. The journey continues by bemo
or taxi.

In the city
Because of the chaotic traffic conditions, the many one-way streets and
lack of parking, it is advisable to
explore the city centre on foot. There
are very good bus and bemo services
from a number of terminals – the
Denpasar Tourist Office can provide
an overview and current information
(see above).

SHOPPING

In spite of the sometimes chaotic
traffic conditions, a shopping tour of
the centre of the Balinese capital is
well worthwhile. Instead of looking for
tourist-oriented articles found in souvenir shops, shop alongside the local
population for things typical of the
country: silk cloth, batik, fruit, vegetables, spices, reasonably priced shoes
and sandals, and electronic items.
Among the most popular shopping
streets that also offer Indonesian
handicrafts are Jl. Gajah Mada, Jl.
Sumatera and Jl. Sulawesi.

Ramayana Bali Mall
On three floors, Denpasar's oldest
shopping mall offers local and Australian branded goods and a large
selection of DVDs and CDs, as well as
a number of cafés and self-service
restaurants.

WHERE TO EAT

▶ Moderate
① ***Atoom Baru***
Jl. Gajah Mada, tel. (03 61) 22 27 88
This is a favourite place to stop while
shopping or visiting the market and
offers a large selection of Chinese
dishes. Try the spicy fish and seafood,
and wash it down with an ice-cold
beer.

▶ Inexpensive
② ***Betty***
Jl. Sumatra 56
Small restaurant, popular with the
locals and independent travellers; Mie
Goreng and other Indonesian (rice)
dishes are served.

WHERE TO STAY

▶ Luxury
① ***Tohpati***
Jl. Bypass 15
Tel. (03 61) 23 62 73, fax 23 24 04
The accommodation consists of 50
rooms in bungalows set in a lush park
on the northeastern edge of town;
fitness centre, tennis, pool.

▶ Mid-range
② ***Pamecutan Palace***
Jl. Thamrin 2, tel. (03 61) 22 34 91
It is quite possible to encounter the
owner of the hotel, who is none other
than King Ida Cokorda Pemecutan XI.
His highness's hotel has a beautiful
Balinese-style garden.

▶ Budget
③ ***Inna Bali***
Jl. Veteran 3
Tel. (03 61) 22 56 81, fax 23 53 47
The former Natour Bali, built in 1927,
is bordered on both sides by a
municipal park; with pool and an
excellent restaurant.

sion that has taken place in and around Denpasar. There are now more than 1,000 people per square kilometre or 2,590 per square mile – in contrast to the western part of the island where only about 250 individuals live in every square kilometre (650 per sq mi). The capital now faces huge problems including environmental pollution, poor air quality, heavy traffic and an excessive number of people seeking to earn a living in the tourist centres close by. As a consequence, Denpasar continues to expand and in some places has merged with neighbouring independent townships.

Pasar Badung, Denpasar's fruit, vegetable and fish market, is full of tasty tropical morsels.

History

The Raja of Badung was one of the first to submit to colonial rule and was prepared to formalize it by signing a treaty 1841. He hoped that by doing this the Dutch would leave the province of Badung in peace and allow him a degree of independence. This proved to be the case, at least for a period of 63 years. But a fateful event took place when the Chinese schooner *Sri Kumala* ran aground off the coast near Denpasar on the night of 27 May 1904. The Balinese looted the ship, whereupon its owner demanded compensation, at first from the Raja Agung Made and, when this proved unsuccessful, from the Dutch. After unproductive negotiations, the Dutch issued the raja with an ultimatum and at the same time brought in troops and surrounded Denpasar. When the raja refused to give in to the ultimatum, they closed in more tightly and began with the invasion on 14 September 1906. The events that followed on that day contributed to the dark memories the Balinese have of the period of Dutch occupation. When the invaders marched up to the palace of the rajas of Badung, the gates opened and a long procession of people slowly moved out toward the foreigners led by the raja himself, carried on a litter. The procession stopped just a few metres away from the Dutch and a Brahma priest took the raja's jewel-encrusted kris (dagger) and thrust it in his ruler's heart. Following this example, one after the other, men, women and children met their death. For a short time the Dutch stood dumbfounded, but then they took up their rifles and commenced shooting all the Balinese who were not victims of this **ritual mass suicide** (puputan). The palace went up in flames and almost burned to the ground.

The example set by the Raja of Badung and his followers was followed the same day by the Raja of Pemecutan and later in prison by the Raja of Tabanan, whom the Dutch had arrested. In 1908 there

Denpasar *Map*

Where to eat
① Atoom Baru
② Betty

Where to stay
① Tohpati
② Pamecutan Palace
③ Inna Bali

was another such puputan in Klungkung in which 250 people died. The Dutch found themselves under international pressure as a result and in 1914 they replaced the military troops with a police force.

What to See in Denpasar

A walking tour of Denpasar is not recommended. First of all, the individual sights are located far apart, and these distances are best covered by taxi. Secondly, a walk through the capital's noise-filled streets, jammed with traffic, creates more pain than pleasure.

Take a taxi

The palace of the prince of Badung, into which a small, friendly hotel has been integrated, can be found in the corner formed by Jalan Thamrin and Jalan Hassannudin. Behind the red brick walls are a number of charming buildings set in a lush tropical garden. The owner of the palace, and consequently the hotel, is King Ida Cokorda Pemecutan XI, whom the Balinese greatly respect. The central government of Indonesia, however, has never recognized his coronation in 1989, which was attended by several dethroned kings from Java and Bali.

★ ★
Puri Pemecutan
🕐
Opening hours:
daily 8am–5pm

The palace complex, which was almost burnt to the ground after the ritual mass suicide of 14 September 1906, was later rebuilt, but on a smaller scale. The richly decorated entrance gate is impressive, as are a number of fine reliefs, the only surviving remains of the original buildings, to be seen in the rear part of the palace grounds. A collection of lontars (Old Balinese texts on palm leaves) that were saved from the fire are kept in one building; in another are historical gamelan instruments. The luxuriantly blossoming garden forms a sharp contrast to the rumble of traffic outside the palace gates.

Measured against international standards, the systems in place at the Bali Provincial State Museum may be found a little lacking. However, the collection is definitely worth a visit. The majority of the exhibits are also labelled in English, making their history, origin and meaning more understandable. The Museum Negeri Propinsi Bali, located in the Jalan Wisnu not far from Puputan Square, primarily displays **Balinese art and architecture**. It is housed in three adjacent buildings whose architecture reflects traditional Balinese building style and which are modelled on both the palace and the temple. The buildings are set in their own grounds in the palace complex entered through a split gate (candi bentar). A second candi bentar opening to an outside street is permanently closed. Next to it stands a kulkul (bell tower).

★ ★
Museum Negeri Propinsi Bali (Bali Provincial State Museum)
🕐
Opening hours:
Tue–Thu 8am–2pm,
Fri 8am–3pm

The tour of the museum is best begun in the rear building, whose exhibits include a Balinese wedding ceremony (front side) and the tooth filing ceremony (rear), both depicted in glass cases. Take a look at the various wooden models (including a royal throne), carved symbols of Hindu deities and some examples of batik and embroidery, as well as the intricately carved window shutters. The middle building, named Gedung Karangasem after its architectural style, contains finds from the Neolithic period. There is a fine suite of seats and some stone figures on the veranda. The building, by the way,

The Art Center displays its treasures in the midst of a tropical park.

was first built by the Dutch in the form of a hall that was open on all sides; the walls were added later.

The third building is richly decorated; it was constructed in the style of the Palace of Tabanan. Inside, in the middle of the room, barong figures are placed on a pedestal. The wooden ceiling beams are very elaborately carved.

Between the buildings is a »shower« that the royal family had installed. It is slightly sunken into the ground, making it easy to miss at first glance.

★ ★
Pura Jagat Natha

Just to the right of the main exit of the Bali Provincial State Museum is the Temple of the Rulers of the Worlds (Pura Jagat Natha). It is dedicated to **Sangyang Widi**, the incarnation of the most supreme gods in Balinese Hinduism: Brahma, Vishnu and Shiva. Brahma is worshipped here as the »god of gods«. The symbols for the deity preserved in the temple – Sangyang Widi depicted as a gleaming golden metallic figure sitting on a seven-tiered throne made of coral stone – are venerated, incidentally, not by isolated groups of people but rather by all Balinese Hindus.

★
Church of St Joseph

Some 550m/600yd north of the Bali Provincial State Museum stands the Catholic church of St Joseph, in which Christian images, for example in the stained glass windows, and Balinese sculptural decorations are colourfully mixed.

Pura Maospahit is one of Denpasar's oldest and most important temples. Its origins date back to the 15th century. As the name indicates, it was founded by the Majapahit dynasty that originally came from Java, and remains their ancestral temple even today. Over the course of time it has been subjected to remodelling and beautification and much of the original furnishings have been lost.

✱ Pura Maospahit
◄ No fixed opening hours

As the main entrance on Jalan Dr. Sutomo is only open on holidays, the entrance in the gang or alleyway running along the left side of the temple complex must be used. The open door can be found by going some way down the alley designated »Gang III«. There is another entrance into the main part of the temple: go to the end of Gang III and then to the right a short way along the enclosure wall.

The temple consists of two parts, separated from one another by a high wall. Entrance to the grounds is through a split gate (candi bentar), which is actually the temple's main attraction. The following deities have been carved on the five pillars (from left to right): the god Sangkara (a manifestation of Shiva); the ancient Indian god of the sky, Indra; the god of the dead, Yama; the god of wind, Bayu; the mythical bird and Vishnu's mount, Garuda; the Indian god Kubera (god of wealth); and the sea god, Waruna. There are some sacral structures in the area to the right inside the temple that do not belong to Pura Maospahit, but rather are part of a family temple. At the rear stands the Gedong Maospahit, a shrine for the veneration of ancestors. The ancestors of the East Javanese Majapahit dynasty are venerated in the closed building next to it. It is worth taking a look at the **three thrones for the gods** (pelinggih) decorated with stag antlers, which are reserved for the ancestors of the Majapahit dynasty.

What makes Denpasar's art centre interesting is its comprehensive collection of Balinese paintings in the main building and an adjoining sales exhibition featuring works by both established and up-and-coming artists. Behind the building is a **lush tropical garden** with small ponds. There is also an open-air stage where dance performances are presented during the annually held »Festival of Arts«, and frequently on other occasions as well.

✱ Taman Wedhi Budaya Art Center

The works of German artist and musician **Walter Spies** (► Famous People) are on display in a small, inconspicuous building on the street leading to the art centre; a brochure is available at the ticket counter.

! Baedeker TIP

Practice makes perfect

Every morning young dance students at the art centre can be seen hard at work, practising and rehearsing. In the early evening (6.30pm) they present the fruits of their labours, performing dances such as the barong and kecak.

The **largest market in the capital** is housed in a four-storey building located at the point where Jalan Gajah Mada (one of Denpasar's main traffic arteries) and Jalan Sulawesi converge. The fresh fruit and vegetable market is in the basement of the building, while articles for everyday use can be purchased on the upper floors. The Pasar Badung has its own house temple (in front of the entrance). Fishmonger's shops can be found on the other side of the building. The reason for them being half hidden is that, according to Balinese-Hindu belief, the sea is occupied by demons and evil spirits; this applies to the creatures caught there too. There are numerous other stalls and street vendors in the area surrounding the market building.

★ ★ Gianyar

M 7

Capital of the administrative district of Gianyar
Distance: 26km/16mi northeast of Denpasar

Region: Central Bali
Altitude: 127m/417ft

In the 17th and 18th centuries Gianyar was the capital of a powerful kingdom. The city is now the capital of the district that bears its name and lies in well irrigated hill country that is intensely cultivated, mainly with rice. Its modest textile and handicraft industries are vital to the region.

The city of Klungkung was the capital of the most powerful realm in Bali from the 15th to the 17th century (▶ Klungkung, History). As Klungkung's authority diminished, the rulers in Gianyar, only 12km/

▶ VISITING GIANYAR

INFORMATION

Gianyar Tourist Office
Jl. 12 B, Gianyar
Tel. (03 61) 94 35 54
Fax 94 34 01

GETTING AROUND

From Denpasar, head in a northeasterly direction to Sakah; turn right here and drive on past Blahbatuh.
There are buses from Denpasar-Kerenang several times daily. Bemos can be found along the road.

**WHERE TO STAY /
WHERE TO EAT**

▶ **Budget / Inexpensive**
Sua Bali
On the outskirts of the village of Kemenuh (on the road from Denpasar to Gianyar near Blahbatuh)
Tel. (03 61) 94 10 50, fax 361 94 10 35
Less a hotel, more a simple place to stay where visitors to Bali can experience socially responsible tourism up close. Experiencing Balinese living and eating and making contact with the local population is easy here.

There seem to be flocks of free-range ducks everywhere.

7.5mi away, were increasing theirs. During the time of the Dutch occupation, Gianyar's princes were able to agree terms with the invaders, with the result that Gianyar was spared from intervention
and the royal family was able to retain its influence.

What to See in and around Gianyar

There is not much left of the former glory of the city of Gianyar.
Modern, functional buildings now dominate the appearance of the
city.

Puri Gianyar, built by Dewa Manggis IV in 1771, faces the central
village square. It is normally not open to the public, but with a little
luck one of the members of the family still living in the palace may
openthe gate. The palace consists of several **traditional Balinese
style** pavilions. If you are given the opportunity to view the interior
of the palace, take a close look at the superb carvings and the figures
in the delightful tropical garden.

★★
Puri Gianyar

◄ No regular
opening hours

Only about 5km/3mi southwest of Gianyar lies the small, quiet market town of Blahbatuh with two particularly interesting temples.
Pura Dalem Blahbatuh is located in Benawah village on the road
leading to Denpasar. Inside is a sitting **Buddha (!) in the midst of
Hindu figures** – an indication of the tolerance Balinese have in religious matters. The second attraction in Blahbatuh is Pura Puseh
Blahbatuh or Pura Gaduh. It contains the enormous **head of a giant,**
which the locals say is a representation of the prince of demons, Jero
Gede Mecaling. He is said to have come to Bali on several occasions
in earlier times from the island of ► Penida, wreaking havoc here
with his demons and devils.

★
Blahbatuh

Gilimanuk

B 3

Region: West Bali	**Altitude:** sea level
Administrative district: Jembrana	**Distance:** 85km/53mi west of Singaraja

Gilimanuk is the most important ferry and commercial port linking Bali and its larger neighbour, the island of Java. The most westerly city in Bali, Gilimanuk lies on the Bali Strait (Selat Bali), which is only 2.5km/1.5mi wide.

Port Gilimanuk must surely be the **city with the least tourist attractions in Bali**. About the only thing that might be of interest to the visitor is the bustling activity around the harbour, mostly centred around ferry traffic. Then there is the night-time market held every evening in the city centre, where there are a few good snack bars. 200m/220yd east of the harbour is the **Museum of Man**, which displays finds excavated in the vicinity of the city including exhibits from prehistoric burial sites, pottery and tools (opening hours: daily 9am–4pm).

▶ GILIMANUK

GETTING AROUND

The road from Denpasar to Gilimanuk runs in a northwesterly direction, in part along the coast (approx. 130km/80mi). There is a regular daily bus and bemo service from Denpasar-Ubung.

The little village of **Palasari** (with Catholic inhabitants) is just a short side trip off the road from Denpasar to Gilimanuk; some 10km/6mi further west is **Blimbingsari**, where mostly Protestants live. Both villages have a small church.

Ferry service Ferries to the neighbouring island of Java (Ketapang Port, approx.
Bali–Java 30–45min) leave from Gilimanuk (turn left at the end of the main street and follow the signs). Reservations can be made and tickets bought at the harbour.

★ ★ Kapal

L 7

Region: Southwest Bali	**Altitude:** 75m/246ft
Administrative district: Badung	**Distance:** 15km/9mi north of Denpasar

There was a time when the people of Kapal were famous for their pottery, but today the little town between Denpasar and Mengwi is better known for its temple figures and decorative items made of cement and stone.

What to See in and around Kapal

Shops open to the street line the main road through the town. On sale, among other things, are stone figures and house temples. Before making any purchase, do consider the substantial weight of most of these otherwise charming and well-worked objects and the prohibitive expense of shipping them back home.

The Pura Sada (tower) of Kapal is one of the most important temples in Bali. It is the **temple of the founding prince of Mengwi**, whose ancestors originally came from Klungkung. The Pura Sada can be reached by following the main road in the direction of Tabanan and then turning left into a narrow lane (200m/220yd). The building that stands today was constructed on old foundation walls, the remains of a shrine built around the 12th century. The temple at first appears to have only two parts, since the outer forecourt with a large waringin tree is not enclosed. The entrance into the first enclosed courtyard of the large complex is through a split gate (candi bentar) with a seven-tiered roof thought to date back to the 14th or 15th century.

In the inner courtyard, slightly to the left, is the Bale Pesamyangan in which the gods are welcomed to the temple. The original of the massive prasada in Majapahit style probably also dated from the 14th or 15th century. It was completely destroyed in a devastating earthquake in 1917 and not rebuilt until 1948–49. Whether its current location corresponds to the original site is uncertain.

The grimacing demon in the upper part of the pagoda is particularly striking. There is a stone basin in the middle symbolizing the abode of the heavenly nymph Widadari, who is considered to be the mediator between the world of the gods and the world of men. To the right of this are **57 stone thrones for the ancestors** of the Mengwi dynasty and on the eastern side there are three throne seats. In the rear of the temple, other shrines and thrones are dedicated to the divine trinity, Brahma – Vishnu – Shiva.

▶ KAPAL

GETTING AROUND

Take the road leading northward from Denpasar in the direction of Singaraja.
Good bus connections from Denpasar-Ubung; bemos run from either Denpasar or Mengwi.

✴ ✴
Pura Sada
(Prasada)

Pura Sada *Plan*

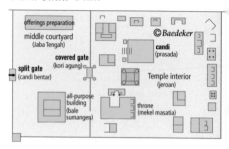

offerings preparation
middle courtyard
(Jaba Tengah)

© Baedeker

candi
(prasada)

covered gate
(kori agung)

split gate
(candi bentar)

Temple interior
(jeroan)

all-purpose
building
(bale
sumangen)

throne
(mekel masatia)

★★
**Pura Desa
and Pura Puseh**

Another village temple that is well worth seeing is located directly on the main road going through Kapal. Actually, there are two temples, Pura Desa and Pura Puseh, but both have been built together in such a way that their original separate identities are only discernable to the initiated. The **richly decorated gate with three entrances**, one reserved for each member of the divine trinity, Brahma – Vishnu – Shiva, is quite unusual. There are superbly detailed reliefs depicting parts of the Tantri animal fables on either side of the gate.

**Sempidi and
Lukluk**

the two small villages of Sempidi and Lukluk, lying outside Kapal in the direction of Denpasar, have lovely village temples with opulently decorated gates and walls.

Klungkung (Semarapura)

N 7

Capital of the administrative district of Klungkung **Population:** 17,000	**Region:** East Bali **Altitude:** up to 160m/525ft **Distance:** 23km/14mi east of Ubud

Klungkung, once the governmental seat of a powerful kingdom, lies at the foot of a region of gently rolling hills. In clear weather, the Gunung Agung volcano forms an impressive backdrop.

Today, Klungkung – which since 1995 has officially gone by the name of **Semarapura** – is a busy town. It forms an important link between central Bali and the eastern part of the island, which for a long time was cut off from the rest of the island, both economically and physically, following the devastating volcanic eruption of 1963 and the accompanying earthquakes.

▶ VISITING KLUNGKUNG

Information

Klungkung Tourist Office
Jl. Untung Surapati 2
Semarapura
Tel. (03 66) 214 48
Fax 228 48

GETTING AROUND

Take the road running east from Denpasar via Gianyar. There is a regular bus service from Denpasar-Kereneng. Bemos can be found along the road.

WHERE TO STAY /
WHERE TO EAT

▶ **Budget / Inexpensive**
**Loji Ramayana
Palace Hotel**
Jl. Diponegoro 152
Tel. (03 66) 210 44
9 rooms around an inner court-yard with modern amenities; restaurant with Chinese cuisine in the garden.

Kerta Gosa was built in the 18th century to serve as the royal court of justice.

At the close of the 15th century, the Hindus in Java were so persecuted that the only option they had was to flee to the neighbouring island of Bali. Among them was Batu Renggong, the son of Prince Widjaya. His father, in order to escape imprisonment, had burned himself alive – a fate his son did not wish to share. With several hundred followers (among them many priests), he fled to Bali, where he built a palace in Gelgel, a small place about 5km/3mi south of Klungkung, declaring himself a Dewa Agung (grand duke) and Gelgel his seat of government. Around 1710, the court moved to the considerably better situated Klungkung, where Prince Di Made, a great-grandson of Widjaya, built a new palace. The **Kerta Gosa Court Hall**, the town's greatest attraction, probably also dates from this period. Klungkung's importance grew so much in the following years that this court hall handled all the important legal disputes on the whole island of Bali and passed judgement on criminals.

Klungkung also played an important role during the attempts by the Dutch to occupy the island. After the Dutch had brought towns in the north like Singaraja and Buleleng under their control, a vanguard led by the merchant **Cornelis de Houtman** reached Klungkung, where they were welcomed as guests by the Dewa Agung, who had a great interest in the European way of life. A little while later, it was agreed to establish trading relations.

In the 18th century, Klungkung increasingly lost its importance and influence to nearby Gianyar. Although the Dewa Agung agreed with the rulers of the neighbouring principalities to take concerted action against the Dutch, he did not have the military means to mount a defence against the threatening invasion. As a consequence, after Buleleng fell in the north and Amlapura suffered the same fate in the east, Klungkung became one of the first regions to be conquered by the Dutch. During the course of the invasion in 1908 a terrible event occurred that still arouses deep sentiment in the Balinese. When the Dutch reached the palace, the gates swung open and a procession of some 250 men, women and children filed out. When they came to a halt in front of the bewildered Dutch, the Dewa Agung plunged a kris into his breast – an example they all followed (▶Denpasar). This act proved insufficient for the Dutch; every Balinese that had not committed suicide or was badly wounded but still alive was cut down in an ensuing hail of bullets from Dutch rifles.

What to See in and around Klungkung

Modern, functional buildings and reconstructions

Not much remains of the splendour of old Klungkung. The Dutch pulled down almost all of the buildings that represented the Dewa Agung's rule, which leaves the present-day appearance of the city dominated for the most part by modern, functional buildings. It was not until the 1980s that some buildings were repaired or reconstructed. They recall the city's grand past, a time when Klungkung was considered to be the centre of art and culture in Bali and brought forth a great number of important painters.

Taman Gili

Spreading out in the centre of town is the Taman Gili (garden of the island), a **well-tended park** whose outline approximately corresponds to that of the Puri Agung, the former royal residence. Standing in the middle of a pond covered in lotus blossom is the Bale Kembang, a small pavilion with beautiful wayang paintings inside.

★ ★
Kerta Gosa

The 18th-century Kerta Gosa courthouse is a marvellous sight to behold, particularly because of its **unique ceiling paintings that are also executed in wayang style**. These were originally painted on canvas, but in the course of being restored in 1960, they were fixed on more durable sheets of cement. In wayang style (a style still used in the paintings of some artists in and around Klungkung), the paintings tell a story in which the same person is always the main character. When a condemned man stood in front of his judges, he only had to raise his head to get an idea of what awaited him after his judgement. Adulterers, for example, had their genitals burned off; women had to look into the faces of their aborted children while walking through an inferno; and thieves were tortured to death in boiling oil.

The accused could see the drastic punishments in store for them in the paintings.

In contrast, heaven and the rewards in store for those who abide by the law during their lives can also be seen. Only the five basic colours were used for the paintings. Standing in the centre of the courthouse are six richly decorated chairs and a rectangular table at which the three judges (Pendand priests) and the assessors sat. There is also a small museum on the premises.

⊙
Opening hours:
daily 8am–5.30pm

Around Klungkung

The small village of Kamasan, some 2km/1.2mi south of Klungkung, is known for its **painters** who still practise the traditional wayang technique of painting. There is also a widely-known art school here that combines traditional and modern painting techniques. Along with textile painting, Kamasar is also noted for its skilled and creative **bronze and silversmiths**.

Kamasan

About 2km/1.2mi beyond Kamasan lies Gelgel. Its former public buildings are gone, and nothing remains of the splendour of this once important place.

Gelgel

The Semis Lukis Klasik Banda museum is in Banda (Jl. Pertigaan), 5km/3mi west of Klungkung. It is also named the **Gunarsa Museum of Classical and Modern Art** because it was founded by the Balinese artist, Dr. Nyoman Gunarsa.
Along with Gunarsa's studio and a collection of his work, objects from the 17th through to the 19th century are shown, along with modern and abstract works.

Banda
⊙
Opening hours:
daily 9am–5pm

A few miles down the road from Klungkung in the direction of Amlapura is the small coastal village of Kusamba with its black beach. The inhabitants of this village live primarily from fishing and salt production. On the way to Kusamba, evidence of the violent volcanic eruption of 1963 is still visible.

Kusamba

✶ ✶ Kubutambahan

L 1

Region: North Bali
Administrative district: Buleleng

Altitude: sea level
Distance: 12km/7.5mi northeast of Singaraja

Kubutambahan is a typical North Balinese city lying in the middle of a region that has scant rainfall yet is intensely cultivated. There is little here to interest the tourist; the absolute highlight is the temple complex of Pura Meduwe Karang with its flowery ornamentation that is characteristic of the region.

What to See in Kubutambahan

★★
Pura Meduwe Karang

Pura Meduwe Karang is definitely worth a visit. This Hindu temple is dedicated to the male counterpart of the rice goddess, Dewi Sri. Translated, the name of the temple means »to whom the earth belongs«. The local population comes here to supplicate for a rich harvest on the surrounding coffee, maize, fruit and vegetable plantations.

Upon entering the tripartite temple, three platforms can be seen in the first courtyard (jaba) with 13 figures in the lower row, 10 in the centre row and another 13 in the back row, all of which represent **characters from the Ramayana epic**.

A four-part split gate (candi bentar) opens into the second courtyard (jaba tengah) with a multitude of figures standing against the wall opposite that separates the third courtyard (jeroan) from the inner sanctum (bebaturan).

In the centre of the shrine is a stepped platform on a square base. Standing on it to the left is a gedong pesimpangan, dedicated to Ratu Ayu Sari (one of the manifestations of the earth mother Ibu Prtiwi) and to the right is a gedong pesimpangan for Ratu Ngurah Sari, the protector of the products of the earth. Don't miss the stone relief of a **man riding a flower-bedecked bicycle** on the right side of the shrine. While the locals insist the carving is at least 400 years old, the general opinion is that it is supposed to be the Dutch ethnologist W. O. J. Nieuwenkamp, which would explain the cyclist's long nose. While doing scientific research in North Bali in 1904, Nieuwenkamp would travel about by bicycle, a form of transportation completely unknown to the population at the time. The relief is no longer in its original condition as it was damaged in an earthquake in 1917. It was altered during later restoration work.

 KUBUTAMBAHAN

GETTING AROUND

Head eastward from Singaraja toward Amlapura. Good bus and bemo connections.

Sambiran

A good 25km/15.5mi east of Singaraja at the village of Pacung a road branches off to the right and leads to Sambiran. The villagers here feel that they are descendents of the Bali Aga, the original inhabitants of Bali, and they speak a **dialect** similar to the Old Javanese language.

A further distinctive feature is their **manner of burying the dead**. While the dead on the rest of Bali (with the exception of Trunyan, ▶Penelokan) are sooner or later cremated, the people of Sambiran toss the bodies of their dead into a ravine outside the village. Sambiran is one of a handful of villages that has resisted Hinuism and continues to follow the ancient Bali-Aga religion of their ancestors.

Kuta

Region: South Bali
Altitude: sea level

Administrative district: Badung
Distance: 9km/5.5mi southwest of Denpasar

Back in the 1960s, Kuta, once a fishing village, came to be a tip known only to the first European travellers. Today it is Bali's best-known holiday resort. Kuta lies on the southwest coast of the island, only a few miles away from the international airport.

It was here in Kuta that the so-called »losmen« and »homestays«, accommodation for tourists that is now typical in Bali, were first created. Today, Kuta has merged with the towns of **Legian** and **Seminyak** to the north, and all year round attracts predominantly younger travellers from Australia, Japan and Europe. **There are more than 500 establishments** offering accommodation in all price categories, including the legendary Poppies, one of the oldest hotels in the centre of Kuta. Set in beautiful tropical grounds, Poppies has been popular with travellers since it first opened. The centre of Kuta received something of a »general overhaul« in 2004, being supplied with a modern sewerage system in the process. With floral arrangements now increasing its attractiveness still further, the busy shopping streets and alleys are a magnet for ever more travellers from the five-star hotels of Nusa Dua. In the evening, Kuta throngs with thousands of visitors from all over the world.

Well-known holiday resort

Sun, sand and sea at Kuta Beach

▶ VISITING KUTA • LEGIAN • SEMINYAK

INFORMATION
Badung Government Tourism Office
Jl. Raya Kuta 2, Kuta
Tel. (03 61) 75 61 75, fax 75 61 76
www.badung.go.id

GETTING AROUND
Kuta lies on the road between the airport and Denpasar. Good bus and bemo service, also to other tourist destinations such as Ubud and Lombok (bus / ferry).

ENTERTAINMENT
Waterbom Park
Both the young and the young at heart enjoy visiting Waterbom Park (Jl. Kartika Plaza, www.waterbom.com) with its numerous waterslides, swimming pools and beach chairs under the palm trees.

Evening entertainment
A range of discos, bars and nightclubs is concentrated in Kuta. The number one for Kuta fans remains the *Hard Rock Café* (Jl. Pantai) with a daily changing programme of live music. There are numerous other nightclubs and bars, including some that are open-fronted, in the Jl. Seminyak.

SHOPPING
Textiles and leather
Kuta, and also to a lesser degree Legian, is the most popular place to shop for textiles in Bali. There is a plethora of boutiques, tailors and open shops selling clothing. You will find both international brand names and cheap copies, as well as batik and fanciful fashions in the Balinese hippy-style, women's suits, trousers and coats fashioned in leather, and silk dresses and shirts.

Bali Mal Galeria
A two-floor shopping centre with numerous boutiques and outlets (Ralph Lauren, Puma, Adidas) selling branded goods at low prices. The spacious Granmedia book shop offers an excellent selection of literature about Bali, including fantastic volumes of photographs. The food court is on the second floor (Jl. Bypass Ngurah Rai, Simpan Dewa Ruci, Kuta).

Kuta Kidz
Imaginative and colourful with a huge selection that excites both children and parents – at low prices (Bemo Corner, Kuta).

Baedeker recommendation

Surfer Girl
Nowhere is the selection wider than here: the collections of 82 manufacturers are on sale (including the labels Billabong, Paul Frank, Body & Soul). Surfer Girl itself has gained cult status; the store's shopping bags are a popular souvenir (Jl. Legian 138, Kuta).

WHERE TO EAT
▶ **Moderate**
Gateway of India
Jl. Abimanyu 10, Semiyak
Tel. (03 61) 73 29 40
Simple décor and furnishings but the best Indian cooking on the southwest coast; try the Kadai Chicken, which is served in a superb sauce.

Padma Club
Jl. Padma, Legian, tel. (03 61) 75 28 85
For years this has been a favourite tourist haunt with moderately good Indonesian cooking; regular live music.

► Inexpensive
TJs Mexican
Poppies Lane I, Kuta
Tel. (03 61) 75 10 93
For more than two decades a faithful community of fans have been enjoying guacamole, tacos and enchiladas here in the centre of Kuta; on Thursday evenings there is a buffet accompanied by mariachi music.

WHERE TO STAY
► Luxury
The Oberoi
Jl. Laksmana, Seminyak
Tel. (03 61) 73 03 61, fax 73 07 91
www.balioberoi.com
This has been one of the finest hotels (75 rooms) on the island for over 30 years; like all of the hotels of the Indian luxury chain, it is a stylish place to stay. A buffet is served three times a week in the Amphitheatre restaurant and Balinese dances are presented. The Kura Kura restaurant, just a few steps away from the sea, is romantic and luxurious.

► Mid-range
Kartika Plaza
Jl. Kartika Plaza, South Kuta
Tel. (03 61) 75 10 67, fax 75 39 88
www.discoverykartikaplaza.com
All rooms with ocean view.

Hard Rock Hotel
Jl. Pantai
Tel. (03 61) 76 18 69, fax 76 18 68
www.hardrockhotels.net/Bali
418 rooms. A few years ago, Asia's first Hard Rock Hotel opened up next to the Hard Rock Café. A must for fans of 40 years of rock'n'roll history, it features the familiar décor and furnishings found everywhere in the world and, as ever, a collection of music memorabilia. There is also a pool and spa.

► Budget
Ramah Village
Gang Keraton, Seminyak
Tel. (03 61) 73 10 71, fax 73 07 93
www.balirama.com
18 cottages, ideal for families and those who prefer self-catering accommodation. These well-kept, nicely furnished bungalows in a variety of sizes (living room, bedroom, kitchen, bathroom and terrace) have a pleasant atmosphere and are rented out at various prices, with a discount for long-term guests.

Delicious assortment of fruit

Kuta Beach The extensive Kuta Beach, on which a spot in the shade is difficult to come by, is separated from the restaurants and hotels by a busy road. True, it doesn't exactly live up to the clichés of a tropical paradise, but it is nevertheless popular for swimming, sunbathing and surfing. It fills up in the late morning, a **meeting place for young, independent travellers**.

! *Baedeker* TIP

For body and soul
Innumerable spas and beauty salons in Kuta offer outstanding massages and beauty treatments at very reasonable prices. One popular establishment is Spa Semara (Jl. Blambangan 4, Prana Spa, Jl. Kuti, Seminyak), whose excellent services include Ayurvedic treatments. It all takes place in high-class and stylish surroundings: the spa's large red building is reminiscent of a north Indian palace.

Kuta is centred around Jalan Legian, which stretches several miles to the north. There are countless boutiques, cafés, restaurants, bars and discotheques here. Reasonably priced, self-made batik fashion wear is sold at open stalls. In the small spas and wellness salons nearby it is possible to enjoy traditional massage and oil cures – and without breaking the bank. Travel agents offer tours of the island as well as international flights, while tattoo studios compete for business. Moving further north, the restaurants and hotels become more expensive.

The **Human Tragedy Monument** commemorates the events of 12 October 2002. It stands on the spot where a bomb attack killed 202 people from 22 countries (▶ History, see p.52).

Jalan Melasti, which runs east-west and crosses Jalan **Legian**, forms the invisible border of Legian. The beach of the same name is broader here and there is no traffic to disturb the peace and quiet. Luxury hotels are to be found in extensive tropical gardens in neighbouring Seminyak further north. The clothing on sale in the shops here is mostly more expensive than in Kuta, but also of higher quality. The Balinese-style teak and rattan furniture available in local outlets is held in high regard by Bali's foreign residents.

A day-to-day sight in Bali, women carrying offerings

★ ★ Lombok (neighbouring island east of Bali, one of the Lesser Sundas)

Indonesian province:
Nusa Tenggara Barat
Population: approx. 2.5 million

Area: 4725 sq km/1812 sq mi
Altitude: 0–3726m/12,225ft

Lombok and Bali were often called the »unequal sisters«, usually in reference to the fact that Lombok remained relatively untouched by international tourism. While Bali became known all over the world, Lombok languished in the shadows. Today, all of that is changing.

Once upon a time, only backpackers ventured to Lombok and those who knew it described the island as »Bali as it once was«. In recent years that has become a thing of the past: the island now boasts a good tourist infrastructure. Visitors to Lombok (Chili Island) should however prepare for its **peculiarities**. Everything is a little quieter and slower here. The population has not been influenced by tourism nearly as much as in Bali and things more or less tolerated or accepted on the neighbouring island can be considered offensive in Lombok. This is particularly true when travelling in the interior of the island and coming into contact with the Sasaks, Lombok's original inhabitants.

With an area of 4725 sq km/1812 sq mi, the island is only slightly smaller than Bali. The two are separated by the 40km/25mi wide and up to 3000m/10,000ft deep Lombok Strait (Selat Lombok), which is at the same time a zoogeographical boundary (**»the Wallace Line«**) separating the Indomalayan and the Australasian flora and fauna. The island's most prominent point is the Gunung Rinjani volcano. At a height of 3726m/12,225ft, it is the third highest elevation in all of Indonesia. Mount Rinjani stretches out in an east-west direction and, counting its foothills, covers almost the whole of the northern half of the island.

? **DID YOU KNOW ...?**

■ ... that Alfred Wallace was a contemporary of the much more famous Charles Darwin and that he also formulated a theory about evolution? He used the knowledge he collected during his extended travels throughout Indonesia to develop his ideas. Wallace discovered stark differences in the biomes of the islands to the north and to the south of the Lombok Strait; tropical vegetation, monkeys, tigers and elephants could be found in Bali and the western islands, while Lombok and the islands to the east have dry vegetation and fauna influenced by Australia, for example, giant lizards and cockatoos.

History Once ruled over by the Balinese princes of the Karangasem dynasty, who considered it merely an adjunct, Lombok was occupied in the mid-17th century by princes from the island of Sulawesi (Celebes). In 1740, the Karangasem dynasty, who dominated eastern Bali

Lombok Map

Laut Bali
(Bali Sea)

Bali

Selat Lombok
(Lombok Strait)

Amoramor
Lebuhan Carik
Bayan
Papak
Batu Koq
Dasankembar
Sendang Gila
Blantung
Sugian
La
Pa
Senaru
Tanjung
Gunung Rinjani
(3726 m/12224 ft)
Sembalun Lawang
Bangsal
Tembabar
Sembalun
Bumbung
Pemenang
Menggala
Sapit
Senggigi
Sidemen
Sesaot
Peseng
Timbanuh
Swela
Lombok
Meninting
Dasangria
Aik
Tetebatu
Aik Mel
Pringgabaya
MATARAM
Selat
Buka
Kutaraja
Ampenan
Cakranegara
Mantang
Lekong
Anjani
Pagutan
Narmada
Rempung
Prampuan
Bengkel
Kopang
Terara
Pancor
Bongor
Kuripan
Batukumbung
Sakra
Selong
Gerung
Sukarara
Praya
Beleka
Labuhan
Haji
Lembar
Batujai
Ganti
Tanjungluar
Bangko
Bangko
Pelangan
Mangkung
Tanahawu
Jerowaru
Sekotong
Silung
Kateng
Sengkol
Batu
Blongas
Blanak
Nampar
Ekas
Peugantap
Kuta
Tanjung
Ringgit
Mawun
Tajung Aan

PROVINCE OF BALI
PROVINZ NUSA TENGGARA BARAT

Selat Atlas
(Alas Strait)

20 km
12,5 miles
© Baedeker

Samudra Indonesia
(Indian Ocean)

(►Amlapura), regained control over the western part of the island. The Muslims from southern Sulawesi, however, continued to rule in East Lombok until 1849 when the Raja of Karangasem incorporated the whole island into his kingdom. In 1838, the united Principality of Lombok was established and five years later the princes of Mataram recognized Dutch sovereignty. In 1891 the Dutch felt compelled to brutally crush a revolt by the Sasak after which the colonial masters were able to incorporate the whole of Lombok into the Dutch East Indies. Lombok proved to be an ideal **base for launching Dutch punitive expeditions** against Bali, which the Sasak rulers willingly supported. They welcomed the Dutch forces as a means of freeing them of Balinese hegemony. Today Lombok is part of the Indonesian province of Nusa Tenggara Barat.

Population Approximately 2.5 million people live on the island of Lombok; 80 percent of them are **Sasak**, the native inhabitants. The Sasak people are thought to have originally come from northwest India, and possibly also from Burma (present-day Myanmar). This occurred some

▶ VISITING LOMBOK

INFORMATION
Lombok Tourism Office
Jl. Langko 70
Mataram
Tel. (03 70) 63 17 30, 63 18 66
www.visitlombok.com

GETTING AROUND

Lombok can be readily reached from Bali either by flying with the Garuda subsidiary »Merpati« (flight time approx. 30min) or crossing over by speedboat (approx. 2.5hrs) or car ferry (approx. 4.5hrs). All of these means of transportation provide services several times a day. The planes land at Mataram airport, only a few miles north of the provincial capital. Boats and ferries out of Padang Bai in Bali arrive in Lombok at Lembar Harbour, some 30km/19mi southwest of Mataram. The central bemo station is 7km/4.5mi from Ampenan and about 2.5km/1.5mi outside Cakranegara.

SHOPPING
Sasak Pottery
A large selection of pottery with traditional as well as modern patterns (Jl. Raya Senggigi, Ampenan, www.sasak-pottery.com).

WHERE TO STAY
▶ Luxury
Sheraton Senggigi Beach Hotel
Senggigi
Tel. (03 70) 69 33 33
Fax 69 32 41
www.sheraton.com/senggigi
The island's first five-star hotel lies directly on the white sands of Senggigi Beach. Warm textiles, chandeliers, rattan and colonial-style furniture dominate the atmosphere of the main building. The 161 rooms are in the low building with a view of either the tropical park or the sea. An evening stroll through the enchantingly illuminated gardens and a dinner in the restaurant can be recommended even to those not staying in the hotel. The buffet next to the pool, accompanied by the strains of gamelan music and dance performances, is particularly nice.

Qunci Villas
Mataram, Senggigi
Tel. (03 70) 69 38 00
Fax 69 38 02
www.quncivillas.com
A small, superb hotel; accommodation is in 20 villas (starting at 40 sq m/ 430 sq ft) with a modern, purist feel; Balinese atmosphere is provided by ikat fabrics, open bathrooms and a view of either the tropical garden or the ocean. After sunset, flickering torches light up the pool and gardens. There are massage pavilions and a top-quality restaurant – the fantastic ambience here makes it well worth the price.

▶ Mid-range
Senggigi Beach Hotel
Jl. Raya Senggigi km 8
Tel. (03 70) 69 32 10
Fax 69 32 00
Spacious, well-tended hotel (148 rooms) consisting of a main building and a number of bungalows in the middle of a 13ha/32ac tropical garden beside the sea. This is an ideal place for divers as a diving base is located in the hotel. Five restaurants and the renowned Mandara Spa round out the facilities offered here.

Puri Mas
Mangsit Beach

Tel. (03 70) 69 38 31
Fax 69 30 23
www.lombokboutiquevilla.com.
Private and personal; the Dutch owner, a former professional dancer, has created a gem of a hotel in the local style; a gate embellished with dramatic woodcarvings leads into an enchanted world. The 17 rooms are spread out among small houses, each with its own veranda and furnished with Indonesian antiques. Hindu deities stand guard over the tropical gardens separated from the ocean by only a narrow strip of beach.

► **Budget**
Senggigi Reef Resort
Jl. Raya Senggigi, Senggigi
Tel. (03 70) 69 33 65
Fax 69 32 36
www.senggigireefresort.com
21 delightful bungalows on the village's beach with facilities for a variety of water sports; the small restaurant serves both Balinese and »American style« breakfasts, fruit juices and dishes typical of the region.

Dharmarie
Senggigi Beach
Tel. (03 70) 69 30 50
Small, low-priced hotel on the beach.

The simple bungalows have air conditioning, and are surrounded by lawns and tropical flowers. There is a reduced rate for those staying longer.

WHERE TO EAT
► **Moderate**

Baedeker recommendation

Asmara
Jl. Raya Senggigi, Senggigi
Tel. (03 70) 69 36 19
Choose a table under the palm trees or in the restaurant located a little higher up at which to enjoy the Indonesian dishes or pizza & pasta served here. There is a pick-up service by car if desired. The restaurant also features a small art gallery.

► **Inexpensive**
Dua Em
Jl. Transmigrasi, Mataram
Tel. (03 70) 69 67 34
At the Dua Em the locals sit shoulder to shoulder with the tourists to enjoy the national dish, ayam taliwang (grilled marinated chicken with spinach).

time around the 14th century. A possible indication of Burmese origin is the great similarity of Sasak traditional clothing with those of mountain tribes living in today's Myanmar (formerly Burma). The Sasak primarily live from agriculture. The large majority of the Sasak people are **Muslims**; only about 10% of Lombok's population profess the Hindu faith, but a variety of influences can still be recognized today in the language, culture and traditions of the island. Some 30,000 Balinese live in Lombok today. Just as in Bali, rice cultivation plays an important role here, but the rice terraces are not nearly as artfully and systematically arranged. In addition, there are vegetable and tobacco plantations, but as the harvests are almost exclusively used for domestic consumption, little produce is exported.

Even though there has been a discernible trend in recent years toward urbanization in Lombok, the majority of the Sasak still live in typical villages. One characteristic feature of these traditional style settlements is the **rice house** (lumbung). Normally square in shape, these houses are constructed exclusively of the natural materials clay and wood and raised up on stilts. The roofs are usually made of grass, but rice straw can be used as well. The lumbung is a very practically designed structure. Domestic and working animals are housed below, the family lives in the middle and provisions are stored under the high, domed roof. Incidentally, Sasak houses are used as models when designing new hotels.

Villages and houses

In contrast to the Balinese, the majority of the population in Lombok had **converted to Islam** by the 16th century. Apart from an insignificant Hindu minority living mainly on the western part of the island, most of the indigenous Sasak today remain faithful to Islam. Occasionally, especially in the mountain villages in the northern part of the island, there are those who profess to the old **Wetu Telu religion**, a form of Islam with elements of an ancestor cult and Hinduism, and which involves the veneration of natural shrines.

Religion

Many beaches are deserted.

Mataram • Ampenan • Cakranegara

Mataram Mataram is the capital of the island of Lombok and the administrative centre of the Indonesian province of Nusa Tenggara Barat.

Although today Mataram and its neighbours, the originally independent towns of Ampenan and Cakranegara, have merged together to the point where their borders have all but disappeared, they have each been able to retain something of their original character. **Ampenan** has remained the harbour because of its location next to the ocean but has largely lost its significance, even though the only airport in Lombok is closest to it.

As has always been the case in **Cakranegara**, the Chinese who settled here over the course of the centuries dominate commercial life in the markets and bazaars, which explains why the locals derisively call the place »Chinatown«.

Finally, Mataram is still considered to be a garden city and is where all of the main agencies of the provincial government have been established. Apart from the museum in Mataram (see below), there is hardly any sight in Ampenan/Mataram/Cakranegara to speak of. There are, however, some easily accessible sights in the surrounding area that are worth the trip.

Small bungalows in the style of traditional rice houses

✳
Mataram Museum
🕐
Opening hours:
Sun–Thu 8am–2pm,
Fri 8am–11am

The Mataram Museum (Jalan Panji Tilarnegara) is a must for anyone interested in the history of Lombok, and particularly in the history of its people. In addition to a number of documents and writings, its exhibits include tools, implements, weapons and examples of the decorative arts. Traditional Sasak house architecture is illustrated with a number of models. Most of the displays are explained in both Indonesian and English.

✳
Meru Temple

The Meru Temple, built in 1720 by the Balinese Prince Karang, is also worth a visit. In the innermost part of the temple are several merus dedicated to the Hindu trinity of Shiva, Vishnu and Brahma.

✳
Lingsar Temple

The Lingsar Temple, located not far north of Cakranegara at the village of Narmada, is venerated by both faithful Hindus and believers in the Wetu Telu religion. On a certain day at the beginning of the rainy season (October–December) the Lingsar Temple attracts throngs of **pilgrims from both religions**. A split gate (candi bentar) opens onto a broad roadway with a pond to the right and left. Standing to the left about halfway down the roadway is a Hindu shrine on a square base (no entry allowed) with four shrines (the one on the left faces Gunung Agung, the abode of the gods on neighbouring Bali). A separate shrine is for members of the Wetu Telu religion. Beyond are pools used by worshippers for their ritual ablutions.

Close to Jalan Seiaparang are the ruins of the Mayura Water Palace built in 1744 as part of the palace of the Bali princes. Standing in the middle of an artificial lake is an open-sided pavilion accessed by means of a narrow causeway. It was used both as a meeting place for the Hindu princes and as a court hall.

Mayura-Water Palace

Northwards along the coast is the Pura Segara or Water Temple. There are several small fishing villages along the way with colourfully painted wooden boats. A Chinese and a Muslim cemetery are located in the vicinity of Pura Segara.

Pura Segara (Water Temple)

Senggigi • Sukarara

Just a few years ago only local children played on the beach here, but now **Senggigi Beach has become a tourist centre** (18km/11mi north of Ampenan). The resort has several decent hotels surrounded by a number of bars and restaurants. The attractions however are limited to the bathing facilities and the beach itself, which is plagued by hordes of peddlers who descend on the holidaymakers, especially in the evening hours.

Senggigi

The small village of Sukarara lies a good 25km/15.5mi southeast of Mataram and is known for its traditional-style hand-woven textiles. These skilfully worked fabrics, often taking months to produce, are offered for sale directly in the village at prices fully justified by the skilled work involved.

Hand-woven fabrics in Sukarara

✱ ✱ Climbing Tour of Gunung Rinjani

An ascent of the Rinjani volcano, the third highest mountain in the Indonesian Archipelago, is one of the most memorable experiences possible in Lombok. Any tour planned for this worthwhile climb should allow for sufficient time to enjoy the magnificent volcanic landscape of the area, which has been a nature reserve since 1984.

Mountain tour lasting several days

There are several different routes to the summit of Gunung Rinjani (3726m/12,224ft), which is revered by both the Sasak and the Balinese as a sacred mountain. The relatively easy climb from Senaru in

Recommended starting point: Senaru

View of the Rinjani volcano and Lake Segara Anak

the central north of the island is recommended. Not only are a number of local guides available here, but it is also highly likely that there are other tourists willing to join forces and form a group. If a guide has been hired, it can be assumed that he will see to arranging the necessary equipment.

A bus or bemo can be taken from Mataram to Anyar. From here it is only a few miles to Senaru. It is best to spend the night in Senaru and get an early start on the 12km/7.5mi hike to Segara Anak Cater Lake the next morning. The ascent, best begun early in the morning before sunrise, is quite easy; just follow any of the mostly well-travelled paths with trail markers beginning in Sengara that are numbered from 1 to 200.

An ascent all the way to the summit of the volcano requires not only ample time but also good physical condition. The summit can be reached from the crater lake in about 4.5 hours. From the summit there is not only a **fantastic view** of the crater lake and the entire island of Lombok, but you can also see all the way to Bali and its highest mountain, Gunung Agung. Except during the rainy season, the descent from the crater's rim down to the crater lake can be made in a good three hours. A trail from the lake leads in about 1.5 hours to a hot spring that is strongly sulphurous and has a temperature upwards of 70°C/158°F; the spring is the source of the small Kali Putih river (white river). Primitive camping sites are provided here, as well as on the shores of the crater lake, making it possible to extend the tour for several days.

Gili Islands

The three small islands of Gili Air, Gili Meno and Gili Trawangan lie only a few miles off the northwest coast of Lombok. They can be reached by boat from the small port town of Pemenang. The crossing takes between 20 minutes and an hour.

The Gilis – as water sports enthusiasts from all over the world have been calling them for ages – offer **fantastic beaches** and an **underwater world that is mostly still intact**. All motorized traffic is banned. The traditional cidomos (horse and cart) serve as transportation. Most of the lodgings offer only modest comfort but are cheap. Incidentally, the best spots for diving and snorkelling are to be found on Gili Trawangan, which, with its 300ha/740ac, is the largest of the Gili Islands. Diving equipment can be hired on the island.

★ ★ Mengwi

L 7

Region: Southwest Bali
Altitude: 95m/310ft

Administrative district: Badung
Distance: 16km/10mi northwest of Denpasar

Mengwi was once the chief town of the principality of the same name. Its rulers played a role in Bali's history insofar as they were continually having to come to terms with other powers – at first in a power struggle with the princes of Klungkung and Gianyar and later with the Dutch colonial rulers, to whom they immediately acquiesced. In 1891 the rulers of Tabanan and Badung divided up the principality amongst themselves, putting an end to its independent status.

What to See in and around Mengwi

Pura Taman Ayun (Garden Temple in the Water) is one of Bali's six state temples making it one of the most important temples on the island. The imposing temple complex is **set on an island in a river**. The inner temple is also surrounded by a moat. Having passed through a split gate (candi bentar), a large fountain dedicated to the underworld can be seen in front of the entrance to the inner temple.

★ ★
Pura Taman Ayun

▶ MENGWI

GETTING AROUND

A road runs northwards from Denpasar in the direction of Singaraja. There is a regular bus service from Denpasar-Ubung, and bemos can be found along the road or at the Denpasar-Ubung bemo station.

The innermost temple, entered through a covered gate (candi korung), has no less than 27 structures of differing importance and purpose.

Pura Taman Ayun is integrated in the network of temples throughout Bali. Its status can be recognized by the gods represented, which include not only those for whom the temple was originally built but also those who come to visit from other shrines during their celebrations. This includes, for instance, the gods who make their home on Gunung Agung and Gunung Batur. A meru next to the enclosure wall is dedicated to the rice goddess Dewi Sri, and the third bale on the left-hand side is held to be home to a number of gods. Pura Taman Ayun was built in 1634 during the reign of Raja Gusti Agung Anom and given its present appearance around 1937.

Taman Ayun appears to be a small island because it is surrounded by wide moats filled with water-lilies.

The museum's two pavilions can be reached by a small ferry. The museum displays pictures and models detailing the Manusia Yadnya ceremonies.

Like so much in Bali, the monkey forest of Sangeh, 20km/13mi from Denpasar and 10km/6mi from Mengwi, has become very commercialized. Even before reaching the forest where **hundreds of monkeys live wild**, visitors are subjected to a plethora of souvenir shops lining the path leading from the car park. According to legend, the monkeys are the living progeny of Hanuman, the monkey king, a central figure in the Indian epic, the Ramayana (► Literature). They are therefore considered sacred, and venerated in Pura Bukit Sari, a temple in the middle of the forest thought to date from the 17th century. Even more impressive than the temple are the massive trees towering around it, which are found nowhere else in Bali. Their origin is unknown.

Beware – the monkeys can sometimes be rather aggressive. This is particularly true of mothers with young. Handbags should be kept closed and cameras put away during the walk through the forest. People who wear glasses should be aware that the monkeys like to play with a »borrowed« pair of glasses. As with the monkeys in the forest of Ubud, it is best to maintain a safe distance to avoid being bitten. Feeding the animals can also present problems. The monkeys have a tendency to grab food out of visitors' hands when they approach with a bag of nuts or bananas. Particularly spirited animals will pursue tourists in order to get at the tasty treats more quickly.

In Marga (15km/9.3mi northwest of Mengwi) is the **Margarana National Memorial** that commemorates the battle for independence against the Dutch on 20 November 1946. Next to it is the cemetery for the 1371 fallen Indonesians and a memorial museum.

✴ ✴ Negara

D 5

Capital of the administrative district of Jembrana
Distance: 33km/20mi southeast of Gilimanuk

Region: West Bali
Altitude: 120m/395ft

Most of Bali's Muslims live in Negara, right in the middle of one of the island's most thinly populated regions. This undoubtedly has to do with its relative proximity to the neighbouring island of Java, which has a predominantly Islamic population. Negara has hardly any tourist attractions but is widely known for the water buffalo races that take place in the city between July and October.

▶ VISITING NEGARA

INFORMATION
Jembrana Government Tourist Office
Jl. Surapati 3, Negara
Tel. (03 65) 410 60

GETTING AROUND
Negara lies 97km/60mi west of Denpasar on the road to Gilimanuk. Buses make the trip regularly from Denpasar-Tegal. It is not advisable to take a bemo from Denpasar; instead take one from Gilimanuk or Pulukan.

WHERE TO EAT
▶ **Inexpensive**
Makan Wirapada
Jl. Ngurah Rai 107
Tel. (03 65) 411 61
Good, basic Indonesian food is served here.

What to See in and around Negara

Negara is a clean little town with a number of attractive houses typical of the type of construction used in this part of Bali. There are several mosques that can be looked at outside of prayer times, but do ask permission to enter first.

★★
Water Buffalo Races

Once a year, the otherwise sleepy little town of Negara really comes to life. For about the last hundred years or so, between July and October, water buffalo races have been held here. Thousands of visitors converge on the city, many of whom are intent on having a flutter. Hotel receptions or the tourist office in Denpasar can supply the exact date. During the races, pairs of buffalos pull two-wheeled carts that carry jockeys trying to urge the clumsy-looking beasts to greater speeds. Amazingly, the water buffalo are capable of reaching speeds of **up to 30mph/50kmh** along the 2.5 km/1.5mi race course.

The speed, running style, strength and colour of the animals are judged.

A small, private **gamelan museum** with a beautiful collection of regional gamelans can be tracked down in **Sangkar Agung** by following the signs saying »Jegog Suar Agung«. The village is only a few miles away from Negara, though reaching it necessitates leaving the main road to Denpasar near Jambrana.

Meanwhile, the main road to Denpasar continues through the small town of Pulukan, which is particularly popular with travellers wishing to get off the beaten track. The lodgings available here are admittedly only modest, but surfers will appreciate the »gnarly« conditions on the beach.

Pulukan

✱ ✱ Peliatan

M 7

Region: Central Bali
Altitude: 66m/217ft

Administrative district: Gianyar
Distance: approx. 2km/1.2mi south of Ubud

Peliatan is popular with visitors to Bali who favour idyllic country charm over the bustle of the tourist centres. It is located halfway between Ubud and Mas. Two of Bali's most famous dance groups call Peliatan home. At certain times their rehearsals in the royal palace of Puri Agung are open to the public.

Peliatan is not a particularly attractive place. Even the local temple is of little cultural or historical significance. An exception is **Pura Pande**, the »Temple of the Blacksmiths«, which has an exceedingly attractive covered gate (candi korung) of red brick and white tuff. Beyond it is a Garuda figure on a wall that protects against demons. Another aling aling stands in front of the flight of steps leading into the inner temple courtyard.

A sight of a special kind is Agung Rai's painting gallery, the largest of its kind in Bali, located on Jalan Rengosekan. Agung Rai (born 1955), a descendant of a royal family, has been a committed collector of Balinese art for many years. It is thanks to him that many local artists have had the opportunity of presenting their work to a wider public and are able to live from the subsequent sales. The owner reinvests the proceeds from the pictures sold in the sales exhibition next door in new paintings, constantly increasing the considerable size of his collection (opening hours: daily 8am–5pm). The **Agung Rai Museum of Art** (ARMA; opening hours: daily 9am–6pm) with works by Walter Spies, Rudolf Bonnet and Le Mayeur (► Baedeker Special p.218) now belongs to the Fine Art Gallery, as do the Café Arma and the extensive grounds of the Kokokan hotel and restaurant in the Puri Indah Garden.

▶ PELIATAN

GETTING AROUND
The road to Peliatan runs to the northeast from Denpasar in the direction of Ubud and Tampaksiring or from Ubud south toward Denpasar. There are good, regular bus and bemo services from Denpasar-Kereneng and Ubud.

✱ ✱
Agung Rai Fine Art Gallery

🕐

Artist in the Agung Rai Museum

Museum Rudana Another art museum focussing on modern art is the Museum Rudana at Jl. Cok Rai Pudak 44. Modern Balinese paintings are displayed on the first two floors and numerous classic works are to be found on the third (opening hours: Mon–Sat 9am–5pm, Sun noon to 5pm, www.museumrudana.com).

✳ Penelokan

Region: North Bali
Altitude: 1452m/4764ft

Administrative district: Bangli
Distance: 40km/25mi north of Ubud

Directly translated, the name Penelokan means something like »beautiful view«. Whoever gave this small village its name was not exaggerating. The panorama enjoyed here consists of a fascinating landscape with Lake Batur stretching out below and the summit of the Gunung Batur volcano towering above.

Once, both Penelokan and the village of Batur (see below) lay directly at the foot of the volcano. The inhabitants patiently accepted the considerable damage caused by the eruptions in 1917 and 1926

▶ VISITING PENELOKAN

GETTING AROUND

To reach Penelokan, take road no. 27 from Denpasar to Bedulu, then no. 31 to Lake Batur. Several buses a day leave from Denpasar-Kereneng. Bemos and buses travelling to Penelekon or Kintamani can be found in all major towns and cities.

WHERE TO EAT

▶ Moderate

Lake View Restaurant
Lake View Hotel, Penelokan, Kintamani
Regional cuisine served in spectacular surroundings with a view of the volcano and crater lake; highly recommended.

WHERE TO STAY

▶ Mid-range

Lake View Hotel
Penelokan, Kintamani
Tel. (03 65) 513 94
www.indo.com/hotels/lakeview
Fantastic location on the rim of the crater; stylishly furnished rooms with a view of the crater lake and Gunung Batur. Hiking tours and excursions in the surrounding area can be booked in the hotel; cultural and musical events are held regularly.

---

before they decided after the latest eruption (1963; about the same time as that of Gunung Agung) to resettle the village on a less dangerous spot higher up on the rim of the crater.

What to See in and around Penelokan

The awe-inspiring view of the volcano, Gunung Batur, and Lake Batur, impressive though it is, is about all that Penelokan has to offer. Any sights of interest were completely destroyed in the eruptions of 1926 and 1963. One of these was a temple dedicated to the goddess Dewi Danu containing a shrine that was highly venerated because of her function as a tutelary of the seas and the waters of Lake Batur. As if by a miracle, it was spared by the flows of lava and is today in Pura Ulun Danu Batur.

◀ Ill. p.155

Because of its strategic location, Penelokan is richly blessed with souvenir shops and stands and countless numbers of souvenir hawkers move from place to place, somewhat pestering the visitors here. A variety of buffets are offered at a number of restaurants.

Penelokan is a good starting point for a four-hour **hike up the Gunung Abangvolcano**, which, at 2153m/7064ft, is a good 400m/1300ft higher than Gunung Batur rising up on the opposite shore of Lake Batur. Gunung Batur can also be easily climbed from Penelokan.

✱ ✱
Gunung Abang

With an area of some 140 sq km/54 sq m, the Batur crater **is one of the world's largest volcanic craters**. It was formed millions of years

✱ ✱
Danau Batur
(crater lake)

ago by the collapse of the magma chamber after the interior of the volcano vent had been partly emptied through an eruption. Lake Batur formed in about the centre of the caldera and today has a maximum depth of 100m/330ft.

★★
Gunung Batur

A hiking tour to the summit of Gunung Batur (also called Gunung Lebah or »Mountain in the Depths«) offers the chance to experience some fabulous landscapes. The climb can be made in three hours at most, even by the less experienced. Good footwear is recommended because of the loose lava rock. Since the mountain is often already veiled in thick clouds in the morning hours, it is best not to set off too late. First, take the road from Penelokan down to Kedisan and follow it to Toya Bungkah, a village on the western shore of the crater lake known for its hot sulphur springs.

A **well marked trail** begins south of Toya Bungkah and leads up Gunung Batur. While hiking through the marvellous scenery, do not stray from the path because the danger of fumaroles lurks on all sides. There is a stunning view from the summit of the barren landscape with its bizarre lava formations, the valley and Gunung Abang opposite.

Great care should be taken when hiking around Gunung Batur, particularly by hikers who suffer from a touch of vertigo: at some points along the ridge they may find themselves looking straight down into frighteningly deep abysses on both sides.

An alternative route up Gunung Batur involves a three-hour climb from the village of Pura Yati. For reasons of safety, it is best to make the ascent **accompanied by a person who knows the territory**. There are plenty of Balinese interested in guiding visitors on the three-hour tour.

Kintamani

6km/4mi along road no. 35 to the northwest of Penelokan, just before reaching the bustling market town of Kintamani sprawled out along the road, lies the village of Batur.

★
Batur (village) ►

The highlight here is the **Pura Ulun Danu Batur** temple complex. The buildings are grouped around a shrine in the form of an eleven-tiered meru dedicated to the goddess of the lakes and rivers, Dewi Danu, that survived the volcanic eruptions of 1926 and 1963. There are several other merus forming an impressive backdrop, especially in the morning and evening.

The temple complex of black lava rock has been in the process of continual expansion for years and will consist of almost 300 buildings when it is finally completed. Of particular note are the demons depicted in the entrance area, which are considered to be guardians and protectors against evil spirits. The temple grounds offer a superb view of the surrounding mountain scenery.

The village of Batur was threatened by the volcanic eruption of 1917 and then partially destroyed nine years later by lava flows. The villagers then abandoned their original village and built new homes on

View of the Batur and Ayung volcanoes from the temple

higher ground, which seemed safer to them. When Gunung Batur erupted once again in 1963, the move proved to have been a wise one. The flow of lava did not reach the new village site. There is reasonably priced accommodation in the village.

Up on Mount Penulisan (1745m/5725ft), some 5km/3mi north of Kintamani, is the temple complex of Pura Tegeh Koripan, the highest lying shrine in Bali. The path up to it has close to 350 steps; it is a climb best made only by visitors in suitable physical condition. The ideal time to visit is either early morning or late afternoon.

★ Pura Tegeh Koripan

The temple complex, which offers a fine view across the surrounding countryside, dates back to the 11th century and probably served as a royal temple of the Warmadewa dynasty from Pejeng. The temple is entered through two split gates. There is an interesting **stone cube** in front of the entrance on the left-hand side along with the surviving fragments of a lingam; both cube and lingam are highly revered. Standing inside the temple are a number of bales containing stone figures, some presumably dating from the Hindu-Javanese period in Bali. Of particular note are the figures of the divine couple, Vishnu and Lakshmi, holding a four-leaf lotus blossom in their hands. Other interesting figures depict Shiva, Parvati, Ganesha and a four-headed Brahma. Standing in the middle of the courtyard is a throne reserved for Shiva, the lord of the mountain, when he attends cult ceremonies.

Trunyan The village of Trunyan on the eastern shore of Lake Batur can be reached in 20 minutes by motorboat from Toya Bungkah. It is inhabited by **Old Balinese** (Bali Aga), who live comparatively traditional lives and have only recently begun taking an interest in tourism. Visitors are now welcomed in the village.

★ ★ Penida (Nusa Penida)

O–Q 9/10

Administrative district: Klungkung
Altitude: 0–529m/1,735ft

Area: 322 sq km/124 sq mi
Population: 49,000

Lying 22km/13.5mi off the southeast coast of Bali is (Nusa) Penida, an island some 8km/5mi long which actually belongs to a group of islands that include the considerably smaller islands of Ceningan and Lembongan located off to the northwest. The islands are populated predominantly by Muslims.

The limestone massif that forms the core of the island of Penida runs in a north-south direction and reaches a height of 529m/1736ft. None of the three islands have any agricultural value as the permeable karst soil is hardly suitable for cultivation. The main source of the modest income there is **fishing**. Penida formerly served as the **place in which condemned prisoners from Klungkung were exiled**. Believing as they do in spirits, the Balinese are highly suspicious of Penida Island. As they tell it, the **giant, Jero Gede Mecaling**, an exceptionally evil spirit, lives on the island and has already managed on a couple of occasions to cross the Badung Strait with his band of evil spirits and wreak terror and destruction in Bali. Only after the Balinese fashioned a similarly looking figure of a demon and set it up on the coast did the giant stay away. Even today, on the eve of Nyepi, the festival celebrating the New Year (► Baedeker-Special p.90), when the Balinese carry a gigantic figure of a demon through their village and then to the shore to burn it there, it is mainly the terrifying giant they have in mind.

Outrigger boats take tourists to Nusa Lembongan.

⏵ VISITING PENIDA • LEMBONGAN

GETTING AROUND

Speedboats make the 40-minute crossing from Padang Bai (southwest of Amlapura) to Toyapakeh several times daily. The outriggers that leave every morning from Kusamba (southeast of Klungkung) to either Sampalan or Toyakapeh take about 2.5 hours.

WHERE TO EAT / WHERE TO STAY

► Mid-range

Nusa Lembongan Resort
Tel. (03 61) 72 58 64, fax 72 58 66, www.nusalembonganresort.com
Along with a beach on Sanghiang Bay and a view of Agung volcano, this hotel offers peace and quiet, rest and a range of water sports. Excellent international dishes can be enjoyed on the terrace with a wonderful view of the beach and ocean. There is also a nice bar close by.

Made's Homestay
Sampalan, tel. (03 66) 296 09
A small street between the market and the harbour leads to this tiny, pleasant hotel (4 rooms) with a pretty garden.

Visitors to Penida are mostly attracted to the northern coast, which is **ideal for surfing and diving**.

What to See on the Island of Penida

Those making the crossing to Penida from Kusamba first set foot on dry land in the island's main town, Sampalan. A lively market is held daily near the harbour, but there is not much else of interest here.

Sampalan

The Pura Ped temple is in the harbour village of west of Sampalan. The holy temple shrine stands in a square, artificial pond about 50m/164 ft from the beach.

Toyapakeh

Located some 5km/3mi southeast of Sampalan is the Goa Karangasari cave with an **underground freshwater lake**. The entrance to the system of caves is somewhat concealed and the cave entrance itself only measures 2.5m/8ft across. Inside, the cave opens up to an impressive 15m/50ft in height with a series of small passages leading off it (bring a powerful torch or hire one from the locals offering their services as guides on the road outside). A walk through the whole cave will lead to the opposite exit in a steep rock wall.

✱ ✱
Goa Karangasari

There are a number of nice beaches on the west coast of Penida. The beach at Toyakapeh is particularly attractive to swimmers, snorkellers and divers, but beware, the tides here are quite strong. Occasionally there are dangerous underwater currents, and sharks are sighted from time to time as well.

Beaches

Seaside cliffs Swimming is not possible on the island's south coast, but the steep cliffs rising sharply up to 200m/656ft above the crashing breakers are impressive.

Lesser Island of Lembongan

Getting there Nusa Lembongan (docking at Jungutbatu) can be reached either from Toyakapeh on Penida or from Sanur (in Bali) by outrigger or small motorboat (indulge in a little haggling over the fare).

★
Beaches The island (population 3500) earns a living from day trippers who come to snorkel, swim, surf, dive and then return to Bali after 5pm. There are few cars; three-wheeled taxis are the main form of transport. The main village on the 4km x 2km/2.5mi x 1.2mi island is **Desa Lembongan**. The houses are enclosed by decorated stone walls. Mangos and banana trees can be seen in the gardens. The women of the island harvest algae from the ocean to use as fertilizer or, finely ground, for cosmetics and medicinal treatments or to sell to chemical factories.

The ruins of a Hindu temple, **Pura Pancak**, are perched on a 50m/164ft-high hill, from which there is a fine panorama of the sea and even the Gunung Agung volcano in Bali. The main attraction, however, is the **»Underground House«**, which took one man 15 years to chisel out beneath the ground. It has rooms, hallways, stairs, a kitchen and a bath, with shafts providing light and air. Reasonable accommodation offering comfort and relaxation can be found in Sanghiang Bay and Nusa Lembongan Resort. A suspension bridge connects Nusa Lembongan to the neighbouring island of Nusa Ceningan.

Sanur

Region: South Bali
Altitude: sea level

Administrative district: Badung
Distance: 7km/4mi southeast of Denpasar

Things are somewhat quieter in Sanur than in Kuta and Legian, even though the town just southeast of Denpasar has experienced a recent boom.

The basis for this boom had been established much earlier, though, when the Grand Bali Beach Hotel was built in 1967, the first hotel in Bali that reached an international standard. This concrete monolith dominated the area and was the reason that the building codes in Bali were changed to restrict the height of new structures to that of the tallest palm tree in the vicinity. A coral reef lies off the beach and can be reached by outriggers (jukung). Sanur's lagoon is good for swimming except at low tide; the current is dangerously strong beyond the reef. Compared to Kuta and Legian, Sanur is considered to be **a somewhat finer class of resort** and, accordingly, luxury hotels line the beaches. That may be the reason that the sand here is also a little cleaner. The **spectacular sunrise on Nusa Penida** is something that should not be missed!   ◄ Tip

Not far from the Grand Bali Beach Hotel is the house of the Belgian painter, Le Mayeur, who died in 1958. It is open daily for tours except Sundays from 10am to 2pm (►Baedeker Special p.218).   **Le Mayeur House**

 VISITING SANUR

INFORMATION

Denpasar Tourist Office
Jl. Surapati 7, Denpasar
Tel. (03 61) 22 36 02, fax 23 45 69

GETTING AROUND

There is a regular bus service from Candi Dasa, Kuta, Lovina, Padangbai and Ubud.
Bemos can be flagged down along Jl. Danau Tambligan and Jl. Danau Poso.

WATER SPORTS

Sanur is a centre for a wide variety of water sports. Besides the beachfront hotels, there are a number of small businesses and private individuals offering diving and snorkelling trips and windsurfing courses. Trips lasting several hours in one of the many outrigger canoes are very popular (do not forget sun protection). Jet skis and paddle boats are also offered for hire. With the capital close by, the beaches are quite busy at weekends and the number of stands offering snacks, batik and arts and crafts, already quite numerous on weekdays, increases even more. Among the places that can be recommended for surfing instruction, diving courses and excursions are: Indonesia Surf Adventure (Jl. Bypass Ngurah Rai, Tel. 03 61/27 00 52) and Ena Dive Centre & Marine Adventure (Jl. Tirta Ening 1, Blajong, tel. 03 61/ 28 88 29).

WHERE TO EAT

► **Expensive**
Lotus Pond
Jl. Raya Sanur
Tel. (03 61) 28 93 98
Dishes from all over Asia, including fish specialities; the bebek betutu (smoked duck) is delicious. Dance performances are often presented.

► **Moderate**
Pergola
Jl. Danau Toba 2
Tel. (03 61) 28 84 62
Modern design and furnishings; the speciality here is grilled fish. Often with live music.

Lovingly painted boats

A young legong dancer

A BALINESE LOVE STORY

One of the most famous love stories between a foreigner and a Balinese was that of the Belgian painter Le Mayeur and the legong dancer Ni Pollok. The couple resided in a villa in Sanur, which was turned into a museum after Ni Pollok died.

It all happened in 1933. Ni Pollok, Bali's foremost legong dancer and a celebrity on the island, turned 16 and was soon to face being too old to dance the legong, because, according to the prevailing opinion, the best dancers were to be found in the age group 12 to 17. When, by chance, the delicate beauty met the Belgian painter Adrien Jean Le Mayeur, who had come to the island a year earlier, the two fell in love with each other. Ni Pollok became Le Mayeur's model and two years later the couple married. The one year that the well-travelled painter had planned to stay on the island became many decades.

school and self-proclaimed hopeless romantic, resolved to design the property in traditional Balinese style. The famous sculptor, Ida Bagus Made Pantri, assisted them in any way he could and, taking their time, they started construction. Time was of such little consequence that it was not until two decades later that the construction team were in agreement – their project was completed.

Set in the midst of a tropical garden with hibiscus and bougainvillea

Careful Planning and Designing of the Villa

Ni Pollok purchased land in Sanur and decided to build a house. She and Le Mayeur, a graduate of a technical

International Esteem and Many Enthusiastic Visitors

Teak and fantastic carvings dominate the interior. Some of the wooden window shutters display scenes from

the Ramayana, the monumental Indian Hindu epic. The completion of a decorated table alone, they say, required more than half a year. Le Mayeur was a perfectionist. He aligned the windows so that each appeared like a painting, framing a section of garden scenery he had created: a special flowering tree, perhaps, or an artwork, or a pond overgrown with lotus.

Mayeur became a renowned and highly regarded artist, whose fame spread far beyond the borders of Indonesia. The exhibitions of his paintings in Singapore (1937), Kuala Lumpur (1941) and Singapore (1941) were extraordinarily great successes. In 1951, *National Geographic* magazine dedicated a story to Le Mayeur and remarked that **the hospitality of the Belgian-Balinese couple was exceptional**. Indeed, numerous visitors, including many foreigners taking a holiday in Bali, came and went to and from the couple's villa, being served trays of delicacies by the lady of the house and her house servants. Le Mayeur and Ni Pollok were even able to welcome Sukarno, Indonesia's first president and the Indian Prime Minister Nehru in Sanur in 1956. Supposedly it was Sukarno who inspired the childless couple to erect a museum on their marvellous property after their deaths.

Art Treasures and Works by Mayeur

The painter died two years later and was buried in Brussels. Ni Pollok lived in Sanur until her death at the age of 70. The Le Mayeur Villa on the beach went to the state, and was made into a museum. Along with a large number of Indonesian art treasures and antiques, there are **88 of Le Mayeur's colourful paintings on display**. The two most famous are of his favourite subject – his wife.

The Le Mayeur Museum is located 200m/220yd north of Grand Bali Beach Hotel in Jl. Hang Tua in Sanur.

Restaurant Penjor
Jl. D. Tamblingan (200m/220yd north of the Hyatt hotel)
Tel. (03 61) 28 82 26
Traditional dances are performed here several times a week at 8pm.

► Inexpensive
Café Batujimbar
Jl. Danau Tambligan 152
Tel. (03 61) 28 73 74
Simple meals served in a courtyard garden.

WHERE TO STAY
► Luxury
Bali Hyatt Hotel
Jl. Danau Tamblingan
Tel. (03 61) 28 12 34
Fax 28 76 93
www.bali.resort.hyatt.com
A successful synthesis of luxury, tropical ambience and Balinese décor, plus an atmosphere that is a balm for body and soul (389 rooms).

Inna Grand Bali Beach Hotel & Spa
Jl. Hang Tuah
Tel. (03 61) 28 85 11, fax 28 79 17
www.innagrandbalibeach.com
There is no avoiding this hotel for most visitors to Bali as a number of airlines have their headquarters here. The hotel (574 rooms) in the only high-rise in Bali has been thoroughly modernized; the rooms are comfortable but unfortunately a bit sterile. There are numerous restaurants, cafés, bars and shops.

Tandjung Sari Hotel
Jl. Danau Tamblingan
Tel. (03 61) 28 84 41, fax 28 79 30
www.tandjungsari.com
Boutique hotel (26 bungalows) in the style of a private hideaway with the charm of old Bali; beach restaurant and an elegantly furnished library.

► Mid-range
Sanur Aerowista
Jl. Danau Tamblingan
Tel. (03 61) 28 80 11
Fax 28 75 66
The attentive child care, ambitious sports programme and first-rate restaurant ensure the custom of an enthusiastic clientele.

Paradise Plaza
Jl. Hang Tuah 46
Tel. (03 61) 28 17 81
Fax 28 17 82
www.sanurparadise.com
This hotel, surrounded by a lot of water, is particularly family-friendly. Children enjoy »Camp Splash« with its variety of water slides and places to play; for the grown-ups there is an excellent spa and nice restaurants.

Baedeker recommendation

Segara Village
Jl. Segara Ayu
Tel. (03 61) 28 84 07
Fax 28 72 42
www.segaravillage.com
Stone gods, floral arrangements, the fragrance of lotus blossoms; this hotel (30 rooms) is designed like a Balinese village and can look back on a 50-year history. The thatched bungalows have modern interiors complemented by Indonesian antiques.

► Budget
Puri Mango Guesthouse
Jl. Danau Toba 15
Tel. (03 61) 28 84 11
Fax 28 85 98
www.purimango.com
Reasonably priced with the essential amenities: beach location, pool and nice restaurant.

The island of Lembongan (►Penida) can be easily reached from Sanur by outrigger or motorboat. The crossing from the north end of the beach takes about an hour.

Bali's oldest artefact is a stone pillarthat can be found on the southern outskirts of town behind Pura Belangjong. It has an inscription in Sanskrit and is estimated to be more than 1000 years old.

A trip to Bali Orchid Garden (3km/1.8mi north) is a wonderful place for an outing. Thousands of the elegant plants can be admired. There is also a shop selling orchids and books on the subject (opening hours: daily 8am–4pm).

Around Sanur

The village of Padang Galak lies only a few miles north of Sanur. Every year in July, Padang Galak attracts tourists and Balinese alike when the large **Kite Festival** takes place. Initially, the object of this event was to give a boost to the flagging art of Balinese kite making, but the contest has developed into a major tourist attraction. The black beach is a favourite meeting place for surfers.

✶✶ Singaraja

Capital of the administrative district of Buleleng
Population: 100,000

Region: North Bali
Altitude: 15m/50ft
Distance: Approx. 80km/50mi north of Denpasar

Singaraja, the governmental seat of the administrative district of Buleleng and the second largest city in Bali, lies on the north coast of the island. There are large-scale coffee plantations in the surrounding fertile countryside. The new seaport further west plays an important role in the commodities trade with other the Indonesian islands.

The area around present-day Singaraja was probably already settled by the 10th century. The settlement did not gain any importance, however, until the reign of Raja Panji Sakti in the 16th century, when the raja had his residence, Singaraja (Lion King), built there in 1604 and the village was named after it. The district of Buleleng takes its name from a cereal grain that was cultivated in the region in the late Middle Ages. Singaraja played no small part in the Dutch efforts to bring Bali under their rule. After several failed attempts, the Dutch managed to capture the stronghold in 1849. The town was later

Singaraja Map

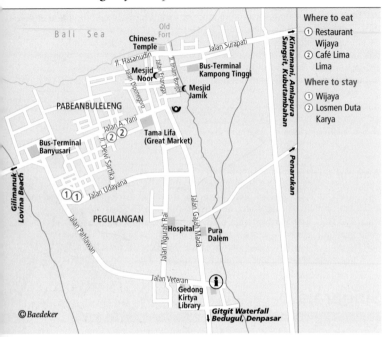

Bali Sea

Old Fort

Chinese-Temple

Jalan Surapati

Jl. Hasanudin

Jalan Pangeran Diponegoro

Jalan Flangga

Jl. Imam Bonjol

Mesjid Noor

Bus-Terminal Kampong Tinggi

Mesjid Jamik

PABEANBULELENG

Kintamani, Amlapura Sangsit, Kuburambahan

Jalan A. Yani

Bus-Terminal Banyusari

Jl. Dewi Sartika

Tama Lifa (Great Market)

Penarukan

Jalan Udayana

Jalan Pahlawan

Jalan Ngurah Rai

PEGULANGAN

Hospital

Pura Dalem

Jalan Gajah Mada

Jalan Veteran

Gedong Kirtya Library

Gitgit Waterfall Bedugul, Denpasar

Gilimanuk Lovina Beach

© Baedeker

Where to eat
① Restaurant Wijaya
② Café Lima Lima

Where to stay
① Wijaya
② Losmen Duta Karya

made the seat of the Dutch colonial government and remained the island's capital until 1946 (after that ▶Denpasar became the capital).

What to See in Singaraja

The original town of Singaraja has **numerous Dutch colonial-style houses**. It lies slightly inland and is bordered to the north by the city districts of Pegulangan and Pabeanbuleleng. The place makes a decidedly quieter impression than the current capital of Denpasar. Pabeanbuleleng boasts a charming Chinese temple (usually closed) at the old harbour, two small mosques and a large, bustling market (Tama Lila) held daily in Jalan Ahmad Yani.

★ ★
Pura Dalem

Pura Dalem, **one of the most interesting Hindu temples in the north of Bali**, can be found in Jalan Gajah Mada. The temple is entered through a small split gate (candi bentar) which leads into the first temple courtyard. To the left is another gate, elaborately decorated, which reveals the second courtyard that is, surprisingly, set 2m/6.5ft lower. Standing to the left is the Bale Gong, and to the right the Bale Pemalaiyagan, in which the gods are welcomed by the worshippers during the temple festivals. On the right side of the wall separating

► VISITING SINGARAJA • LOVINA

INFORMATION
Buleleng Tourist Office
Jl. Veteran 23, Singaraja
Tel. (03 62) 251 41

GETTING AROUND
Take the road running north from Denpasar to Singaraja, passing through Sempidi, Mengwi and Bedugul or – an infinitely more attractive route – travel from Denpasar first through Kapal, then westward via Antosari to Pengastulan and then continue along the coast past Lovina Beach. There is a daily bus service from Denpasar-Ubung.
Bemos ply the coastal road to Lovina Beach.

NIGHTLIFE
Although much tamer than the »Bermuda Triangle« of Kuta, Lovina offers sufficient opportunities to hear live music in the evenings. Restaurants, bars and cafés all offer music events that change weekly.

SHOPPING
There are numerous snack stands at the night market at Banyusari bus station (Jl. J. A. Yani). Fish dishes are also available here.

WHERE TO EAT
Most of the restaurants in Singaraja are on Jl. J.A. Yani, the main street, and serve Chinese food.

► Moderate
① Restaurant Wijaya
Singaraja, Jl. J. Sudirman
Tel. (03 62) 219 15
Non-residents also like to dine in the best hotel in town; sandwiches, soups and salads are on the menu along with the Indonesian dishes.

Kwizien
Lovina, Jl. Raya Kaliasem
Tel. (03 62) 420 31
The focus here is on European food; from Norwegian salmon, Greek salads and lamb dishes to pasta and French vol-au-vents. There is also an exquisite picture gallery.

► Inexpensive
Bali Apik
Lovina, Jl. Bina Ria
Kalibukbuk
Tel. (03 62) 410 50
Young, independent travellers meet here for the delicious breakfast and low-priced snacks.

② Café Lima Lima
Singaraja, Jl. J. A. Yani
The food here is fresh and simple.

WHERE TO STAY
► Luxury
Most visitors prefer the hotels in Lovina because they are quieter, more comfortable and better value for money.

Puri Bagus
Lovina, Jl. Raya Kalibukbuk
Tel. (03 62) 214 30, fax 226 27
www.bagus-discovery.com
This was the first luxury hotel in the area. 40 Balinese-style villas with palm leaf covered roofs, open-air restaurant in a spacious tropical garden on the coast on the outskirts of town, plus a diverse programme of tours.

Damai Lovina Villas
Lovina, Kayuputih
Jl. Damai
Tel. (03 62) 410 08, fax 410 09
www.damai.com

The more discriminating independent travellers who appreciate the tranquil and exquisite atmosphere of the eight villas with colonial furnishings come here. Ambitious cuisine that combines elements of Balinese and Australian cooking. The only drawback is the location – away from the beach in the hills overlooking the sea.

► **Mid-range**

① *Wijaya*
Singaraja, Jl. J. Sudirman 74
Tel. (03 62) 219 15, Fax 258 17
26 rooms (with bath and air-conditioning) arranged around an inner courtyard; there are also less expensive rooms.

Rambutan Cottages
Lovina, Kalibukbuk
Tel. (03 62) 413 88, fax 416 21
www.rambutan.org
Popular, family-run hotel (30 rooms) surrounded by tropical vegetation, only a few hundred feet away from the black-sand beach. Some rooms have air-conditioning; those with just a fan are cheaper. Beautiful tropical garden with two pools. Balinese evenings and dance performances take place in the restaurant.

► **Budget**

② *Losmen Duta Karya*
Singaraja, Jl. J. A. Yani 59
Tel. (03 62) 214 67
12 rooms with bath and air-conditioning or fans, small inner courtyard, and attentive service.

Aditya Bungalows
Lovina, Kaliasem
Tel. (03 62) 410 59
Fax 413 42
Small bungalows (80 rooms) directly on the beach. This well kept hotel has basic furnishings, a quiet atmosphere, a swimming pool and a popular restaurant with a view of the ocean. There are many more inexpensive lodgings (homestays, losmen) in the centre of Lovina.

---

the first and second courtyards is a wooden seat for the priests with a stand for the offerings. Five steps at the end of the temple lead up to a stone terrace with gedongs for a number of different deities. Take a look at the finely executed **erotic reliefs** throughout the whole temple complex.

★ ★
**Gedong Kirtya
Library**

⏱
Opening hours:
Mon–Fri 8am–2pm,
Sat 8am–noon

The Gedong Kirtya Library stands at the east end of Jalan Veteran in the Sasana Budaya complex, the old palace of the kingdom of Buleleng in the south of the city. A visit can be recommended to those with a burning interest in Balinese history and some knowledge of Dutch.
Besides **some 3,000 manuscripts written on lontar palm leaves**, the library founded by the Dutch in 1928 also houses countless diaries, newspapers and periodicals as well as 8200 historical books from the period of the Dutch occupation. Only the palm leaf manuscripts are stored in sheet metal boxes, everything else is stacked on open shelves – and pretty haphazardly at that, seemingly lacking any form of classification. Those with time to spare or wishing to use a rainy

day to explore the history of the island just might make one or the other revealing discovery in the Gedong Kirtya Library. The supervisory staff allows access to almost everything in the library. It is customary to sign the guest book before leaving and a donation is obligatory.

Around Singaraja

A little less than 10km/6mi west-southwest of Singaraja, stretched along the Bali Sea coastline, is the seaside resort of Lovina Beach with a number of new hotels. Even if the quality of the beach is not particularly outstanding – it is **quite narrow and its sands are dark** – a beach holiday here has its attractions as it is much quieter than the overcrowded beaches in the south of the island.

Lovina Beach

Lovina is made up of several villages, which are **predominantly visited by independent travellers** looking to book several days of cheap lodging. Guesthouses, small hotels and restaurants line Jl. Raya Singaraja, the main street in the town centre, as well as the road leading to the beach, Jl. Rambutan. Bordering to the east is the village of Banyualit, where the hotels are crammed along Jl. Lovina. Brightly coloured fishing boats lie on the beaches and »beach boys« urge the tourists to buy souvenirs, take a tour on the water or head into the mountains. Snorkel tours to the clear waters of the offshore **coral reef** are proffered on the beach. Other boat owners specialize in **dolphin watching**. Usually during the course of such a one-hour tour dolphins will be sighted, and they then accompany the boat.

Lovina

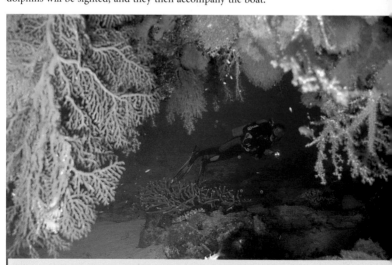

Divers and snorkellers are drawn to the coral reef off the coast.

Komala Tirtha can be found by turning off the main road from Lovina Beach shortly before coming to Singaraja and following the signs for a few miles. Komala Tirtha has a hot sulphur spring and enjoys a delightful setting in a forest. Visitors can bathe in the spring's pool for a small fee.

Gitgit Waterfall

Gitgit Waterfall is located **in dense jungle** in Bedugul near the village of Gitgit, located some 10km/6mi inland to the southeast of Singaraja. A path, about 800m/2625ft long with a number of steps, leads from the car park past rice fields, clove trees and through tropical vegetation. There are stalls offering food to feed the numerous monkey families, along with patchwork quilts and handicrafts. The spray from the waterfall can already be felt just beyond the ticket booth were the admission fee is paid. The cataract plummets from a height of about 35m/115ft into a gorge with a stream. »Showering« and swimming are allowed.

Sangsit

Standing near the village of Sangsit, about 6km/4mi northeast of Singaraja, is the lavishly decorated **Pura Beji**, a temple dedicated to the

Worshippers at a ceremony honouring the sea gods, during which the water is made sacred.

fertility and rice goddess Dewi Sri. It belongs to a rice farmers' cooperative (subak) and exhibits **both Hindu and Chinese-style elements**. The tripartite split gate opening into the inner temple courtyard is lavishly ornamented. The faces of grimacing demons framed by finely crafted lotus blossoms can be made out on its exterior. Beyond is an aling aling, a protective wall to keep out demons, flanked by two snakes. The diversity of architectural ornamentation typical of northern Bali is continued inside. Rising above the temple complex is the gedong of the goddess Dewi Sri. Three figures from the Ramayana can be seen to the right and left on the exterior wall when leaving the temple.

Though the other temple in Sangsit, **Pura Dalem**, is otherwise plain, the finely detailed stone reliefs are noteworthy.

About 10km/6mi down the road that branches off to the south in Sangsit is the village of Sawan, which is known for producing **gongs**, a musical instrument used in gamelan orchestras.

Sawan

Sukawati

M 8

Region: Central Bali
Altitude: 95m/312ft
Distance: approx. 17km/10.5mi
northeast of Denpasar

Administrative district: Gianyar
population: 12,000

Sukawati is two towns in one. Centuries ago it grew so closely together with Batuan, the town bordering to the north, that only people from the two towns can tell where the boundaries between them are. Prince Marakata issued a decree in 1022 ordering that the towns be separated, but nothing much really happened. Today, the large number of Chinese living in Sukawati are putting their stamp on the town.

Sukawati and Batuan are **renowned for their many craftsmen**, who offer their wares in the shops lining the thoroughfares. The production of decorative arts has a tradition here. In former times, noted artists stayed in the royal palace of Sukawati. The **Art Market** (Pagar Seni) in downtown Sukawati is an interesting place to visit: numerous dealers offer sculptures, puppets, woodcarvings, fans, costumes and all manner of other goods here in a two-storey building.

Old tradition

 ▶ SUKAWATI

GETTING AROUND
Head northeast from Denpasar in the direction of Gianyar. There is a regular bus service from Denpasar-Kereneng. Bemos can be found along the roads out of Denpasar and Gianyar.

An appealing hotchpotch of art objects

Batuan style   The town of Batuan has garnered a certain amount of fame through the distinctive style of painting named after it. This style, which gained significance around 1920, has its focus not so much on religious mythical subject matter but rather on **expressionistic depictions** of the life of the Balinese people. Up until then, artists had considered and painted objects only as a decorative accessory to the much more important underlying intent; now the focus shifted and they concentrated their attention on the person or landscape as subject matter. It is assumed that the impetus for this change in style during the Dutch colonial period was primarily the new rulers, who commissioned works from the local artists and made European painting techniques and equipment available to them.

The Batuan style later gained greater influence when painters were among the first tourists arriving in Bali from around the world, and they instructed the islanders. Two of them were the highly esteemed painters Walter Spies (►Famous People) and Rudolf Bonnet.

Around Suka-wati/Batuan   Other villages with numerous arts and crafts shops can be found in the vicinity of Sukawati and Batuan, for example, in **Puaya**.

★ ★ Tabanan

**Capital of the administrative
district of Tabanan
Population:** 12,000

Region: South Bali
Altitude: 105m/345ft
Distance: 24km/15mi northwest of
Denpasar

**Tabanan, the capital of the district of the same name, is located in
the fertile region north of Denpasar known as the »Rice Basket of
Bali«.**

What to See in and around Tabanan

Tabanan's rulers played an important role during the Dutch attempts
to occupy Bali. A powerful principality since its founding, Tabanan
was able to maintain its power over the centuries and under its ruler
Gusti Pandji Sakti (*c*1700) became one of the most influential principalities in Bali. When the Dutch landed on the coast on 22 June
1846, the Balinese defences lasted only a few days, though it must be
said the rulers had gone into hiding in the hills. It is recorded that
one of the rajas said: »While I live the state shall never recognize the
sovereignty of the Netherlands! Rather let the kris decide.« And decide it did! When the Dutch finally succeeded in taking Tabanan and
stood before the palace, the members of the royal family seized the
kris and committed ritual suicide (puputan).

History

▶ VISITING TABANAN

INFORMATION
Tabanan Tourist Office
Jl. Gunung Agung
Tel. (03 61) 81 16 02
Fax 81 27 03

GETTING AROUND
Tabanan can be reached from Denpasar by taking the road to Gilimanuk
and Negara. There are good connections daily by bus and bemo from
Denpasar-Ubung.

WHERE TO EAT
▶ **Inexpensive**
There are some simple warungs
downtown and around the
market.

WHERE TO STAY
▶ **Mid-range**
Puri Anyar
Kerambitan (west of Tabanan)
Puri Anyar is a 17th-century palace.
Guests and visitors are regularly
treated to »Palace Nights« featuring
traditional dancing and Indonesian
specialities from the kitchen.

Temples, markets and music

The city has a number of temple complexes, but the really special sights are more to be found in the surrounding area. The busy market (pasar) near the bemo station is worth a visit. Tabanan is otherwise known for having a **good gamelan orchestra**. There is also a Christian mission station. On the eastern edge of town is the small but interesting **Museum Subak** with displays featuring models and farming implements that illustrate rice cultivation in Bali (no regular opening hours).

✱ ✱ Countryside

The road heading north from Tabanan toward Singaraja passes through a truly **breathtaking landscape of rolling hills** with artfully arranged rice terraces and little villages with friendly inhabitants. It is worth taking a little extra time on this route to enjoy the many impressive sights this charming countryside has to offer.

✱ ✱ Krambitan

A few miles seaward down the road in the opposite direction from Tabanan is Krambitan, a village of considerable size. There are two interesting former royal residences here, Puri Anyar and Puri Gede. Both palaces lie directly on the road. **Puri Anyar** is actually a faithful reproduction of the original 17th-century building that was destroyed for the most part during an earthquake. It is now a hotel with rooms offering a view of a magnificent tropical garden. Under normal circumstances, non-residents may enter the compound and its several courtyards.

The second palace in Krambitan, **Puri Gede**, stands opposite Puri Anyar. It was built in the 18th century in typical Bali style (tours by prior appointment, tel. 03 61 / 81 26 68).

> ## ❗ *Baedeker* TIP
>
> ### A visit to the spice garden
> Pepper, vanilla, ginger, cinnamon and cocoa; Balinese spice gardens will whisk you away to an aromatic world of intoxicating fragrances. Exotic shrubbery and vegetation abound; take a sniff here and a whiff there, sample strange fruit with a completely unknown name or sip a cup of freshly prepared cocoa. Ready packaged spices, coffees and teas can be purchased afterwards.

✱ ✱ Pura Luhur Batukau

One of the island's six state temples, Pura Luhur Batukau, is located at the foot of Bali's second tallest mountain, the 2276m/7468ft-high Gunung Batukau. The temple is located about 28km/17mi from Tabanan along a well developed road. The expansive temple complex was built in a **romantic jungle setting**. The central shrine faces Gunung Batukau.

A small pura dalem stands to the left of the entrance into the first temple precinct. The stone throne for the goddess Batari Uma (here in the manifestation of Durga) with a Vishnu figure mounted on the mythical bird, Garuda, is worth a closer look. The temple is divided into two courtyards and on both sides of the first one are bales that are used for preparing the flower and fruit offerings. A traditional split gate (candi bentar) with ornate reliefs forms the entrance to the second section. Towering upwards inside the second courtyard are several merus with a varying number of pagoda roofs (tumpang) dedicated to different deities. The highest (centre) has seven steps and belongs to Batara Panji Sakti. Left of it is a meru with three tumpangs dedicated to the gods of the five directions, Shiva, Vishnu, Ishvara, Brahma and Mahadevi. Pura Batukau attracts thousands of pilgrims from all over the island who make offerings to the gods for several days every year in March. At those times, the otherwise seemingly remote temple is festooned with colour.

Bubbling away some 7km/4.5mi south of the tiny town of Wangayegede are the hot sulphur springs of Yeh Panas. A **spaciously designed bathing complex** has recently been built here and provides a large pool for bathing and swimming. In addition, private fenced-in »séparées« with effervescent baths can be hired.

✱
Yeh Panas Hot Springs

The only way to walk to the »land in the middle of the sea« with dry feet is during low tide.

★★
Pura Tanah Lot

If there is one sight among Bali's innumerable attractions that no visitor should miss, then it is surely Pura Tanah Lot. Every evening, coach-loads of tourists bussed in from Kuta, Legian and Sanur file through a labyrinth of lanes, full of souvenir dealers, to experience one of nature's grand spectacles. The **fascinating sunset** behind the backdrop of the relatively small temple on the rocky cliffs off the coast is a sight to behold. Pura Tanah Lot, which can be reached on foot at low tide, was erected by Pedanda Sakti Bau Rauh. Forced to flee to Bali from religious persecution on the neighbouring island of Java, he erected several temples on the island. There is a shrine in his honour in Pura Tanah Lot. The highest structure in the temple complex, which is closed to non-believers, is a five-step meru (tumpang), the seat of the divine trinity. The faithful believe that a sacred snake

Best view ▶

has its home in one of the other shrines. The best view of the temple and the sunset is from a specially built **visitors' terrace**. As it is usually full to the last seat, it is advisable to get there early before the tour operators' large omnibuses arrive.

★★ Tampaksiring

M 6

Region: Central Bali	**Administrative district:** Gianyar
Altitude: 630m/2065ft	**Distance:** 78km/48mi northeast of Denpasar

If it were not for Tirtha Empul, one of Bali's most important spring temples, the modest market village of Tampaksiring would never appear on any tourist map. Having said that, the villagers of Tampaksiring are also known for their fine wood and horn carvings that can be purchased all over Bali but are best bought right here in the village where they are the cheapest.

What to See in and around Tampaksiring

★
Pura Desa

Tampaksiring has a **Vishnu shrine**, Pura Desa. The complex, which has two courtyards, lies on the main road heading north; in the first courtyard stand a couple of pavilions decorated with beautiful carvings and reliefs.

★
Pujung

Like Tampaksiring, the small village of Pujungis known for the **high quality of its wood carving**. The countryside around Pujung is fantastic, above all when bathed in the light of early morning. It is worth getting up early just to enjoy a walk here at that time of day.

★★
Gunung Kawi

2.5km/1.5mi down the road heading south from Tampaksiring towards Gianyar is an **unusual kind of religious architectural site**. Deep down below in the narrow valley of the river Pakerisan is an ensemble of three groups of rooms or cells resembling a hermitage and another three groups of monuments all hewn from rock. The Balinese call the site Gunung Kawi, which means »Mountain of the Poets«. According to a number of inscriptions, Anak Wungsu, once the ruler of a large part of Java, along with his four wives and another four concubines, is commemorated here – legend has it that the eight women were voluntarily burned to death after Anak's death. If this is true, then the complex assuredly dates back to the 11th century, either to the time Anak was alive or relatively shortly after his death.

The narrow footpath from Tampaksiring down to Gunung Kawi first leads to a group of four monuments. The small Pakerisan river cuts through particularly appealing terrain at this point.

To the left on the opposite river bank is the group of five monuments; the one positioned a bit higher up could have been for Anak Wungsu. To the right of the group of five is a complex with monks' cells and in the middle is a monolith whose significance has yet to be determined. A tenth monument (thought to be for one of Anak's high officials) can be found by following the Pakerisan gorge further southward. There are more monks' cells (second and third hermitages) carved out of rock above the river on the east bank as well as some a little further south of the tenth monument.

▶ TAMPAKSIRING

GETTING AROUND

To reach Tampaksirin, take the road from Denpasar in a northerly direction via Celuk. There is a daily bus service from Denpasar. Good connections by bus and bemo from Ubud.

The terraced complex of the **spring sanctuary** Pura Gunung Kawi Sebatu is best reached by turning right just outside of Tampaksiring and following the signs (approx. 2.5km/1.5mi). Three pools form an ensemble. Added to that is the shrine in the shape of a square pond, in the centre of which stands a small, open shrine with a stone throne. Even though the finely-worked **water spouts** are overgrown with thick moss, the exceptional quality of their craftsmanship is recognizable. The actual spring temple of Pura Sakti Puseh, standing to the side, is always closed.

✷
Pura Gunung Kawi Sebatu

The origin of the Pura Tirtha Empul spring sanctuary is tied to a legend. It seems at one time there was a great drought when the demon Vitra had gained power over all of the water in the lakes and rivers and kept them locked away. This brought Indra into action, who thrust a lance into the ground where Tirtha Empul stands today and once again opened the springs. Indra has been considered the »protector of water« ever since.

✷ ✷
Pura Tirtha Empul

The centrepiece of the spring temple is a lake whose waters, flowing through a total of **31 elaborately designed spouts**, feed four bathing

31 waterspouts feed the bathing pools of Pura Tirtha Empul.

basins. The left pool is reserved for men and the right one is for women to perform ritual ablutions. Once a year, the villagers symbolically cleanse their pots, bowls and water jugs. The »five holy waters«, Pari Suda, Panglukatan, Sudamala, Tirtha Teteg and Bayan Coko, are collected in the small basin to the far right. A gedong standing in the pool's centre is reserved for the god of the spring shrine. Many visitors take the holy water with them from the spring for use in rituals such as rites of passage.

Wisma Negara (Sukarno's former summer residence) Located above the spring temple is Wisma Negara. The founder of the Indonesian state, President Sukarno (►Famous People), had the palace built as his summer residence in the 1950s. It has two sections separated by a narrow valley cleft but connected by a footbridge. Today the modern furnished building serves as an **Indonesian government guesthouse**. It is occasionally open for tours, but identification papers are requires. Its extensive park offers a nice view of the spring temple down below in the valley.

★ Taro One of the oldest settlements in Bali is Taro (10km/6mi northwest of Tampaksiring). It has an impressive temple, **Pura Gunung Raung**, whose form is supposed to resemble the mountain of the same name in East Java. The place is also noted for its **albino cows**, which are loaned out for religious ceremonies. They can be seen grazing south of the village just outside the **Elephant Safari Park**, where it is possible to take a look at the countryside from the back of a Sumatra elephant.

✦ ✦ Tenganan

P 6

Region: East Bali
Altitude: 242m/794ft
Distance: 4km/2.5mi north of
Candi Dasar

Administrative district: Karangasem
Population: approx. 450

The inhabitants of the village of Tenganan have a special ethnicity. Up until the 1980s, this tiny fraction of the Balinese population lived in total seclusion. Tenganan lies at the southern foot of the central volcanic massif whose highest elevation is Gunung Agung.

The inhabitants of Tenangan claim to have been created by the god Indra himself and to be a chosen people. As proof of this, they refer to the »Usana Bali«, the Balinese story of creation written on palm leaves as early as the 14th century, which mentions that there are exactly 30 families in the village who are the **descendents of the gods**. The **Bali Aga** (original Balinese) of Tenganan form an independent community – much like those in Trunyan (►Penelokan) – consisting of a number of groups organized according to strict rules.

Special inhabitants

There is no private property here; everything belongs to the community. As early as about the age of eight, boys and girls must, after a transitional period of a year, join a group (Truna or Daha). From then on, the parents and family play only a minor role. The group assumes the responsibility of raising them to be fully-fledged members of the community (krama desa). Factors such as age, sex, profession and abilities are decisive when they are later sorted into the

▶ TENGANAN

GETTING AROUND

Travel from Candi Dasa in a northwesterly direction. There is no regular bus or bemo service. Motorbike taxis (ojek) are usually waiting along the road.

»right« group, where they remain for the rest of their lives. As the »darlings of the gods«, the Tenananians see the purpose of their lives not in physical labour but rather in leisure – and in preserving old traditions and arts and crafts. They let others work for them. The rice fields around the village are cultivated by outsiders who relinquish a part of the harvest as rent. This leaves the villagers free to devote their time to playing gamelan music, weaving artistic textiles – this is the only place where the **art of the double ikat** is still practiced (► Arts and Crafts: Textiles) – or to copying ancient manuscripts.

Whoever leaves the community (e.g. marries a person from another village), loses all rights enjoyed as a native of the village. Although

The textiles from Tenganan produced with the double ikat process are known worldwide and treasured by collectors.

still tolerated in Tenganan, they must move to the eastern part of the village, the Banjar Pande. They are also no longer permitted to participate in religious ceremonies.

What to See in and around Tenganan

★ ★
General layout of the village

As recently as the 1980s, Tenganan was a village where visitors were highly unwelcome, but since then the Bali Aga have come to realize that good money can be made with tourism and the prosperity they already enjoy can be increased even more. Naturally, visitors are still banned from the village's sacred temple compounds.

No motor vehicle traffic is allowed in Tenganan. The village consists of three avenues running parallel to each other in an imaginary line from Gunung Agung to the sea. Lining these streets are the kampongs (family compounds) with their rice-straw thatched residential and functional buildings. It is quite possible nowadays for the

! **Baedeker TIP**

The art of the double ikat

The women of Tenganan are masters in the art of weaving cloths on their looms with threads that have been pre-dyed in such a way as to produce a traditional pattern. The parts that are not meant to be dyed are tied tightly in knots (ikat). Ikat cloths are precious works of art whose production takes many months, even years in the case of cloths with complicated patterns used for rituals. Simpler quality cloth is available for purchase at markets.

residents to invite visitors in to take a look around. In the western part of the village are those buildings in which groups of boys and girls meet, as well as the Bale Agung, where the married, full members of the village community gather. Further up from the village stand the shrines dedicated to the Old Balinese Prince Pangus, Pura Sembangan and Pura Santi, the seat of the deities of Gunung Agung.

West of the river lies the villageDau Tenganan, which bears similarities to Tenganan and can be visited by car. Turn left 1.5km/0.9mi along the route between the main road and Tenangan and follow the road for another 1.5km/1mi.

Dau Tenganan

★ ★ Ubud

M 7

Region: Central Bali
Altitude: 92m/302ft
Distance: 25km/15.5mi north-northeast of Denpasar

Administrative district: Gianyar
Population: 16,000

Ubud, Bali's »artistic heart« in the centre of the island, nestles in a very appealing tropical setting with deep green rice terraces and almost impenetrable forests and wild gorges. The irrigation of the soil, principally achieved by means of an ingenious system of canals, has enabled Ubud's population to live from farming for centuries. Today, however, the livelihood of the city's inhabitants is based largely on tourism.

Ubud is considered to be Bali's centre of art and culture. Many of the artists living here still derive inspiration from the beautiful landscape all around the city. Some of them – including painters, sculptors, and woodcarvers – have joined together in **artists' communities**. Ubud and it environs are regarded as the »shopping centre« for traditional Balinese arts and crafts. With a little luck, it is still possible to acquire one or the other authentic antique and take them home – after obtaining the necessary export permits. Aside from the numerous artistic attractions, Ubud itself has only a few sites of historical and cultural interest. However thanks to all the accommodation available, it is an **ideal base for daytrips** into the surrounding countryside to visit, for example, the monkey forest, the white herons of Petulu or the craftsmen of Mas.

Bali's centre of art and culture

What to See in and around Ubud

There are a number of attractive temples in the city with a variety of temple festivals and other ceremonies throughout the year.

Temples

▶ VISITING UBUD

INFORMATION

Ubud Tourist Office
Jl. Raya, Ubud
Tel. (03 61) 97 32 85

GETTING AROUND

The road from Denpasar to Ubud runs northeast through Kesiman and Sukawati. There is a bus service several times daily from Denpasar-Kereneng; bemos also leave regularly from Denpasar.

EVENTS

Ubud is the centre of traditional cultural events. Every evening, either in one of the twelve large temples located in and around Ubud, in a park or in a magnificently furnished hotel, a ceremony or performance is held beneath the night sky. These include kekac, fire and trance dances, gamelan music, Ramayana ballets and legong dances. The variety is considerable and the events that take place are of exacting artistic quality. A list is available in the tourist office on Jalan Raya.

WELLNESS

Balinese massages

Numerous hotels and guesthouses in Ubud offer Balinese massages; there are even spas that specialize in them. Plenty of advice and addresses can be obtained just by walking along the streets of the city centre. Some of the most beautiful and most expensive spas are in the five-star hotels. Make your appointment early, as some treatments can only be booked when there is little demand from the hotel guests. One recommended establishment is *Nur's Beauty Salon* (Jl. Hanoman 28, Padan Tegal), run very successfully for more than 25 years by the Javanese owner, Nur.

Sri Guru, a »healer« famous in Bali, has been in the business just as long. The master himself can be found working along with his many personally trained employees at *Ubud Body Works* (Jl. Hanoman 25, www.ubud bodyworkscentre.com), where creams, soaps and massage oils, as well as Jamu herbal medicines, popular throughout Indonesia, can be purchased.

SHOPPING

Many craftsmen

The region is a true Eldorado for aficionados of the decorative arts. Ubud is famous for the high quality of

Batubulan has a huge selection of sculptures.

the paintings on show in the city, while outstanding silversmiths are at home in the village of Celuk, Mas has its woodcarvers, and Batubulan is the village of stonemasons.

WHERE TO EAT

► Expensive

① *Ary's Warung*
Jl. Raya Ubud
Tel. (03 61) 97 50 53
The specialities served in Ary's Warung can be enjoyed on two floors: the lower floor is the place to meet for a Balinese lunch, above is a veranda that takes on a special atmosphere after sunset.

► Moderate

② *Batan Waru*
Jl. Dewi Sita
Tel. (03 61) 97 75 28
Delicious Indonesian cooking in an unusual setting. The restaurant has been built over a crystal-clear, bubbling brook.

► Inexpensive

③ *Pesto Café*
Jl. Raya Campuhan
Tel. (03 61) 97 58 88
In the immediate vicinity of the famous Tjampuhan Hotel, Balinese and Mediterranean dishes (although without pesto!) as well as vegetarian snacks are served in the Pesto Café.

Ubud Map

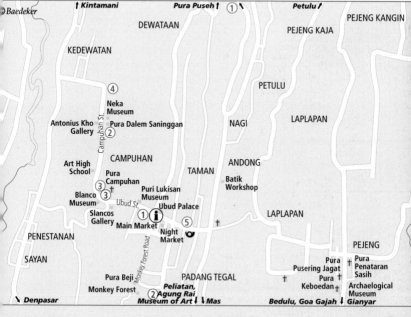

Where to eat
① Ary's Warung
② Batan Waru
③ Pesto Café

Where to stay
① Bagus Jati
② Pita Maha Resort & Spa
③ Tjampuhan
④ Ulun Ubud
⑤ Puri Saren Agung

WHERE TO STAY
▶ Luxury
① *Bagus Jati*
Br. Jati, Desa Sebatu
Kecamatan Tegallalang
Tel. (03 61) 97 88 85
Fax 742 58 63
www.bagusjati.com
In Hindu mythology, Jati is a holy place, separated from the world. This spa retreat (8 villas) does its utmost to live up to this description. Set in the midst of breathtaking natural surroundings with views of tropical forests, volcanoes and peaceful valleys, the private villas are not only spaciously and luxuriously designed, but each has its own spa area, where massages can be enjoyed. The hotel's health centre also offers massages.

② *Pita Maha Resort & Spa*
Jl. Sanggingan
Tel. (03 61) 97 43 30
Fax 97 43 29
www.slh.com/pitamaha
24 traditional Bali-style villas, furnished with exquisite arts and crafts from Ubud. Enchanting and tranquil location in the hills above the town.

Four Seasons at Sayan
Gianyar 80571
Tel. (03 61) 97 75 77
Fax 97 75 88
www.fourseasons.com
Spectacularly constructed building in the mountains on the outskirts of the village of Sayan not far from Ubud. The open hotel lobby is entered by way of a bridge (18 suites and 36 villas) with a view of rice terraces and coconut palms; the other floors of the terraced building are beneath the lobby. There is a round pool that appears to float above the Ayung river valley.

▶ Mid-range

Baedeker recommendation

③ *Tjampuhan*
Jl. Raya Campuhan
Tel. (03 61) 97 53 68
Fax 97 51 37
www.tjampuhan.com
A monument to the local hotel industry. Although this hotel, owned by the royal family, is getting on in years, it is still one of the most stylish lodgings in the village, and rich in tradition to boot. Numerous stone stairways link the 63 cottages set in the midst of dense greenery with the hotel compound. There is a famous spa with a natural stone grotto and spring-water pool.

④ *Ulun Ubud*
Jl. Raya Sanggingan
Tel. (03 61) 97 50 24
fax 97 55 24
www.ulunubud.com
Charming hotel styled as a Balinese village, set in lush, natural surroundings. There is a dramatic view from the rooms of the Tjampuhan river flowing far below. Colonial ambience abounds with four-poster beds, mosquito nets and antiques.

▶ Budget
⑤ *Puri Saren Agung*
Jl. Raya Ubud
Tel. (03 61) 97 51 75
Fax 97 51 37
Stylish and at the same time reasonably priced, the accommodation is basic in the royal palace in the centre of Ubud. Some rooms have antique furniture. It is lively here and not always quiet – but guaranteed to be unforgettable.

The museum (Jl. Campuhan, Samnggigan) named after the Balinese painter Suteja Neka (born 1939) will particularly appeal to those with a special interest in the development of **painting in Bali**. Neka inherited his artistic talent in part from his father, who, although a gifted sculptor and an active member of Bali's first artistic society, did not gain much of a reputation until his later years. Suteja Neka's breakthrough came in 1966, when his and his father's works were ex-hibited at the opening of a hotel in Sanur. He subsequently taught young Balinese the basics of paint-ing. In addition, he collected art works in Bali, including pictures by **Walter Spies** (► Famous Peo-ple), Rudolf Bonnet and Miguel Covarrubias, as well as numerous works by Balinese artists.

The Neka Art Museum has a total exhibition area of 6900 sq m/ 74,300 sq ft, spread out over four buildings standing in a beautiful garden. Temporary exhibitions are featured in a fifth building. A richly illustrated museum guide that not only provides information about the works on show but also in-cludes the artists' biographies is available at the ticket office.

★ ★
Neka Museum
Opening hours:
Mon–Sat 9am–5pm,
Sun noon–5pm
www.museumneka.com

> **Baedeker TIP**
>
> **Yoga, dance or Balinese cuisine**
> Ubud is a stronghold of exciting courses, workshops and seminars on Balinese culture. The local tourist information office can provide a list of events, which is also posted in cafés and restaurants. The programme ranges from one hour lectures to events lasting several days as well as courses attended weekly.

Art lovers should not miss visiting the house of the painter **Antonio Maria Blanco** (► Famous People), who died in 1999. The house stands in a magnificent tropical garden not far west of the city centre. The museum provides a glimpse of the multi-faceted work of the exalted artist, who, during his lifetime, understood exceptionally well how to reach a worldwide, artistically-minded public.

Blanco's property, which was provided him by the son of a Balinese prince, is now the centre of the **Blanco Art Foundation**. It supports many talented young artists; one of the ways it achieves this is by or-ganizing group exhibitions. The private Museum Puri Lukisan (Pal-ace of Painting) in the main road, Jl. Raya Ubud, was founded in 1954 with the support of the Dutch painter Rudolf Bonnet (died 1978), who also became its first curator. It is dedicated to the history and tradition of Balinese painting and woodcarving. The museum, with its museum shop and café, has irregular opening hours (www.mpl-ubud.com).

★
Blanco Museum
Opening hours:
daily 9am–5pm
www.blancobali.com

Museum Puri Lukisan

The Monkey Forest can be easily reached on foot. It is located south of the city centre and although not nearly as large as the forest of Sangeh (►Mengwi), it is situated in a more beautiful landscape. After leaving the unavoidable peanut and souvenir peddlers behind, the path leads to an enormous waringin tree with a stone monkey sitting underneath.

Monkey Forest

Pura Dalem Agung Padang Tegal, the **shrine** in the monkey forest, always has hundreds of little monkeys romping about on it. They are eager to take any food offered but occasionally can become aggressive. Spectacle wearers in particular should be on their guard. The monkeys have even been known to grab the contents of trouser pockets and handbags. The temple is a good example of southern Balinese religious architecture. Take a closer look at the covered gate (candi korung) and the bell tower (kulkul) with its phallus-shaped clapper, resting on a stepped base and richly decorated with reliefs.

Around Ubud

Petulu   Bird-watchers should not miss making a detour to Petulu, which is only about 3km/2mi north of Ubud. Towards evening, huge flocks of white herons, held sacred by the Balinese, settle on the trees in the vicinity.

Market scene (Neka Museum Ubud)

Several groups of long-tailed macaques live in an open range zoo at the end of Monkey Forest road.

A good 4km/2.5mi south of Ubud is the small village of Mas, which is first and foremost famous for its exceptionally skilled inhabitants. The shops and showrooms of numerous **woodcarvers**, sculptors and other craftsmen can be found scattered along the main road. The workshops, in which it is possible to watch the artists at work, are often right next-door. Some woodcarvers teach courses, both for beginners and the advanced. Toward the end of the village are the shops of the furniture makers, who produce tables, chairs and sitting room suites of bamboo and rattan.

Mas

Terms from Mythology, Religion, Art and Everyday Life

The following specialist terms are intended to provide a little support to visitors to Bali. A list of the most common terms has been selected from the large number that exist.

Adat Ancient traditional common law

Aling-aling A wall that provides protection against demons. Such shoulder-high walls usually stand behind covered gates (►Candi Korung).

Atap Palm-leaf roof

Bade Cremation tower. The body of the deceased is carried in procession to the place of cremation in a bade.

Bahasa Indonesia National language of Indonesia

Bale Pavilion-like buildings within a kampong (traditional family compound) or a temple. A bale is usually open on all sides; the roof is supported by pillars. Normally a temple has not just one but several bales.

Bale Agung Pavilion in which the elders or married men of a village gather.

Bale Banjar Pavilion in which the members of a ►banjarmeet.

Bale Gong Large pavilion in the middle courtyard of the temple's (normally) three courtyards. The ►gamelan plays here during temple festivals; the musical instruments are also stored here.

Bale Pesamyangan Pavilion within a temple. The gods are welcomed here at the beginning of a temple festival. As the faithful never know how many gods are coming to visit, the Bale Pesamyangan is accordingly spaciously designed.

Bale Pesimpangan This is where the gods stay who do not permanently reside in the temple, but are rather just visiting (►Gedong Penimpanan).

Bale Piasan Pavilion in which the offerings are placed or prepared.

Bali Aga Old Balinese

Banjar Section of a village (►Desa). The members of a banjar are all the married men in a section or neighbourhood in the village. All important matters concerning the banjar (including also disputes among the members) are discussed and decided upon in regular meetings. The decisions of the banjar, normally reached by a majority, are binding for all members.

Banyan Holy trees with wide-spreading branches and aerial prop roots

Baris Ritual warrior collective dance performed by men

Barong Mythical creature in Hindu mythology. In contrast to the witch ►Rangda, Barong embodies the world-healing principle.

Basuki Snake god of the underworld

Bayu Indian deity (god of wind)

Bedawang Turtle as symbol of the underworld; one of the ten incarnations of the god Vishnu. One or two snakes are wrapped about it and it always forms the foundation of a lotus throne (►Padmasana).

Bemo Public minibus

Brahma Creator of the world; one of three ►Trimurti

Buddha Siddharta Gautama Shakya, founder of Buddhism; the »Awakened (or Enlightened) One«, who, on his own account, recognized the emptiness of the world.

Bukit Hill

Candi Gate

Candi Bentar Split gate. Its origin is traced back to the following legend. When the mountain of the gods, Mahameru, was transported to the island of Bali, it broke in two, forming Agung and Gunung Batur. The split gate symbolically stands for these holy mountains in Bali. Its shape, growing narrower at the top, resembles a mountain cut through the centre, splitting apart into two equally large parts.

Candi Korung Covered gate. It usually forms the entrance to the innermost area of the temple and is customarily extremely richly decorated. Guardian witches or hideous demon faces (►Raksasa) are often put on the sides of the candi korung or kori agung; these are meant to keep the spirits from the underworld away from the temple area. The covered gate also stands symbolically for the three passages of the life of a Hindu: birth – death – rebirth.

Chakra Disc, symbol of Vishnu; wheel of the teachings of Buddha

Cidomo Horse cart

Cili Fertility symbol for the rice goddess ►Dewi Sri; usually arranged in flowers, depicted with grains of rice or painted

Danan Lake

Desa Village community. A desa consists of several ►banjars.

Dewi Danu Tutelary goddess of water

Durga Hindu supreme mother goddess appearing in many forms (usually kindly and punishing forms)

Dewi Sri Tutelary goddess of the rice plant

Eka dasa rudra The largest and most holy festival in Bali; it is a cleansing ritual for the whole universe to renew its balance and is usually performed every 100 years in Besakih.

Gamelan Orchestra with up to 40 musicians. Primarily gongs and drums are used to make the music; occasionally stringed instruments are also employed.

Ganesha Elephant-headed Hindu god; son of Shiva

Garuda Mythical bird-like creature, Vishnu's mount; national symbol of Indonesia and of the state airline

Gedong Enclosed pavilion

Gedong Agung Edifice for honouring the ancestors

Gedong Penimpanan Small structure in which everything is kept that is suited to providing shelter for the gods and deities during their visits to earth.

Goa Cave

Ganung Mountain, volcano

Hanuman (Hanoman) Son of the wind god, monkey general in the Ramayana

Ikat Term for style of weaving using resist dying on either the warp or weft; tied surfaces take on no colour. Interweaving warp and weft that are both tied-dyed creates double ikat.

Indra Indian deity (god of the wind)

Jaba First courtyard in a temple complex

Jaba Tengah Second courtyard in a temple complex

Jamu Traditional medicine based on herbs (▸Baedeker Special p.122)

Jalan (Jl.) Street

Jeroan Third, innermost courtyard in a temple complex

Jukung Double-outrigger canoe

Kali Terrifying manifestation of ▸Devi

Kampong Balinese family compound (in a garden); actually a Javanese one-floor straw hut

Karma Sum total of all good and bad deeds; effect of fate

Kecak Dance telling the story of the Ramayana performed in the middle of a circle formed by the chorus.

Kori Agung ▸Candi Korung

Kris Mythical dagger (cf. p.65)

Krishna Eighth incarnation of Vishnu

Kulkul Bell tower; a resonating wooden gong (often hollowed-out logs) used as »bells«. A kulkul not only serves to call the faithful to a temple festival, it is also an important part of a well-devised alarm system. For example it is used as a fire alarm.

Laut Ocean

Legong Classic dance performed by three young girls and considered to be the quintessence of grace.

Linga(m) Phallic-shaped symbol in stone or wood; the word comes from Sanskrit and means »mark« or »sign«. The lingam symbolizes the god ▸Shiva.

Losmen Inexpensive accommodation; guesthouse

Lumbung Rice granary

Mahabharata Indian epic. A kind of chivalric poem in 110,000 double verses; it tells the story of the battle of the Pandava and Kaurava for domination over the area around present-day Delhi.

Meru World mountain; a pagoda on a base with roofs stacked on top of each other like storeys

Nyepi Balinese New Year's festival (▸Baedeker-Special p.122)

Odalan Temple anniversary (birthday)

Oggo Oggo Papier-mâché monster used to drive away evil spirits during the New Year's celebration (▸Baedeker-Special p.122).

Padmasana Lotus throne, on which the god Shiva rests in his manifestation as the sun god Surya. The backrest of a padmasana is always arranged facing Gunung Agung; it is always supported by the gigantic underworld turtle, ▸Bedawang.

Padur Raksa Special form of ▸Candi Korung

Panca Sila The five principles that form the socio-political basis of the Republic of Indonesia (Belief, Nationalism, Democracy, Humanity, a Just and Affluent Society)

Pelinggih Shrine for a deity that enjoys permanent right of residence in a temple; the ▸Bale Pesimpangan is for gods that only come to visit.

Prasada A special form of ►candi; a prasada has similarities to a pagoda and symbolizes the veneration of the ancestors of a royal house.

Puputan Ritual suicide

Pura Temple (Sanskrit)

Pura Dalem, Pura Desa, Pura Puseh A village's three temples; Pura Dalem is dedicated to the god Shiva, Pura Desa to the god Vishnu and Pura Puseh to the creator god, Brahma. Pura Desa (temple of life) is the most important; the ceremony of cremation takes place in Pura Dalem, the underworld temple (sometimes also the temple of the ancestors).

Pura Subak Small temple. The place of offering for the members of a ►subak.

Puri Palace of a noble family

Raja King, prince

Raksasa Demon figure, demon mask

Rama One of the main deities in Hinduism and the seventh incarnation of the god Vishnu. Rama is considered to be the most ideal of all rulers because of his moral and ethical perfection.

Ramayana Indian epic; the Ramayana (= »in praise of Rama«) was written possibly as early as the third century BC and tells the story of the god ►Rama in 24,000 four-lined stanzas.

Rangda Witch figure; she embodies the principle of destruction and is one of the manifestations of the world-destroyer Shiva.

Saka Balinese calendar, based on the lunar year.

Samsara Cycle of existence; cycle of birth, decay and death (rebirth)

Sangyang Basuki Snake in the underworld

Sangyang Widi The supreme divine principle; created in the course of the changes in Hinduism on Bali toward monotheism, the belief in one single god that possess the attributes of all the Hindu gods.

Sarong Sheet of batik cloth wrapped around the hips

Sawah Artificially irrigated area used for rice cultivation, usually arranged in the form of terraces

Shiva World destroyer; one of the three ►Trimurti

Selendang Hip sash worn when visiting a temple or a shawl worn over the shoulders

Subak A cooperative-like union; the subak is a union of rice farmers who irrigate their fields from the same main canal. The subak has the task of organizing the work on the rice fields and maintaining the irrigation system in a functioning state; the income generated by a subak is divided equally among the members and a reserve is set aside for harder times.

Sungai River

Taman Park, garden

Tirt(h)a Holy water

Trimurti Divine trinity of the Hindu supreme deities ►Brahma, ►Vishnu and ►Shiva

Tumpang Steps in the upper part of a pagoda, roof

Vishnu Preserver of the universe; one of the three ►Trimurti

Wada Cremation tower; like the ►bade, the wada serves for carrying the body of the deceased in procession to the place of cremation, but is reserved exclusively for the members of the rice-farmer caste Jaba.

Waringin-Baum Holy tree (usually within a temple)

Warung Café, restaurant, chemist's shop, food store

Wayang Theatrical play, theatre

Wayang Kulit Shadow theatre; the puppeteer sits or kneels behind a screen illuminated from behind by a lamp, handling up to ten figures at a time.

Wayang Topeng Theatrical performance with masks; the actors wear masks fashioned from wood, exchanging them frequently during the play (often based on the time when Bali was ruled by princes).

Wetu Telu religion Islamic faith with Hinduistic and animistic influences; has many adherents in Lombok

Yoni Symbol for the vagina; counterpart of the ►lingam

Yonilingam The ►lingam united with the ►yoni; takes the form of a basin with an outlet for the sacrificial water

INDEX

LIST OF MAPS AND ILLUSTRATIONS

PHOTO CREDITS

PUBLISHER'S INFORMATION

Illustrations etc: 141 illustrations, 20 maps and diagrams, one large island map
Text: Heiner F. Gstaltmayr
Revisions and updates:
Birgit Müller-Wöbcke
Editing: Baedeker editorial team (Robert Taylor)
Translation: David Andersen
Cartography: Franz Huber, München MAIRDUMONT, Ostfildern (Island map)
3D illustrations: jangled nerves, Stuttgart
Design: independent Medien-Design, Munich; Kathrin Schemel

Phrasebook in cooperation with Ernst Klett Sprachen GmbH, Stuttgart, editors PONS Dictionaries

Editor-in-chief: Rainer Eisenschmid, Baedeker Ostfildern

1st edition 2009
Based on Baedeker Allianz Reiseführer »Bali«, 6. Auflage 2008

Copyright: Karl Baedeker Verlag, Ostfildern
Publication rights: MAIRDUMONT GmbH & Co; Ostfildern

Printed in China

DEAR READER,

We would like to thank you for choosing this Baedeker travel guide. It will be a reliable companion on your travels and will not disappoint you.
This book describes the major sights, of course, but it also recommends the best pubs and beach bars, as well as hotels in the luxury and budget categories, and includes tips about where to eat or go shopping and much more, helping to make your trip an enjoyable experience. Our author Heiner F. Gstaltmayr ensures the quality of this information by making regular journeys to Bali and putting all his know-how into this book.

Nevertheless, experience shows us that it is impossible to rule out errors and changes made after the book goes to press, for which Baedeker accepts no liability. Please send us your criticisms, corrections and suggestions for improvement: we appreciate your contribution. Contact us by post or e-mail, or phone us:

▶ **Verlag Karl Baedeker GmbH**
Editorial department
Postfach 3162
73751 Ostfildern
Germany
Tel. 49-711-4502-262, fax -343
www.baedeker.com
www.baedeker.co.uk
E-Mail: baedeker@mairdumont.com

Baedeker Travel Guides in English at a glance:

▶ Andalusia
▶ Bali
▶ Barcelona
▶ Berlin
▶ Brazil
▶ Budapest
▶ Dubai · Emirates
▶ Egypt
▶ Florida
▶ Ireland
▶ Italy
▶ London

▶ Mexico
▶ New York
▶ Paris
▶ Portugal
▶ Prague
▶ Rome
▶ South Africa
▶ Spain
▶ Thailand
▶ Tuscany
▶ Venice
▶ Vienna